Percy Greg

Without God

Negative Science and Natural Ethics

Percy Greg

Without God

Negative Science and Natural Ethics

ISBN/EAN: 9783743305953

Manufactured in Europe, USA, Canada, Australia, Japa

Cover: Foto ©ninafisch / pixelio.de

Manufactured and distributed by brebook publishing software (www.brebook.com)

Percy Greg

Without God

WITHOUT GOD:

NEGATIVE SCIENCE AND NATURAL ETHICS.

WITHOUT GOD:

NEGATIVE SCIENCE AND NATURAL ETHICS.

BY

PERCY GREG

AUTHOR OF
"THE DEVIL'S ADVOCATE," "ACROSS THE ZODIAC,"
&c., &c.

> "What can ye give us for a Faith so lost,
> For love of Duty and delight in Prayer?
> How are we wiser that our minds are tost
> By winds of knowledge on a sea of care?"
> LORD HOUGHTON'S *Palm Leaves*.

LONDON:
HURST AND BLACKETT, PUBLISHERS,
13, GREAT MARLBOROUGH STREET.
1883.

All rights reserved.

CONTENTS.

CHAPTER		PAGE
	INTRODUCTORY	1
I.	THE CYNIC COSMOGONY	9
II.	NEW LAMPS FOR OLD	30
III.	CHANCE OR CREATION	58
IV.	THE PARADOX OF POSITIVISM	79
V.	MORALS OF PROBABILITY	123
VI.	WOMAN'S FUTURE WITHOUT FAITH	156
VII.	DESPAIR	176
VIII.	INVERTED MORAL ASPECTS	198
IX.	THE INVENTED DEITY	218
X.	'BY THEIR FRUITS'	246
XI.	THIN ICE AND SNOW-BRIDGES	281
XII.	CÆTERUM CENSEO	312

WITHOUT GOD.

INTRODUCTORY.

I INCLINE to think that the progress of scepticism, and still more that sort of half-acknowledged ascendancy which doubt, if not disbelief, seems now-a-days to assert, are due in no small measure to a double misconception. The character and foundations of unbelief, Agnosticism—whatever term may least offensively describe that of whose diffusion we are all conscious—has greatly changed of late. It rests more and more upon grounds intelligible to, but not appreciable by, the general public; upon reasonings whose force they can feel, but whose truth they cannot judge, whose exact weight they cannot measure. It rests, first, upon Biblical criticism of the destructive character; criticism which tends to do away with the apparent force of the Christian evidences by suggesting that the records were written at a comparatively late period, and when there had been time for the growth of what is now called a myth. But secondly, and far more strongly, it rests upon the recent progress of science, and especially upon the Darwinian theory of Development. The public can well understand that, if the Gospels were written in the second century, we have no contemporaneous first-hand testimony to the facts of the Apostolic history. They can understand that the Darwinian system, in its received form, does away with the firmest basis of Natural Religion, the argument from design. But they cannot estimate for themselves either the evidence to the date of the Gospels, or the evidence which proves the truth of Evolution, hardly even the bearing of Evolution upon the question of intelligent Creation. They are therefore chiefly influenced by the judgment of those whom they believe to be competent judges; and a great advantage is given to Unbelief by the general assumptions that most impartial critics have given up the Apostolic origin of the Gospels, and that most men of science have given up Creation.

Both assumptions are greatly exaggerated. With the first I do not pretend to deal here; I will only say that very competent critics believe, on grounds which seem to me very strong, that at least one history of Christ's ministry, miracles, and resurrection—probably one or more of those we now possess—was written before the destruction of Jerusalem. On the other and deeper question, I have perhaps as little authority to speak. But, as one of that unlearned public which has a sufficient general knowledge to form some idea of the force and bearing of the evidence, and as having discussed it with many men from many points, I would wish to warn those who have had less leisure for such studies against yielding too far or too fast to the fame rather than to the force of the evidence. The authority is indeed overwhelming; but let us be sure how far that authority goes. It is an unfortunate consequence of the sharp line drawn between orthodoxy and infidelity that men who repudiate the former are supposed to go all lengths with the latter; and do not always care to point out, sometimes hardly care to perceive, how far their convictions really carry them. Very few men, probably, who have carefully studied the subject, doubt the gradual development of species, the generation of races as of individuals by natural law. I am sure that it is possible to accept by far the larger and surer part of the recent conclusions of science without losing faith either in

Providence or in Creation; nay, while finding in Evolution itself the most striking and impressive evidence of Creative power and wisdom. For more than one strong reason, I could not venture to offer to the many thousands of men who stand much in my own position any confident conclusion, any creed of my own. The form of conversation affords not merely the most convenient, but I think the most truthful, method of laying before my readers the various suggestions which, as the fruit of many years of reading and of thought, may be interesting to those whose minds have been turned in the same direction, but who may have had less time or inclination to work out the results to which, like myself, they feel themselves tending. That form is in some cases especially suited to represent the one conviction I have reached—that there is still a great deal to be said on both sides of the question; a fact too generally overlooked. In a still greater number of instances it affords the best way of putting objections, or of showing where I think that defects of proof or exaggerated inferences may be found in arguments whose general tendency it is impossible to controvert.

I admit that the method is open to the objection taken by one of my critics, that it enables a writer to evade responsibility, to throw out opinions without pledging himself to their truth, or to any distinct belief on the subject thereof; but I hardly expected that such a charge would have been preferred against myself. Those who know me well will allow that I have always had the courage of my convictions, however unpopular, however contrary to my own interests. One of the many personal friends to whom I have been for a quarter of a century keenly opposed in politics defined my course in life as that of a man who 'always chose the side on which his bread was not buttered.' I may have chosen my side too hastily and supported it too vehemently and consistently: I cannot think that I ever flinched from saying in the strongest terms what it seemed right to say, because such outspoken frankness involved, sometimes, more than mere professional loss and injury, mere personal unpopularity and social discredit. Nor am I aware that I have grown more prudent in growing older. An anonymous writer all my life, the anonymity has been not my fault but the inevitable misfortune of my profession. I never wrote what I would not have signed; I would give not a little to have signed all I ever wrote. It would hardly have consisted with the purpose and method either of the 'Devil's Advocate' or the present work to express a strong personal judgment on the various issues raised therein. But, after all, in only one instance have I found my own opinion on any such issue seriously misconceived. In that instance it was my object to indicate at once the great force of the arguments on either side, and the impossibility of bringing them to any common measure. Staunch advocates of either view ascribed to me a strong bias in favour of the opposite conclusion; and both parties were, in different degrees and in a different sense, entirely mistaken.

Perhaps it seems to my critics impossible to believe that, in the present self-satisfied and optimist age, I can really be what the tendency of these works leads them quite justly to call me —a pessimist. Nevertheless, I do believe that for the present all seems to be going to the worse in this worst of all intelligible worlds. Disbelieving in the wisdom of the Many, I disbelieve above all in that extraordinary paradox so popular with the Liberalism of to-day, which affirms that the more ignorant, the less informed, the less leisurely a class may be—the less time they have to think, and the less material on which to form a judgment—the sounder their judgment will be. I cannot therefore hope much, I cannot but dread much, from the inevitable ascendancy of democracy, and government and legislation controlled not by the few wise and well-informed but by the many ignorant and foolish. I see nothing in history, nothing in the nature of things to prove that progress is the constant and certain law of human society. A civilization almost as highly developed as that of the penultimate generation preceded a sudden lapse into centuries of barbarism. The same thing, if we may trust to the evidence of pre-historic monuments, has occurred more than once in the course of human existence ; and I do not see why it may not recur. The present temper of the democracy of Europe seems to render its recurrence very possible. Envy of wealth, jealousy of intelligence, antipathy to an intellectual even more than to an hereditary aristocracy, seem to threaten property, leisure, and education with serious danger. And the destruction of private property, or such interference with personal freedom in its acquisition and disposal as should tend to discourage accumulation or compel equal distribution, would, I believe, suffice in a single century to destroy all that civilization has achieved and to plunge us back into the darkness of the middle ages. And, be it remembered, we should then have a population of the twentieth century with the resources of the twelfth.

I see also in the present tendencies of opinion

a great and real danger to morality, a danger more certain, more immediate, and subtler than that which seems to threaten property and order. I believe firmly that there can be no general—national—universal morality without religion. Religion without a God—a God impersonal or unknowable—are to me contradictions in terms. I admit that many whom I should call Atheists, perhaps a majority of those who avow themselves Atheists, are eminently honest and virtuous men. But I hold, for reasons given hereafter, that their morality contradicts their Atheism: that they have no logical right to their virtues, and that, in the course of half a century at most, their logic will be too strong for their ethical instincts and their unconscious Christian traditions. If I am right in believing that no true morality can long survive Religion, and if they be right in believing that Religion cannot survive enlightenment, Pessimism is not the paradox it seems. Raise the intellectual level of mankind to the highest attainable point—a race which has ceased to be a law to itself or to take a law from above is surely on the high-road to ruin.

CHAPTER I.

THE CYNIC COSMOGONY.

AFTER a quarter of a century of hard professional work, those whom I had served so long having no further need of me, I had, for the first time in my life, nothing to do, and leisure to do it. It followed that, within a twelvemonth, rest and change were once more insisted upon; and once more, in the nick of time, came a letter from the friend whose home offered all the charms a friend's house can possess under such circumstances. At Ferndale Holm there had always reigned a peace and harmony which communicated their influence to the most worried or restless guest; beauty and pleasantness within doors and without, an intellectual activity sure to afford sufficient interest to a wearied mind without setting it too hard at work. I never care to take a prominent part in the conversation there; I never fail to find it worth remembering.

Cleveland wrote:

'I do not repent allowing you to publish your record of our talk, though you have made us terribly long and prosy. I wished you had suppressed Ida altogether, till I read Miss S——'s criticism in the *Androgynist*. Surely none but a strong-minded woman could have committed so unwomanly a mistake in such supreme unconsciousness of self-exposure? Of course, it was because my home is so happy that I could afford to ridicule the disorder, anarchy, extravagance of ordinary married life. I could speak of women as they deserve, because no one could dream that I spoke with "personal querulousness." I forgive Miss S——, however, for the sake of the most pertinent criticism I have seen on our views —the reminder that the working-man can marry early because he grows poorer rather than richer after middle life; *i.e.*, of course, if he means always to live from hand to mouth. It is amusing to see how critics contradict each other; half of them commend you for bringing out our individualities so clearly, the other half complain that you have wholly failed to do so. The truth, I suppose, is this: you have given our several thoughts and characters distinctly enough, but you have clothed all with your own style and language, which, if it be lucid and precise, as they say, is so at an alarming expense of words.'

It happened that, on the evening of my arrival, I was the only guest. We naturally recurred to the topic on which Cleveland's letter had touched, and my hostess observed:

'You said little yourself, and you have left out most of what you did say. But the passage that has called forth the most earnest, most fundamental criticism was your own, and I should like to know exactly what you meant by it. You said, "I believe in, I care for, the utmost development of the highest intellectual and moral forms of manhood infinitely more than I believe in, or desire to help forward, the gradual elevation to such low standard as they may possibly reach of mankind at large. And, if the latter be indeed a task imposed on humanity, it will best be achieved, unconsciously, in striving after the former." Your most thoughtful critic assumes your meaning to be that the aristocracy of intellect will do their duty best by caring only for the culture of their own mental and moral powers, the highest development of their own nature; that they should be indifferent or even adverse to the gradual diffusion of intelligence, enlightenment, and happiness among the

Many. That seems a fair construction of your words; and yet I seemed to understand and agree with your thought at the time; but, as translated, it sounds heartless and untrue as unchristian.'

I hardly knew how to reply, and was relieved when Cleveland took up the challenge.

'Unchristian! Of course. Our friend delights to repeat that he is not a Christian. He used to call himself a Moslem, till I teased him into reading the Koran. I think that cured him. But if on this point he contradicted Christ, he certainly agreed with Nature. According to Darwin, the development of species has proceeded through a perpetually repeated sacrifice of the race to the perfection of its *élite*. This is the aristocratic principle carried to its logical extreme; and you may be content'—turning to me—'not to be wiser than your Creator.'

A.—' I had that truth in mind; and it has profoundly influenced all my views upon the philosophy of life. Providence evidently cares nothing for the many, all for the few. Ten thousand minnows perish to feed one salmon; millions of millions of minnows are born only to be prematurely destroyed in evolving a trout. Natural Selection means that, in the scheme of Providence, the quantity of life is nothing, the quality everything. The millions are created for the one.'

Ida.—' Surely you exaggerate even the hard and heartless view of Natural order assumed by the new pessimist philosophy?'

Cleveland.—' Not at all; and whatever else may be doubtful in their scheme, this, I fear, is beyond question. The law of Malthus applies to the brute creation in all its literal ugliness; the destructive check is enforced to the uttermost. One may hope that the necessary havoc causes comparatively little suffering, the brutes being spared the horrors of anticipation. But the evolutionary method requires that in each successive generation ten should be born to perish that one, a little the best, may find room to live.'

Ida.—' Is it so, as matter of fact? Is not the absence of any real proof of such lavish waste a weak point in Mr. Darwin's scheme? And if it were true of the brutes, can we apply such a doctrine to mankind? Are the most valuable human lives really worth scores of the least valuable; is there so great a difference between man and man?'

A.—' Is there not? Is not one Darwin worth a thousand Australian savages or a hundred Dorsetshire peasants? At any rate, the evidence of human history corroborates that derived from the development of species. The scheme of Providence is the same in both cases. Civilization has been achieved by the extirpation of incoherent inferior or weaker races to make room for the stronger; for those which, if not at the moment superior, were capable of higher ultimate culture.'

Ida.—' But is it not true that a caste which acts on such a principle must be demoralized by its cold-blooded egotism?'

A.—' I don't think so. It is conscious departure from an ideal standard, rather than the honest acceptance of a stern and selfish one, that really demoralizes. Men who will sacrifice their immediate desires to any end, though it be not a very generous one, will keep that tough fibre of manhood which is the actual as well as the etymological foundation of virtue.'

Ida.—' Surely an imperfect fidelity to a high standard is better than the attainment of a low one?'

A.—' But I don't admit mine to be low. The mass of our species can only reach a standard so low that it is hardly worth labouring to lift them to it. My idea is that the influence and example of a really great intellectual aristocracy would do more, even for the masses, than the widest diffusion of the highest civilization of which the "vulgar herd" is capable in the absence of such example. At any rate, *I* care more for a dozen great independent individual minds than for all the millions of a populace like that of France or America; millions of a few low types, whose aim and tendency is to repress independence and to crush out individuality. But I was speaking of the ultimate purpose of thinkers, the aim and ideal of philosophy, not the practical object of government. A ruling aristocracy, intellectual or other, is bound to govern for the benefit of its subjects. The essential idea of Aristocracy is that all authority is trust, never to be turned to the advantage of its holders. It is because Democracy forgets this that a democratic age is so impatient of all authority, from that of the father and husband to that of the Prince and the Church.'

Cleveland.—' You seem half-afraid of your own paradox. Within a species, as in the wider comparison between distinct species, we may think as Providence evidently acts—may weigh lives and not count them, measure their value by capacity for use or enjoyment. Carry out the contrary idea logically to its extreme, and it culminates in that strange combination of asceticism, benevolence, and uncleanness which leads the Fakir to cherish his fleas, and renders all life equally sacred to the Brahmin. It deserves notice that this idea of the sacredness of life for its own sake belongs essentially to the lower and weaker human races. The arch-aristocracy of mankind, the Anglo-Saxon branch of the Teutonic race, entertain no such idea. We frame insensibly a distinct scale of animated existence, ranking the creatures in a natural hierarchy, and never hesitating to sacrifice the lower to the higher. We feel horror in seeing a rabbit given over to a snake; it is the sacrifice of a higher life to a lower. We should be impelled to rescue a monkey or an elephant from a tiger; but we should help a seal to catch fish rather than the fish to escape. We should feed a robin with worms, or an owl with mice, and feel no scruple; and so we should slaughter any number of the noblest beasts to save the lowest savages from starvation. So, again, we feel with Tatnall when, witnessing our defeat by the Chinese, he declared that blood was thicker than water. Few of us but would help a German or American against Chinese or Malays, without stopping to inquire into the merits of the quarrel. We should *feel*, if we had no time to *think*, that the life of one European was worth those of a score of Tasmanians or Siamese. Those who believe in Providence can hardly maintain that the course of Providence, which from the *alga* to the Aryan is one continuous sacrifice of the many to the few, is essentially wrong.'

A.—' But our critic would say that there exists

an immeasurable gulf between human and animal life; that they are not on the same plane; that there is no such distinction of capabilities between the highest and lowest man as, for example, between the monkey and the serpent.'

Cleveland.—'Just because there is so much in man that is not in the highest brutes, the gulf between the highest and lowest men is wider than any that exists below mankind; and the potential capacity of man renders almost indefinitely great the difference between the limited development possible to all the race and the ultimate range of the highest minds. Grant, what I do not believe for a moment, that the lowest level of humanity is, or one day will be, as far above the noblest dog as the dog is above the turtle. But the distance between the turtle and the dog is a limited, if a very wide one; the distance between the turtle and the Australian (say) twice or thrice as great, but still a measurable definite quantity. The difference between the average and the ultimately attainable manhood is indefinite, if not infinite. In power of doing, enjoying, above all of being, the cultivated posterity of the finest natures of to-day will transcend the unimproving successors of the animal men of this age more, far more, widely than these the lower animals; and it is by those capacities that the worth of existences, mortal or immortal, must be estimated.'

'Is the difference between man and man really so great?' Mrs. Cleveland asked, thoughtfully and doubtfully.

Cleveland.—'I think so, shocking as the truth is to many feelings and associations I should wish to respect. The average human animal can find, apparently can conceive no greater, keener enjoyment than to animalize himself to the utmost; to eat or drink himself into a state in which his intellectual faculties are almost annulled, the state of a pig dozing after a full meal. Where in Nature can you find a gulf so vast, a contrast so absolute, as between this average man and the poet or philosopher, whose happiness consists in the most intense exertion of the intellectual, or the highest, most sustained aspiration of the spiritual powers?'

A.—'So far as I can remember my own meaning, I think I had in view, though somewhat indefinitely, the ultimate state of the world. I fancy two conceivable forms which the "federation of mankind" may take. It may be a democracy, formed by the fusion of all races, of a type not exceeding the European peasant or artisan of to-day; or it may be an intellectual aristocracy cultivated to the highest point of which human faculties are capable, the descendants of the *élite* of the Aryan races, resting upon a population such as the Chinese, well-fed, well-clothed, lightly worked, and content to be—not hewers of wood and drawers of water, that will be done by machinery, but—purveyors to those who will direct, govern, and organise them. Personally, I must say I infinitely prefer the latter prospect to the former.'

Cleveland.—' And it seems better to accord with the purposes of Providence. With mankind, as with the brutes, He seems to intend that the superior races shall replenish the earth and possess it; those of the inferior only surviving which are suited to some form of servitude or subordination; the rest being extirpated, sometimes by war, sometimes by that strange decay which always befalls an untameable race in the presence of a high civilization.'

Ida.—' You are almost as cynical as Lestrange himself. I should like to hear what he would say to your doctrine.'

Cleveland.—' He would say not that I underrate the average man, but that I enormously exaggerate the worth of the highest; that no man rises very much above the level of canine virtue or elephantine intelligence.'

A.—' I wonder whether, in a million years, an

elephant could be taught to edit the *Courier?*'

Cleveland.—' Lestrange would say that no elephant would stoop to it. You know you will meet him here to-morrow? There is a flavour of prussic acid about his talk, stronger, I think, than in his writings; and his spirit is more intensely bitter than either.'

Ida.—' Double distilled essence of strychnine. I am so sorry for him. Even if I did not know what his life has been, I should pity a man who has nothing in earth or heaven to believe, to hope, or to love.'

A.—' That may be true of his writings; but is it true of the man himself?'

Cleveland.—' Too true. Not that he is selfish or unfeeling in act; that makes it all the sadder to

> ". . . . mark
> A bright soul driven,
> Fiend-goaded, down the endless dark,
> From hope and heaven."

One whom thought has robbed of faith in God, experience of faith in man; for whom, in his own words, Creation is a chimera and the Creator a dream, the universe a colossal blunder and life a bungle in detail. What restrains him from suicide, if suicide were ever matter of logic, it would be hard to understand. He neither cares for fame nor enjoys pleasure; his hatred of men is strongly tinctured with contempt, his contempt for women embittered by dislike; and yet I think he never wronged the one or dealt hardly with the other. For him existence is, and must be to the end, almost hopeless suffering; and yet annihilation is to him, as to many happier men, its nightmare horror.'

A.—'How, then, does he contrive to work as he has worked, certainly, for the last five years?'

Cleveland.—'Opium. His is one of those rare constitutions in which opium acts solely upon the nerves, dulling or extinguishing the sense of pain without stupifying, nay, while apparently intensifying, the intellectual power. Of physical exertion, either on that account or from sheer weakness, he seems incapable. I have known him shrink for a week from the effort of writing a letter with his own hand; but we both know how many hours of hard sustained mental labour he must go through every day.'

A.—'It has always seemed to me that opium may become to the intellectual what alcohol is to the animal man. There are more constitutions than you seem to think in which it produces that condition of lucid, serene, clear-sighted reverie of which you seem to speak. And yet the intelligence of the alcoholic nations surely surpasses that of the narcotist races of the East?'

Cleveland.—' Perhaps neither the Asiatic nor the Teuton, save in a few exceptional instances, appreciates greatly the intellectual influence of his favourite stimulant. Certainly it does not seem that the Chinese or Turkish opiatist is given to intellectual lucidity; possibly it is only on brains naturally more active and powerful that the drug exerts a clarifying influence. But opium is the delight of a dreamy and sluggish, alcohol of a strong and sensual temperament; the one suits an indolent, the other an active nature in its hour of reaction or repose.'

'Is it possible,' I suggested, 'that opium and other narcotics which are now, I fear, coming dangerously into fashion, suit another and later stage of human development, as alcohol suited an earlier?'

Cleveland.—' Possible, I should say, but dubious. The sleeplessness of men of intellect, now-a-days, is that on which bromide of potash appears best calculated to act. It proceeds from overwrought nerves that will not stop working, will not cease to stimulate the brain; and these stilled, people sleep, or should sleep. But the narcotism of to-day prevails most among women, who have no business with such nervous over-activity. They are not forced, like us, into over-excitement by the necessity of brain work, but seek it in pleasure and as pleasure. Their sleeplessness, as a rule, means voluntary late hours, dissipation, idleness; the remedy would be fresh air, exercise, and home duty. Not always, Ida, of course. God help the women whose sleepless nights mean harassed, over-wearing days! though even these don't trust to the natural corrective —fresh air—as they might. Women who *must* overwork or overworry themselves are even more to be pitied than men. But I fancy that most of the female narcotists of to-day would, to begin with, have preferred wine and brandy to chloral, —which, by the way, is far worse than either opium or alcohol,—and only took to drugs because they were afraid or ashamed to drink alcohol enough.'

'Algernon, don't go off on that score,' urged his wife. 'You see that the "shrieking sisterhood" fancy that your criticisms on feminine follies must be embittered by personal experience; and I could not bear that even the *Androgynist* should hint that your wife must be . . .'

The pause was very characteristic. The speaker, if any of her sex, might righteously and fearlessly 'cast the first stone' at unwomanly vices or unfeminine pretensions; but her pure, delicate womanhood asserted itself more truly and gracefully by an instinctive shrinking from subjects which it must surely soil the innocence and blunt the sensitive spiritual refinement of woman to contemplate so closely as is now the fashion of the sex.

'I did not understand Mr. ——'s question,' she continued. 'I wish you would explain and answer it.'

Cleveland.—'It has been suggested with some plausibility that the first use of stimulants—at least, the first feeling that rendered them a sort of necessity, an object of eager desire—was due to the native cowardice of man. Races too simple to deny their real feelings—too little disciplined to suppress their instincts in obedience to that public opinion which Darwinian or Evolutionist ethics suppose to have been the original basis of what we call the sense of honour—felt the need of artificial hardihood, of Dutch courage. [If so, by the way, one might find therein a motive for the limitation of the privilege of intoxication to the fighting sex, even among tribes too degraded to possess a sense of feminine delicacy.] Savages could exist only by bravery; and yet they were not brave. It is among races not living in a state of constant warfare—races like the Bengalees, the industrious Chinese, the Mound-builders of North America, who must apparently have been a powerful, well-organized, civilized, agricultural nation—that we find the milder, non-provocative stimulants, like tea, coffee and tobacco, originating. In later days, among races which, if warlike, wage war in numbers and under regular discipline, the fierce uncertain ungovernable daring inspired by bhang or brandy is worse than useless. Accordingly we find Spartans and Romans famous for sobriety; and the fierce Vikings and Berserkers, whose heaven was a perpetual drunken orgie, became in a very few generations signal examples of temperance when, converted from lawless rovers into a feudal chivalry, they fought in regular squadrons instead of battling man to man or crew to crew on board their small ships. Now that we begin to find our brains not too sluggish but too active, our nerves so sensitive that even intense pleasure or exciting interest leaves behind a sense not of lassitude and dulness but of restlessness— not of negative but of positive pain—sedatives rather than stimulants become the object of our instinctive craving. I don't say that this is the whole truth, but it is one side of the truth. And so it is among the brain-workers or brain-exciters —the votaries of intellectual toil or intellectual pleasure—that temperance in alcohol and indulgence in narcotics prevail. The navvy still finds his delight in strong drink; the animal man still craves for that which most quickly and thoroughly brutalizes him.'

A.—'How does that theory consist with the student's preference for stimulating champagne, the navvy's predilection for stupifying beer or porter?'

'One takes champagne still,' said Cleveland, smiling, 'to give one "Dutch courage" for the tongue-warfare of the dinner-table or the fatigues of the ball-room. Our *craving*, when it becomes such, is, if not generally yet in an increasing degree, a craving for relaxation, not stimulation of the nerves.'

Ida.—' But, Algernon, surely savages are not so deficient in courage? I always thought they were naturally and individually braver than civilized men. Look at the Red Indian's daring and endurance, the Asiatic's indifference to death.'

Cleveland.—' The Asiatic is inferior in fighting courage—that which is needed by savage tribes—to the European. He will die readily enough; but he dies *too* readily; he lacks the nerve to escape death by defying it. I speak comparatively, of course, and generally, for some Asiatic races are among the bravest in the world. But I doubt if even the American Indian were really in courage —which is distinct from mere indifference to pain

—the equal of the Aryan. He would never fight where he could murder; never fight on equal terms where he could steal an advantage. He would never have attacked like the Zulus, utterly indifferent to the waste of life, fortifications he could not reach under a fire that slaughtered in a few hours four times the number of the defenders. Hurons and Mohicans would never have closed on the Martini rifles at Isandula. Perhaps the very small numbers of the several tribes, rendering each individual warrior of importance to his clan, contributed to this carefulness of life. But, again, the Indians had advanced, morally, beyond the point at which men could openly resort to spirits to keep up their courage: and their warfare required sobriety. Ida, most men are cowards; the courage they display is artificial, due to the insensible teaching of boyhood on the point of honour, or to the direct discipline of soldiership. Three in four would run away, when danger is very great and very close, *if they dared*. The best soldiers do run when it reaches a certain point; and that though the actual risk of running is greater than that of going on—it is *after* the ranks give way that the chief slaughter occurs. The heroes of old did not affect indifference, as everybody does now-a-days. Achilles avowed an intense dread of death; Hector ran away in sight of both armies; Paris was scarcely ashamed of flagrant cowardice.'

Ida.—' But what tortures the Indians endured unflinchingly.'

Cleveland.—'Yes. I believe that there is even more difference between man and man in the power of feeling pain than in the power of bearing it. Women are supposed more sensitive than men, because, as a rule, they scream or faint sooner. But experiment has shown that their sensation is less keen than ours. Their power of endurance is sooner exhausted; but under equal inflictions I suspect they actually feel less. So the Indian feels less than the white man, and therefore endures better. But when it is a question, not of torture brief and intense, but of prolonged suffering which is more equally felt, he yields sooner. Fatigue and hardships are best borne by the strongest, the most perfectly organized, not the least but the most sensitive men and races. In Arctic and desert expeditions, Englishmen hold out better than Russians or Africans, and English officers than English seamen. Endurance is proportioned to vitality; and vitality involves capacity alike of enjoyment and suffering.'

A.—'I don't know how far I agree with you, and it don't matter. I was surprised to be rebuked for not summing up and passing judgment on our discussions; not giving my own opinions. What do they signify? It is not as if I were one whose personal authority carried weight without my reasons, or added weight to them. And, if all we can say on either side has been said, my personal "I think the Noes have it" would be as mere a form as Mr. Speaker's.'

CHAPTER II.

NEW LAMPS FOR OLD.

NOTHING about Lestrange surprised me so much as the fact that at the age of fifty, after thirty years of very hard work and very feeble health, after five of most arduous and anxious labour amid constant physical pain, he was not merely living, but so intensely, consciously, actively alive. The only change perceptible to me—who had not seen him since the last bitter experience which might have driven a strong sensitive nature mad with rage or pain—was a certain disposition, till thoroughly roused, to leave the forward part in argument to others; contributing a few strong, concise, intensely bitter cynicisms, often very pertinent and sometimes startling, as his share of the conversation. Cleveland told me that Ferndale Holm was the only house into which he had entered for many years, perhaps because the only one where his story was so well-known that he could neither suppose himself suspected or received on sufferance—the effect of persistent calumny on one who could neither vindicate nor avenge himself without destroying others. Whether time, suffering, or drugs had so calmed all physical expression of his naturally impatient, impetuous, disputative, though not unkindly temper, as I had known it of old, I could not judge.

Sterne and Vere spent with us the first evening after his arrival; a long one, for in winter Cleveland liked to dine an hour or so after darkness had set in. We gathered round the library fire; for he chose, when no other lady was in the house, that his wife should be able to join without constraint or awkwardness in these conversations, and for that reason had made the library a sort of neutral ground indoors, like the arbour wherein our summer sittings were held—the only room in the house wherein tobacco and embroidery were both at home, affording to either sex that kind of inert physical occupation which furthers conversation by removing from silence the appearance of constraint.

'Have you written anything lately?' Lestrange enquired of our host. 'To me your books read like fragments; and, as I have seen nothing of yours in print for three years, I have been hoping that you would fill up the various gaps and give us your philosophy of life as a whole.'

A.—'I am afraid there was but too much ground for my original fears when first you settled here. You are neither challenged nor stimulated to think out your ideas, and your life is too pleasant not to render you idle.'

Ida.—'I wish you were right. Algernon thinks his friends' society too profitable to write much when the house is full. But these are his holidays; at other times he is very busy. He gives up two or three afternoon hours to my amusement, and lets me share his lighter studies in the evening. But he works steadily till two o'clock on fine days, and all day, or nearly so, when the weather is quite impracticable.'

'Two or three hours of pure enjoyment are as much as I can appreciate in one day,' Cleveland answered; a compliment spoken with a quiet sincerity which, even after eight or ten years of wedded life, called a flush of pleasure to the fair cheek of the young matron.

Lestrange.—'But what have you done with the fruit of three years' work? We shall look for something worthy of so long an incubation.'

Cleveland.—'A very short one, if I had meditated anything really new. My first work digested the fruits of twenty years' experience.'

A.—' At the rate of ten or twenty lines a day!'

Cleveland.—' I don't write so fast as you do, even when I actually begin to compose for the public. But Lestrange imputes to me an ambition beyond my scope. Fifty years, the utmost extent of a working life, would be short enough if I seriously aimed at reducing to system what you are pleased to call my philosophy of life; and the critics would tell me it was but a negative quantity after all.'

Lestrange.—' So much the better. The first thing is to clear the foundation; and your life would be the most useful philosopher ever spent if, instead of building another scheme on the crumbling ruins of antiquated dogmas, you would make a clean sweep down to the solid rock in some small part of the ground now cumbered with the rubbish of ancient Cyclopean falsehood, and the flimsy, hastily-constructed sheds which modern impatience has run up out of the rotten materials of antiquity.'

Sterne.—' Cleveland is too much afraid of their fall. He seems chiefly concerned to warn the world how many precious things, living and dead, would be crushed and lost for ever under the ruins.'

Lestrange.—' We must clear away those ruins before we can recover the buried treasures.'

D

Cleveland.—' Aye. But ruinous as great part of the structure may be, it shelters too many living souls, covers too many irremovable and irreplaceable images of truth and beauty to be recklessly dealt with. Not till I see the way to build a stable edifice, in which future generations may live securely and happily, will I lend a hand to destroy what the past has bequeathed to us.'

Sterne.—' It is tumbling about your ears.'

Cleveland.—' Much of it, no doubt. But I am much more sure that the destroyers are utterly ignorant of the first principles of architecture than that the great works of the Cyclopes and the Titans will not yet last our time and our children's.'

Lestrange.—' I hate rottenness, old or new.'

Cleveland.—' Grant that you are right—I know that the new is rotten to the core : I am not so sure of the old. It may be that the stones are sound, though encrusted with decay and ill-cemented. Repair may be possible ; at present reconstruction is not. I will not help to break with the past till I find some prophet who can foresee the future more clearly than myself.'

Sterne.—' Truth is always a safe guide.'

Cleveland.—' Is it? Why? I, who believe in a superintending, directing Providence, might reasonably think so. I may believe that He has so ordered things that right-doing and true-speaking must always lead us aright. But you, who hold that Man has nothing to look to beyond himself, what right have you to feel sure that by pure chance we may not have blundered on to safe ground; that the Many may not as yet be too childish to be safely trusted with anything so explosive as political, so keen-edged as scientific truth?'

Lestrange.—'What is truth? A duller than Pilate could have asked the question; a greater than Moses, a wiser than Solomon, failed to answer it.'

Vere.—'Or refused the answer to such as Pilate.'

Cleveland.—'Are you right there? Was it not His invariable practice to answer questions irrespective of the good faith of the questioner? This one stands alone without reply, without explanation of the silence. The fact is suggestive, if not significant.'

'Pilate would not wait,' interposed his wife, quietly.

Cleveland.—'It is not so recorded. And if an answer had been offered, Pilate, who was in no hurry to condemn his prisoner, would have been willing enough to hear how the Jewish peasant would answer a question that had puzzled the chiefs of all the Hellenic schools.'

Vere.—'My own faith apart, as mere matter of intellectual appreciation, I vastly prefer the old prophets to the new. When men of profound learning and brilliant ability seek spiritual consolation in a fourth dimension of space, and a basis of morals in the tribal conscience of savages, can we part with the old creeds for such substitutes? Can we feel any reliance on guides so evidently groping in the dark, chasing such intellectual will-o'-the-wisps?'

Lestrange.—'As if bewildered in a maze of words;—given up to believe a lie, and serve them right!'

A.—'I lost my way in the curvature of space, and got hopelessly out of my depth in the regions where triangles may have three right angles, and two and two make five. Is it nonsense or profundity?'

Cleveland.—'Bottomless bathos. I thought over it for months, and only came to that conclusion when I found mathematicians, perfectly competent to sound its depths, pronouncing them mere obscurity.'

A.—'Surely that was obvious? Curvature implies a surface, and a surface something outside of it; whereas there can be nothing outside of space. And the fourth dimension is, I think, impossible as well as inconceivable. I cannot admit that we fail to conceive it simply because we live in a space of three dimensions; as creatures living in a line, or a surface, might fail to comprehend another dimension. Any intelligent being, any creature capable of mathematical reasoning must see that a moving line describes a surface, a moving surface describes a solid. It is not only that we cannot conceive of something else described by a solid; we know that, move it as you will, it describes only, invariably, some form of solid figure. Turn it in what direction, move it at what rate you please, it gives you still three dimensions, and no more.'

Cleveland.—' Yes, that answer is, I believe, really as conclusive as it seems; but, because it seemed so conclusive, I felt very distrustful of it, till I saw it confirmed by authority.'

A.—' Why so ?'

Cleveland.—' Obviously because its truth is *too* obvious.'

Ida.—' Oh, Algernon, what an extravagance !'

Cleveland.—' Not at all, Ida. When I find a master in his art uttering what reads like sheer nonsense, the last inference I am entitled to draw is that it *is* nonsense. The more absurd it looks, the less likely is it that he overlooked the absurdity.'

A.—'But if Clifford did see the obvious answer to his theory, why did he not explain it?'

Cleveland.—'Perhaps because the rejoinder seemed to him still more obvious. I thought so, till I found the objection was as apparent and as conclusive to scholars as to dunces.'

Vere.—'Clifford's reasoning on the numerical question seemed to me to prove its own fallacy.'

Cleveland.—'I think so. I should say that two and two are four; and, *being* four, not *making* four, can nowhere and in no case be five, which is four *plus* one. Contradictions cannot co-exist either in Mars or in Sirius. In no world can B be equal to A, and also to A *plus* C, unless C = o. If we know that the angles of a plane triangle can in no world exceed two right angles, all Clifford's Atheistic reasoning crumbles into dust. Moreover, on the one point where I can test his reasoning perfectly, I can see its fallacy. My own conception of a mathematical line has no such relations to pencil lines more or less fine as he insists it must have; it is the conception either of a direction or a boundary: and, in mathematical understanding, a circle is not a more or less close approximation to a perfectly even line perfectly equidistant from a centre; it *is* that line, and nothing else.'

Sterne.—'To turn your own argument against

you, how came a master to make a mistake which a tyro can detect on such a point?'

Cleveland.—' Because here he was going beyond the true limits of his science. Once passing from true mathematics into metaphysics, and reasoning not on the properties of figures, but on those of thought—once outside his own sphere—he was misled by a metaphysical fallacy common enough among clever men, and fatal to the clearest intellect as to the dullest. He assumed first that his own methods of imagination must be the universal ones. Then, trying to define his own methods of imagination in his own mind, he was evidently biassed by a strong predetermination to find them such as alone would square with his fundamental axiom—that there exist no axioms, no necessary or universal truths, or that if there are we cannot possibly know them as such.'

Sterne.—' But why should he be so bent on holding that?'

Cleveland.—' Read his essays carefully, and you will see from what point he started. Like most vehement controversialists, he began where he appeared to end. In no writer of the day is so much to be read between the lines. Clifford was not a reluctantly convinced, but a fanatically impassioned Atheist. He hated God as our friend here hates democracy, or as a modern Radical hates liberty. He saw the close connection between the idea of universal truth and the idea of an Universal Mind. He perceived that, if we allow any part of the laws of human thought to be laws of thought itself, we can in so far justify an anthropomorphic conception of God. His mathematical negations are all directed against the assumption that, if God think at all, He must to some extent think as we do. In proportion as we believe our own minds to be typical, our own methods of thought to be necessary, the idea of a personal Creator working by those methods becomes probable, or, at any rate, consistent. His object throughout was to depreciate or rather deny the validity of induction from human to universal thought, from the necessities of human conception to actual facts—seeing that human thought almost necessarily points to a God who can be called good and wise in a sense intelligible to humanity; to an Universe organised and governed by laws imposed by a supreme Intelligence.'

Sterne.—' Why do you say that he hated the thought of God ?'

Cleveland—' Because he sneered at, ridiculed, parodied it with a persistent passionate violence and bitterness in and out of season ; because his hatred blinded him to the plainest facts of history and of social life. His ferocious denunciation of a priesthood, his sympathy with persecution directed against Catholics, his idolatry of our Father Man, the bad taste of his blasphemous perversions or caricatures of Theistical phraseology, are all the errors of a man blinded by passionate animosity, not of an intellect gone astray in an earnest unbiassed search after truth. And this is the characteristic temper of modern Agnosticism. The Atheist, who took that name frankly, was content to see no God, no proof of one. The Agnostic, who has not the courage to assume an unpopular title that properly belongs to him, is passionately, enthusiastically resolute to hunt God, if not out of the Universe, certainly out of the mind and thought of Man. The Atheist of the last generation was a true Agnostic. He said that the Creator and the supposed spiritual world were simply outside of our cognizance. The Agnostic of to-day implies in every line not that we do not know of their existence, but that we know them not to exist.'

Sterne.—' The name matters very little.'

Cleveland.—' Nothing, except that it indicates the spirit.'

Lestrange.—' Well, I am an Atheist, and will not stoop to call myself an Agnostic. I have no patience with them, and have, I think, won my right to despise that want of courage, that lack of faith in their own unbelief which make them borrow or steal the language of falsehood to hide the nakedness of truth. The Christian phraseology is to my mind offensive, exaggerated, inflated, even in its proper place. In Agnostic use it would be ridiculous if it were not palpably dishonest. But I can understand strong intellectual indignation against the illusions that mislead such men as yourself and Vere; the nonsense that he believes of which no evidence should have convinced him, the mass of belief you retain after rejecting all the evidence.'

Cleveland.—' You mean that Theism has borrowed its belief from Christianity, rejecting the Christian evidence in order to get rid of the Christian theology?'

Lestrange.—' Or along with it; yes. Vere builds an edifice of falsehood, absurdity, and immorality on a foundation of solid logic if not of solid fact. You rebuild his structure in a form of grand simplicity that almost deserves to be true; but you knock the foundation from under it. You rest the Universe upon an elephant; but you deny the elephant his necessary pedestal in the tortoise.'

'Accepting his evidence,' said I, 'where is

Vere's belief absurd? I could accept the creed; it is the history that I cannot believe.'

Sterne.—' Which of the creeds?'

A.—' Well—not the Athanasian.'

Sterne.—' No, we won't debate that till we find a theologian who can understand or a sceptic who can translate it. But take the fundamental doctrine of Protestantism and of St. Paul, a doctrine certainly as well supported by the Master's own words as any other. How can Vere believe that belief is the supreme moral merit, and that he that believeth not shall be damned?'

Vere.—' You know that the last clause is of dubious authenticity; and you know, too, that the word we translate "believe" has a strong moral significance. Perhaps the strongest of the Master's own sayings in this direction is that "he that despiseth Me despiseth Him that sent me."'

'I find greater difficulty,' interposed Cleveland, ' in the preceding clause.'

Vere.—' True; because we do not know what the Apostles were or how they presented their Master.'

Lestrange.—' We know what should cure priests and preachers of quoting that text on their own behalf. Of those to whom it was applied, Judas was one, and Paul was not.'

Vere.—' Exceedingly true. I wish we all

always remembered that. But assume the Master Himself, with His credentials and the generation He addressed. Is it not fairly obvious that he who adhered to the Scribes or to Epicurus, to the gods of Egypt or Greece, or even to the Deity conceived and worshipped in the Jewish Temple, as against Him and the Father He preached, was despising not only the prophet but the Power that sent Him? Is not an intense moral darkness implied in such rejection, if we take for granted the presence of evidence sufficient to satisfy that generation that a prophet of extraordinary, unheard-of powers was before them—if we allow that His credentials were as authentic as His doctrine was transcendant?'

Cleveland.—' What did they think of His credentials?'

Vere.—' The Jews seem to have accepted them. Their answer was not, "He does not cast out devils," but "He casteth them out through Beelzebub, the prince of devils." Now what must have been the moral state of those who could attribute His doctrine and His life to Hell rather than to Heaven?'

Sterne.—' I don't see how miracles could prove the reality of claims to divine authority or direct inspiration.'

Vere.—' Perhaps not, logically. But take the

whole evidence together: the teacher of a doctrine of unrivalled moral excellence, leading a life of absolutely unselfish devotion, affirms that He has received special authority from above, and displays control over Nature, physical and spiritual, as evidence thereof. It is conceivable of course that He might possess the power without the enlightenment, as it is conceivable that the credentials of a foreign minister should be forged. But if every other particular authenticated the mission, if the envoy really seemed possessed of the mind of his Government, if, where its conduct and its views had puzzled us, he explained them in a consistent, satisfactory manner—still more if he proved himself able to dispose of its fleets and armies—should we not think it unreasonable scepticism to reject his letters because we were unacquainted with his Sovereign's seal?'

Cleveland.—' In what sense, then, do you hold that miracles vindicate a claim to Divine inspiration?'

Vere.—' A single miracle, or a single class of miracles—such, for instance, as the power of healing disease—might prove no more than extraordinary personal gifts; a general power over Nature, a power to raise the dead, to check a storm, to restore a perished sense—above all, to multiply matter—seems almost necessarily to have been specially bestowed by the Author of Nature. If the alleged ambassador puts forth these powers as credentials, declares that He did receive them from the Creator, and for the purpose of authenticating His mission, and if it be very difficult to suspect Him of deliberate lying—then I think the miracles, or rather the power to work them, a very strong confirmation of His claim.'

Cleveland.—' Sceptic as you are, Lestrange, would the miracles have made no impression on you? And is there not strong evidence for some, and especially for the very greatest of them ?'

Lestrange.—' Strong evidence, perhaps, for marvels of some kind ; evidence that the disciples believed their Master possessed of preternatural powers. Grant the miracles of healing, though they are not so clearly proved as hundreds of similar miracles, in which few educated Englishmen believe. Grant all of which we have primary or secondary evidence, all that St. Paul affirms—that is, the Resurrection, the apparition of the crucified Master to his followers on several occasions shortly after death. The last has been obviously magnified and distorted into the present doctrine of the Resurrection.'

Vere.—' Obviously ?'

Lestrange.—' Well, let me state my case, and then judge whether, if you heard the story for the first time, you would not think it a myth developed by the ignorance and superstitions of the age. With all the enlightenment of Athens and Rome, the age was, especially in Asia, thoroughly superstitious. There is abundant proof that Asiatics in general, and Jews in particular, were predisposed not merely to accept but to look for marvels of theurgy and new religious developments. Remember Apollonius; remember the expectation of the Messiah—the fierce theological fanaticism which was evidently seething in the Jewish mind from the time of the Maccabees to the fall of Jerusalem. Remember the phantasies which almost made a Messiah of Vespasian himself. The corruption of Judaism in the age of Tiberius was a soil in which myths would spring up like fungi, and grow to incredible size and monstrous shape even in a few years. Grant, if you will have it so, that one of the Gospels was written between A.D. 70 and A.D. 80. I don't believe it for a moment, but grant it. And I say that forty years would suffice for a far huger growth than that of the present bodily Resurrection out of a mere apparition. And not only it might, but we can see that it did thus grow. Note the enormous difference between the simple apparition frequently repeated—the mere ghost-story—of St. Paul, and the Resurrection and Ascension of the Gospels and the Creeds.'

Cleveland.—' It might be so; how can you see that it was so?'

Lestrange.—' Note what had been added during some twenty-five or thirty years. St. Paul tells nothing that might not be told to-day, except perhaps the apparition to five hundred Brethren at once. The story, as we find it in the Gospels, could not possibly find believers to-day; the credulity of the very ignorant would be dispelled by universal ridicule and contempt. I waive the absurd, impossible story of the guard frightened from their duty, and reporting themselves to have slept on their post. But consider the crucified, tortured frame—tortured to death, with its wounds unhealed—reanimated and able to go about as if unwounded. Consider the miracle involved in the absence of corruption in such a climate. Observe that the Resurgent is sometimes a disembodied spirit, sometimes a fleshly form. He passes through closed doors, He disappears at will; what is more marvellous, with the marks of the thorns on His brow, of the nails in hands and feet, of the spear-wound in the side, He is never seen or never recognised or noticed by the Jews. *There* is a continuous, constant miracle; fancy such a form passing unobserved through the streets of a busy city! But again, He eats and drinks, He is touched and His wounds examined. Finally, He reappears in the body in Galilee, and still with this fleshly form ascends into Heaven. Is not the last incident decisive? It is the conception of an ignorant, thoughtless peasantry; a sect composed of utterly uneducated, credulous, muddle-headed slaves and artizans, who fancy that the sky is a solid vault some four miles above their heads, beyond which lies a physical, material Paradise—a city with streets, and gates, and walls; a garden with trees, rivers, lawns, and flowers; with houses of stone to shelter the earthly body, waters wherein it may bathe, banks whereon it may rest. The idea sprang, like the tales of fairyland, from imaginations thoroughly childish. To us the idea of a physical ascent into Heaven is not impossible only, but inconceivable. But to those among whom the myth grew up it was conceivable and natural; nay, the only conceivable story, the form which St. Paul's narrative must inevitably take in their minds. To their imagination a disembodied spirit was hardly intelligible; a life that had laid aside the flesh and the senses was but a dream, a vision—a spiritual world as dreary as the Homeric Hades.'

Vere was silent, and Lestrange presently turned to Cleveland.

'And you, Cleveland, who would I think give

everything except your conscience and your self-respect to believe, would the miracles have convinced you? What would they have proved? Are you one of those, not a few of whom I have heard wish earnestly that they had lived in that age, could have seen and interrogated the Master, could have witnessed with their own eyes the marvels they cannot accept on report?'

'Yes,' replied Cleveland, slowly and thoughtfully, 'I could have wished to see the miracles; that multiplication of matter especially which seems to me more incredible, so to speak, than the restoration of the dead. But the miracles could never have satisfied me; could, at most, have impressed me with the gifts, perhaps the superhuman authority of one who wielded so unparalleled a power over Nature. But what I would fain have seen, have known, is not the works, but the man. The miracles could not prove Him incapable either of deception or self-deception. There is nothing in preternatural power, in superhuman influence over Nature that necessarily implies superhuman virtue. Let the miracles be ever so real, they indicate rather the magician than the prophet. Prove what they may, they do not prove His truth or His wisdom. They might be genuine, and He none the less an impostor. But to have known Him for three years, and not to know whether He were true or false, sane or self-deceived—*that* were impossible.'

Vere.—' Do you doubt it now ?'

Cleveland.—' Doubt His veracity, or His sanity? No. So little, that, if even now I could ask the questions which I wonder that His disciples never put, I think I should be satisfied; but, in their place, knowing Him as they did, assurance would be perfect.'

Lestrange.—' And your questions ?'

Cleveland.—' How did He know? Had He seen the Father face to face? Had He heard from the still small Voice the truth He taught? Or was it spoken only to His conscience as to ours, if in far clearer, stronger tones? Had He seen the Heaven He promised, the Hell He threatened? In one word, could He give a reason, a proof, though it rested only on His own word, of His mission; explain in what sense He called Himself the Son of God ?'

Lestrange.—'And you would have believed Him ?'

Cleveland.—' I think so. His was a nature that must have been transparent, in so far as it was human; one of which none who had known Him well could be in doubt.'

Vere.—' Then why press your questions? Why not be content with what He has told you ?'

Cleveland.—'Simply because, till He tells me how He knew it, I doubt whether He knew it at all. That He was mistaken upon points of fact seems to me all but certain; and He who believed in demoniacal possession, who was all but certainly deceived when he seemed to recognize the presence of Satan, might be equally deceived when he heard from within the Voice of God.'

A.—'You have a craving for something like Mahomet's assurance, the actual audible Voice of Gabriel, the midnight journey through the Heavens?'

Cleveland.—'If you choose so to put it. Mahomet's account of his inspiration convinces me that he was not inspired. Another might have given an account thereof which would have borne the stamp of truth as strongly as the Koran bears the brand of falsehood on its face.'

Sterne.—'It may be. At any rate most, probably all, disbelievers disbelieve the miracles. But, putting those apart, what is your view of the sense attached by St. Paul and by his Master to the doctrine of condemnation for unbelief? They did lay a great, almost a paramount, stress on the word sometimes translated "faith" and sometimes "belief."'

Vere.—'Yes. I was dealing with the negative,

the condemnation sometimes apparently passed on those who reject Him. But I do not think we are entitled, much less obliged, to attach that condemnation to all who in any age should reject the essentials of Christianity along with and because of the external falsehood in which they might be involved, overlaid, concealed. I see no reason to think that either the Apostle or his Master held *extra Ecclesiam nulla salus;* and even that arrogant phrase does not mean *extra Ecclesiam universa perditio.* Remember that the Catholic Church does not hold that doctrine in the Protestant form, does not damn those who reject, but only those who apostatize from the truth. She pronounces on the final perdition of no soul but that of Iscariot. She allows for "invincible ignorance," a term wide enough to cover all the honest reasons for which the truth may be rejected by those to whom it is imperfectly or unconvincingly presented.'

Sterne.—' Yes; but that loophole proves the existence of the wall. If the Master had not apparently excluded unbelievers from Heaven, the charity of the Church would not have been tasked to provide a side entrance for them.'

Vere.—' You forget that the Church took the canon of Scripture as it stands, with the doubtful termination of St. Mark. And again, though unquestionably the word translated "damned" carries with it the sense of condemnation, I question whether, at least in the Gospels, it bears the technical sense it has in theology. Its proper meaning is "judged;" and every truth, a great religious truth above all, does in some sense judge those to whom it is presented for acceptance or rejection.'

Sterne.—' Still, if Christ Himself or St. Paul did not expressly condemn unbelief as the unpardonable sin, they did treat belief as the highest of all merits, the passport to salvation.'

Vere.—' Well, accept my rendering of that assertion. They regarded faith as the passport to the Kingdom of Heaven.'

Sterne.—' I hardly see the difference.'

Vere.—' Salvation with them did not mean escape from everlasting fire. The Kingdom of Heaven for them existed on earth as well as beyond the grave. It was a moral paradise into which men could enter here, to remain therein for ever, as well as an external brotherhood, militant here and triumphant in Heaven. Faith—personal devotion to Christ as the visible, intelligible incarnation, representation of the Father—was naturally the first essential all-embracing condition of admission therein. I take the doctrine as a whole to be this. Absolute trust in, obedience to, devotion to God—all, and something more than all, that is meant by loyalty to such an earthly sovereign as the Arthur or Charlemagne of poetry—is the essence of religion, the foundation of morality. No external code can supersede this; and this given, an external code is hardly needed. But the Deity Himself is neither perceptible nor intelligible to human senses, to human minds. What He is in His relation to Man we see in His incarnate Son; and to Him our religious fealty is accordingly due. That fealty, including trust, self-surrender, self-sacrifice rather than mere belief—"the devils also believe and tremble"—is the spirit, the life, the way. He who has that has everything else; he who lacks that may struggle hard to keep the Law, may fight his way through the darkness till, like the lawyer of the Gospel, he is not far from the Kingdom of Heaven; but, after all, till he has gained the faith in question, he is less than the least of those who through that faith have really entered the Kingdom.'

Cleveland.—'Does that doctrine seem nonsense, Sterne?'

Sterne was silent.

'Sound sense, but very unsound theology,' replied Lestrange. 'And how about the rich man?'

Vere.—'Christianity has made it possible for the cable to pass through the needle's eye. But consider what the life, what the position of a rich man under the Roman despotism and without the guidance of Christian charity must have been; what temptations to vice, sensuality, selfishness, what absence of all humanizing, softening influences; what use any one of us so brought up would probably have made of wealth; and then say whether the metaphor was so greatly exaggerated. Remember that there were rich men among the disciples. Neither Zaccheus nor Joseph of Arimathea was called on to give all his goods to the poor.'

Sterne.—'But you must admit your Master to have been a very unsound political economist, if not a Communist.'

Vere.—'I could prove, I think, in five minutes that neither He nor His disciples were Communists. They preached alms-giving; but in those days I suspect there were few "sturdy beggars." The misery of the poor and the selfishness of the rich were such that there was no need to insist on judicious limitations of liberality. But the appointment of deacons, carefully studied, indicates an anxiety on the part of the early Church that her alms should be properly distributed. Take Christ's maxims fairly and as a whole, apply them to the state of society with which He had to deal, qualify them simply by the changed circumstances of our own race, climate, and age, and I believe that every one of them will be found sound and practicable; unless we hold that He really forbade forcible resistance to wrong for ever and on principle. Remember, we are directed as Christians to look to the spirit and not to the letter, to consider not the outward act but the inward temper that is commanded or forbidden.'

'And the casting out devils?' enquired Lestrange.

'That,' said Vere, 'is the one thing I cannot pretend to explain to my own satisfaction. If that were your sole difficulty, how long would it keep you without the pale?'

CHAPTER III.

CHANCE OR CREATION.

'WELL,' interposed Cleveland, 'is it my turn yet? Are you satisfied that Vere's Christianity is not untenable nonsense?'

Lestrange.—' I thought his creed was Christian, and therefore absurd; I find that it is neither. But for you, you have borrowed all that you believe from him, and swept away all the ground on which he or any other man has a right to believe it.'

Cleveland.—'You forget that there were Theists before Christ, and even before Moses. Historically as well as logically, God existed and reigned in the thoughts of men before prophets claimed to derive authority from Him. Inspiration assumes, takes for granted, the inspiring Power; each founder of a religion has built on foundations laid in the conscience and convictions of men.'

Lestrange.—' Granted. But in every case the religion-maker sweeps into oblivion that preexisting conception from which he borrows. Socrates derived his Gods from pre-Homeric poets whose Zeus was the blue vault of Heaven. Christ and Mahomet borrowed from Moses, as you from them; and Moses elevated some local tribe idol into a supreme, but hardly a sole, Deity.'

Cleveland.—' It would be a very long and very tedious matter to ascertain how much truth there is in your assertions. No doubt each successive teacher has improved on the conception of the Deity which he found existing in his time. What of that ?'

Sterne.—' Ay; but Lestrange's objection goes further and deeper. He denies your right to a God whose existence and attributes you take from a creed of which you deny the authority. Moses or his disciples say, "There is a God who spoke on Sinai, and made a covenant in the tent of Abraham." Christ says, "There is a Father, of whom I am the Son and visible image." Mohammed says, "There is a God whose angel Gabriel came to dictate the Koran." How do you know there is a God? Each of these answers the question in his own way, and those who accept his answer must believe in his Deity. But you deny the authority; you affirm that God never lunched with Abraham, talked face to face or back to back with Moses; that Christ never saw the Father; that Mohammed was an epileptic, if not an impostor. You say in every case the God of these men was an illusion.'

Cleveland.—' No, by no means.'

Sterne.—' The God in whom they believed was an illusion. At least, all they know of Him, all their grounds for believing in Him, as they have given them, were utter deceptions. Why, then, and by what right do you, who deny the evidence, insist on retaining the verdict?'

Cleveland.—' Because the verdict was not given upon the evidence; the evidence was framed to justify and strengthen a verdict pronounced by the universal conviction of mankind. As you yourself admit, every one of these arch-prophets found a Deity already established in the popular conscience and conviction. Whence came that?'

Lestrange.—' Your God is not the one they found, but the one they invented, or successively developed.'

Cleveland.—' We believe that the God of all is the same, more and more clearly seen as mankind became more capable of distinguishing instinctively the higher from the lower views of His nature; discerned most clearly in each generation by those who spiritually were most in advance of their age.'

Sterne.—' But your God is not, has nothing to do with, the God who was before Abraham. Look back to the foundation of this universal belief, and it is one we know to be false. The primitive Deity is a personification of natural forces, a plural Deity to begin with. Wind, fire, sea, all forces not incarnate in living creatures, and therefore embodied by man's imagination in human shape, or at least endowed with human thought and feeling—these are the first Gods. As these are found to be more or less closely connected, independent Gods are blended, till we get the Elohim of Scripture, a plural noun with a singular grammatical construction. And at last these are identified with the Power which, after ages of sun and star worship, is supposed to have made the sun and stars. You know, then, how your Deity has been invented, or rather has grown up in the fancy of man. You know Him to be the development of an idea originally false as well as barbaric, an idea which has not become true by being refined and civilized. At what point has truth come in, or where do you find authority for believing that all these successive false prophets have blundered on one and the same truth ?'

Vere.—' You remember Napoleon's "You may talk as you please, gentlemen, but who made all that?"'

Lestrange.—' Why should "all that" have been made? Why not have grown like a tree, which it resembles much more than it resembles any of those human structures from the analogy of which you reason that it must have an intelligent constructor?'

Cleveland.—'No doubt it has grown, as did the tree, by law; and the law had a law-giver. I need not repeat my argument* that, as we know the existing Universe must have had a beginning in time, there must have been a date at which the law of its growth was first impressed upon it from without. But I should like to insist a little more fully on the marvellous evidences, not merely of order, but of design, of the adaptation of order to a remote purpose, that seems to me so forcibly to indicate an intelligent foreseeing Designer. The more one thinks over the extremely complicated character of that adaptation to which Darwin ascribes the gradual evolution of the immense variety of existence, the less does it seem possible to accept the idea that all this adaptation is the work of mere chance. I know the Evolutionists would

* 'The Devil's Advocate,' vol. 2, p. 219.

not allow the word; but it does fairly represent not the method, but the origin of the method in which they believe. But accept their doctrine to the full, admit the utmost that their extremest *doctrinaires* pretend not to demonstrate, but to hope that posterity may one day demonstrate. Allow them more than this—given that Evolution, which I must call fortuitous, accounts for everything that on their principles it could possibly have produced—is there not something in the order of Creation which it could not have evolved? Variation and Natural Selection, the correlation of parts, are by the essential nature of their action confessedly limited to contemporaneous influence. They can work upon the present, they can use the materials furnished by the past; but they cannot look forward a single step, they cannot provide for the future. Now, is it or is it not the case that such provision for the future has been made?'

Sterne.—'I should say not. But let us see clearly what you mean.'

Cleveland.—' Wallace points out that in the formation of Man himself there are indications of foresight, of a provision for something not to be realised for ages; that Man, the first man, was endowed with powers, potentialities, that he did not want and could not use for thousands of generations. The brain of the rudest man is nearer that of the philosopher than the brain of the ape; the life, the intellectual needs of the primitive man—if, as Evolutionists teach, the primitive man was something lower than the lowest existing savage—are far nearer those of the ape than those of a Newton or a Cuvier, or even an average Anglo-Saxon gentleman of this nineteenth century. The primitive man, then, was endowed with a brain pre-adapted to the wants of civilization, a brain capable of becoming as soon as opportunity offered that of civilized humanity. More than that, every modification of his structure, if it took place piecemeal, by tiny steps, as Evolutionists teach, must have been for the moment a disadvantage. The half-developed man, not yet standing fully erect, not yet capable of trapping, hunting, taming animals, making weapons, using fire, but deprived of the ape's use of the foot, of the ape's arboreal skill and habits and of the ape's hairy covering, was an inferior animal to the ourang-outang or the gorilla. He was in process of adaptation to something foreseen as higher. In a word, he is unintelligible, unmeaning, contradictory to the whole scheme of Evolution, unless as the intended, foreseen, designed embryo of the civilized man. Not only so; the world was pre-adapted to Man and to civilization. He was not brought into it till multitudes of creatures with whom he could not have contended had been extirpated. He was preserved apart—one must suppose in some land as completely isolated as was till lately the Australian continent—till he had developed skill, courage, powers that could resist the destructive might of the tiger, the lion, the elephant, the rhinoceros; that could baffle the serpent, could tame the canine and bovine races, could hunt down the deer. The earth was clothed with forests, but with forests adapted to his use, forests of an order far superior to those of a former age, forests affording timber as well as fuel. Civilized man would in time have denuded the soil of these, and might probably have done so in many parts before he discovered the fatal consequences, and learnt to replace them; he might have made the whole earth a desert, as he has made parts of it—but that the forests of former ages, not then fit for his use, had been buried for millions of years, and by that burial converted into the most useful form of fuel. Not only had the races with which he could not have contended been swept away, but those he needed had been produced and during ages adapted to his use. Had Man come into being while the great Saurians dominated the earth and the waters, he must have been annihilated. Had he

F

been contemporary with the earlier pachyderms, whole stages of his progress to civilization would have been impracticable. He was reserved for the time when the beasts he could not tame had dwindled, and those he could tame had grown to serviceable form, size, and variety; till the surface of the earth itself had been also, in a sense, tamed and subdued to his use. The same foresight may be discerned, I think, even in the history of human races; in the isolation of some, the extirpation of others, the preservation, first by separation then by collision, of those, by no means always the highest at the time, which were capable of the highest ultimate development. Evolution could by no means have adapted the world to Man—could hardly even have adapted Man to the world—as has been actually done.'

Sterne.—' I think you lay far too much stress on what may have been, perhaps was, mere coincidence. But I don't want to discuss the evidences of design now. My point is that on evidences of supposed design—that is, on the discovery in Nature of something seemingly analogous to human design—you have built an inference utterly unwarrantable, an anthropomorphic Designer. You cannot reason out your God by any tenable process of logic from this basis, even if we admitted it to the full.'

Ida.—' Does not design imply a designer?'

Sterne.—' In verbal logic, yes, Mrs. Cleveland; but verbal logic is always liable to fallacies. We must not take words for things. What we see is pre-adaptation—not the mere suitability of two coincident and interdependent things, but their gradual adaptation to one another before they came to operate on each other. At least, that is what your husband claims, and what I admit for the sake of the argument. *We* pre-adapt only by design, by a careful study, consideration of the objects we intend to effect and of the means by which we can make the laws of Nature accomplish them. But because this is our only experience of pre-adaptation, because *we* can only attain certain ends by design, we have no right to infer that the attainment of similar ends, even by somewhat analogous methods, must be the result of thought like ours exerted by a Being somewhat like ourselves. We have no right to infer design, or consciousness, or personality from such evidences, any more than to infer a brain or a hand.'

Ida.—' But as we know and can conceive of no such thing as unconscious design, hardly undesigned pre-adaptation, are we not forced to that inference?'

Lestrange.—' I should say not, Mrs. Cleveland, even if your negation were absolutely true. We have no right to reason from one case to all, from one example of a designing pre-adapting Being to universal necessities, absolute essential conditions of design or pre-adaptation throughout the Universe. If Man be the only pre-adapting being we know, that gives us no right to infer that every pre-adapting Power in the Universe must resemble Man in any given particular. If we infer personality, why not corporeality; if consciousness, why not a nervous system—especially as the supposed pre-adaptor may not work as we do under laws pre-imposed by an independent Power?'

A.—'In short, design means merely man's method of adapting, or rather of inducing natural forces to adapt, independent things to one another. We know no other case of adaptation, but there may be millions in the universe, and each of them utterly unlike ours?'

Sterne.—'But we do. Bees, beavers, birds, insects of all kinds, adapt most skilfully, most accurately; often—or at any rate sometimes—to results they will never see. Their adaptation, at least in the last case, can hardly be intelligent, is probably not conscious. We can, then, conceive of unconscious adaptation, for we see it, at any rate in the case of creatures which build a home and store it with food for the young they will never behold.'

Ida.—'No. We can conceive no other origin for the unconscious adaptation of the insects' cell to the life of an offspring it will never see, but either its own memory, which makes the adaptation conscious, or the guidance of an instinct implanted by One who has planned the result.'

Sterne.—'We may not be able to conceive—that is, to understand—how the wasp's instinct works, how it was brought to work. But we see that *there* is a design quite as striking as anything so called in Nature, but unconscious on the part of the immediate designer. Why may not the Power that has adapted Man to Nature have worked rather as the wasp works than as man does?'

Cleveland.—'You can hardly imagine the lower Power creating, governing, providing for the higher.'

Sterne.—'How do we know that conscious is superior to unconscious action? One of the greatest, most general objects of human effort is to turn conscious into unconscious action, to teach the child or the soldier to do unconsciously, by force of habit, what at first had to be done by conscious exertion.'

Ida.—'Yes, because conscious effort is so difficult a thing, so precious a resource that we wish to economise it, to reserve it for the highest purposes.'

Cleveland.—' " A Creator unconscious of creating!" A most complicated, elaborate, perfect system of machinery working together in all its parts, self-constructed, or constructed by a Power that did not know what it was doing! Is it possible to believe, to conceive such a thing?'

Sterne.—' It sounds, it looks absurd, because it is so utterly contrary to our own experience. But it accords more or less with the experience of other creatures: and, if there were nothing like it within the reach of our senses, it would still be monstrous to infer that all action throughout the Universe must resemble the patterns of the Earth; that there can be no minds utterly, essentially different from ours—no operations resembling those of our minds accomplished by what we could not understand or should not speak of as mind at all.'

Lestrange.—' But you may carry the argument further and deeper. Admit that adaptation proves design, design intelligence; there you must stop. All that Cleveland's evidence, accepted as he puts it, goes to prove, all that his own argument even indicates, is an Intelligence somewhere that, somehow, has had something to do with the arrangement of this world, perhaps of the Universe. From this you leap the stupendous gulf to a God closely resembling the God and Father of Jesus Christ; a personal, manlike, benevolent, beneficent, sympathising Being, watching, guiding, co-operating with, rewarding, punishing His human creatures. We guess at the shadow of a Demiurgus, and you infer the full portrait of a Jehovah as clearly, distinctly, personally known to us as St. Francis Xavier or St. Bernard.'

Cleveland.—' No. I infer Providence from totally different considerations.'

Lestrange.—' Aye; but what right have you to identify the human Providence with the universal Demiurgus? Both are guesses from one point of contact only. You fill-in all the features of each from your imagination, and blend the two together.'

Ida.—' Surely both, at any rate, display infinite power, infinite goodness, infinite wisdom? It is difficult to conceive two such Beings in one Universe.'

Lestrange.—' I don't know, considering how different the supposed spheres. But I deny all the three attributes. Infinite power need not have recourse to design; infinite goodness would hardly work out its ends through such infinite vice and suffering, and infinite wisdom would not have made such a mess of the whole, such a multitude of mistakes in detail. Nothing in the Universe is perfect, and many of Nature's most striking achievements contrast unfavourably with what Man has even now accomplished. Do you know that a great scientist said of the human eye, "If any optician sent me such an instrument I should send it back, and tell him that he had yet to learn the rudiments of his business"?'

Mrs. Cleveland seemed pained and startled: and Lestrange, observing this, ceased somewhat abruptly, with the first of what might have been a long list of instances.

Cleveland.—'You forget that the eye is not merely a telescopic lens; it has other work to do, other conditions to fulfil. No optician could replace the simplest, most rudimentary eye that God has given to the meanest of His creatures. And if Evolution have done much to endanger theology, it has answered once and for ever the argument from imperfection. Nothing is meant to be perfect; only all to approach by very, very slow steps more and more nearly to perfection.'

Lestrange.—'Aye; but such is not the method of a perfect artificer.'

Cleveland.—'How can you tell that, till you know what his object was? If that object were moral, not physical, and the effort more important than the attainment, your whole argument, with all the thousand examples by which you would have reinforced it, falls to the ground.'

Sterne and Vero had left us, and Lestrange, fatigued and drowsy, had sunk into silence and apparent reverie.

'How is it,' I asked Cleveland, 'that such arguments make so little impression? Logically, I think, Sterne and Lestrange have overthrown your case as a Theist more completely than Vero answered their case against Christianity. And yet I don't suppose either you or I will think to-morrow otherwise than as we thought yesterday upon the subject. How is it that, on these topics, no proof seems to convince anybody; that you hardly find—what, if logic governed our conclusions, as I suppose it ought, should be so common—a convinced Atheist who would give everything in this world to recover his belief in God; or an educated sceptic converted to Christianity by force of evidence?'

This roused Lestrange for a moment.

'Men believe,' he said, 'because they will, disbelieve because they must. But in either case the force of contradiction and the habit of controversy enlist their temper in the service of their creed.'

He sank back into silence, and, after a pause of some minutes, Cleveland replied :

'That is true, but not the truth. Probably no man would be converted to the Thirty-nine

Articles by dint of dry reasoning. But, once led to accept Christianity by evidence, and the Church of England from taste, he would identify the two so thoroughly that he could not separate them again in his own mind, much less in arguing with others. We believe what we are educated to believe; even when we yield that belief to force of argument, it is seldom to the arguments we allege in justification of the change. Conversion, outside the scope of scientific demonstration, is generally gradual and in great measure insensible. Lastly, I doubt if any of us know exactly why we believe anything.'

A.—'Then our belief is worth nothing.'

Cleveland.—'Not necessarily. We must believe something, and something must be true. The inference is that a man's judgment is worth more, counts for more, than his arguments; that the authority of a really sound careful thinker is worth far more than his reasoning, however powerful that may be. He has reached his conclusions, probably, partly by instinct, partly by a process of inference half the steps of which he has forgotten before he reached the end. He simply cannot give us his method; what is of weight is the conclusion attained by a mind whose workings we know to be on the whole sounder and clearer than our own.'

A.—'Then do you believe in God because you were taught to do so? Surely such a belief is worth nothing, being mere matter of chance; and as you must be conscious that it is worth nothing, it can hardly be real belief.'

Cleveland.—'No, that is not exactly the truth. My belief may be worth nothing: the belief of the human race is worth a good deal, unless you can see how they came to believe a lie. "I believe because I do" is justly called a woman's reason when given by an individual: when given by mankind at large it is perhaps the strongest of all possible reasons. Then it means "I being man believe because, being man, I could not do otherwise."'

Again Lestrange woke up.

'I have heard you say that the majority are nearly always wrong. Multiply nothing by a thousand millions, it remains nothing. The creed of one fool does not acquire value if it become the creed of all the other fools in creation: it has the *minus* sign before it still.'

Once more there was silence, which Cleveland presently broke again, in a tone more hesitating than usual.

'If it were true that human belief in an unseen Power were merely the personification of natural forces, then the almost universal human belief in a Deity might, probably would, be as worthless as your logic pronounces it. But it is not a case of the belief of fools traced to some palpable folly; the belief is more universal than that tendency to personification to which it is ascribed. That tendency is, I think, but one form of an universal instinct; and the instinct does not, as on Lestrange's theory it should, grow weaker with civilization and enlightenment. On the contrary, it is, as a natural instinct should be, indefinite and comparatively undeveloped in the feeblest, shallowest order of minds; it is rudimentary among what we may call the rudimentary races, it gains force and clearness among the higher. It is accepted with a wonderful facility, a facility which at least indicates its adaptation to the whole tone of natural human thought, by all. Those who *can* reason themselves out of it are a minority; those to whom the belief is not much more natural than the disbelief are very few indeed.'

A.—' Would you say, then, that you believe because you think the Creator has implanted an instinctive belief in His own existence in human nature at large ?'

Cleveland.—' No. I believe because I cannot help it. I believe as I might feel sure in the dark that my wife, though silent and motionless, was in the room with me. But if all external reasoning and evidence went to contradict that belief, I might be persuaded that it was erroneous; as, searching round and speaking without finding her or obtaining an answer, I might feel satisfied that my instinctive sense of her presence had deceived me. Our logical arguments are edifying, not fundamental; defences put up to protect the natural growth. When they are destroyed the plant is more open to attack, to injury, but its life is in no wise dependent on or derived from them. Evidence from various quarters confirms my belief. I find that the idea of God explains mysteries of creation, of external nature, of human life, of personal experience that no other theory accounts for so well. Now many of the strongest, most assured convictions of philosophers and scientists rest precisely on this kind of reasoning. We have been accustomed to account for half a dozen different series of phenomena in different natural spheres by distinct theories. We find one hypothesis which will explain them all, which reconciles differences or apparent contradictions, and simplifies complicated explanations. A hypothesis which does this in two or three distinct fields of speculation is accepted with almost implicit confidence. And with reason. The chance that an explanation of one case is false, though satisfactory, may be two or three to one. Two or three keys may fit one lock. But the chance that one falsehood should satisfactorily explain two independent facts is very small. The chances against its explaining three or four are so great as almost to amount to certainty.'

Ida.—' In short, your reasons are not the reasons why you believe, but why you ought to believe ?'

Cleveland.—' Evidences of title, not the origin of the right.'

CHAPTER IV.

THE PARADOX OF POSITIVISM.

ON another occasion Merton, the Agnostic and Positivist, had joined our party. Our talk had turned chiefly upon the politics of the day, and from thence had diverged to the electioneering scandals exposed by recent investigation.

Sterne.—' You must, I think, admit one merit in democracy; it tends to do away with corruption.'

Cleveland.—' Quite the reverse. England has for a century seen no corruption comparable to that of America, from the installation of Lincoln to that of Hayes.'

Sterne.—' How do you account for that? You will say, of course, that American statesmen are corrupt because they are poor and are not gentlemen. But why is their corruption tolerated, condoned by the populace which suffers by it?'

Cleveland.—' For two reasons. First, the populace don't feel: The whole amount known or believed to be directly stolen hardly increases appreciably the weight of taxation; and a large proportion of the voters scarcely feel taxation at all. That this last is a real reason you see in the case of New York. Corruption there was carried further, was more open, more shameless, than anywhere else, because the taxation fell on the rich, and the Many were content to see the rich Few plundered for the benefit, not of themselves, but of their like. The voters from the courts, alleys and garrets of the Empire City were well content to see the heavy taxation of the Fifth Avenue increased to make fortunes for men who had emerged from the courts and alleys themselves. Secondly, I take it, the mass of Americans felt that, in the position and with the opportunities of Grant's Ministers, Congressmen and contractors, they would themselves have been at least equally corrupt.'

Sterne.—' Well, democratic governments may be corrupt; they will always tend to be so till democracies can make up their minds to pay salaries proportionate to the incomes of those with whom their rulers mix in society. But I was speaking of the wider, more extensive influence that poisons the source, not the extremities; of the political system that corrupts electors by the hundred or the thousand, not a few fortunate legislators and contractors. Democracy abolishes that.'

Cleveland.—' Yes; you can poison a pond, but not an ocean.'

Sterne.—' Well, it is worth all the evils you ascribe to democracy to get rid of that rottenness and dishonesty.'

' Why is bribery wrong ?' interposed Lestrange. ' It is nonsense to talk of corrupting the electors of Deal and Sandwich. It is contrary to fact to speak of bribing men to vote against their convictions. Either they have no convictions, or they take a bribe from their own side, or they take bribes from both sides and vote for that in which they believe. And the worst cant of all is that which acquits the extortioners and raves at those who submit to extortion, which pardons those who sell their trust and damns those who buy support for truth. As well blame a prince for enlisting mercenaries to defend his country from invasion !'

Sterne.—' One pardons the corrupt elector on account of his ignorance. He knows not what he does. The candidate or the agent is a party to the crime, knowing it to be one.'

Lestrange.—' He knows nothing of the sort; nor do I. Here are five hundred men who have no opinions, and no right to any. The law gives them great power to injure their country: I give them five shillings a head to serve her. Where is the sin?'

Sterne.—'You give them money not to serve their country, but to put you into Parliament.'

Lestrange.—'That may be true of the candidate, though not always. But men bribe out of their own pockets for the candidate of their party—that is, for what they believe to be the public interest.'

Sterne.—But they are encouraging, they are accomplices in, a breach of trust.'

Lestrange.—'I don't see it. It is clear that the bribe does not induce anybody to vote against his conscience or his convictions. The bribed voter is not capable of judging between Tory and Liberal. He sees two respectable gentlemen, either of them equally fit, in his opinion, to legislate for the country; one of whom will give him five shillings, the other seven shillings. He can see no higher interest at stake; why should he not be guided by his own?'

Cleveland.—'Clearly, because the vote is a trust to be exercised for the public interest.'

Sterne.—'Then he has no right to vote at all.'

Lestrange.—'But the law says he has. Democracy has enfranchised hundreds of thousands who understand much better the merits of Bass's and Alsop's beer than those of Beaconsfield or Gladstone. Surely it is a right and patriotic thing to bribe men not to injure their country, as it would be a right thing to bribe men not to torture animals, to buy off captives from torture or slavery?'

Cleveland.—' It can never be right to break the law.'

Lestrange.—' True. I am glad to think that you have there some sort of basis for a moral code, when, as will soon happen if Agnosticism become fashionable, there is no other left.'

Sterne.—' Do you really believe, then, that duty depends on Deity? Did God make right and wrong, and could He unmake them? If so, it is absurd to speak of Him as good, since good is simply His will. If to be good in man is merely to obey the will of God, then goodness in God merely means pleasing Himself.'

Cleveland.—' So it does in good men. God is good because it pleases Him to benefit His creatures.'

Sterne.—' Then the man who pleases to benefit his fellow-creatures is good, whether God exists or not?'

Lestrange.—' Yes; but why should a man be good, if there be no God to whom he owes a duty?'

Sterne.—' He owes it to his fellow-men, as you have just implied that God owes it to His creatures.'

Lestrange.—'Not at all. I did not make men, and should have been heartily ashamed of them if I had. I am not responsible for them or to them. They have done nothing for me; why should I suffer, deny myself or labour for their advantage?'

Sterne.—' And why should you to please God?'

Cleveland.—' For one reason, obviously—because He can and will punish me if I don't.'

Sterne.—' A very poor and miserable reason !'

Cleveland.—' But practical, which no motive that ignores God is. And more, much more than mere fear of Hell or Purgatory is involved in it. Against Divine justice I have no pride, no sense of self-respect, no feeling of resentment or contempt as for a human tribunal, to support me. My conscience sides with Him.'

Merton.—' So, if there be no God, conscience will punish him who serves or disserves man.'

Lestrange.—' No God, no conscience.'

Merton.—' How so?'

Lestrange.—' Without God, what is conscience? What do you make of it?'

Merton—' Religion and morality are both independent of a personal Deity—Religion as loyalty to the highest ideal we can form; Conscience, fidelity to our own sense of right.'

Cleveland.—' And what is right?'

Merton.—' That which will advance the interests of humanity. Man the future, the highest possible development of mankind, is a sufficient object of worship and service. Man, after all, made Jehovah in his image, after his likeness; and God is merely our ideal of humanity as it might and ought to be.'

Lestrange.—' And never will or can.'

Merton.—' Why not?'

Cleveland.—' Well, for two reasons. First, because man is so essentially selfish that all improvement, all great achievement, all progress physical and even moral, is due to self-interest; all civilization has been achieved by men aiming at wealth, or fame, or power. Secondly, because while God is patient because eternal, man and mankind are and must be impatient because their time is short. Your deified humanity has, after all, but a very limited time to exist, and there is no reason to suppose that its deification will be accomplished before its race is run.'

Ida.—' What do you mean?'

Cleveland.—' One of the best founded tenets of the new school is that not only the existence of the world, but that of life on its surface, and that of each individual species, is confined within narrow and successively narrower limits. Say that the earth may have a separate existence of a thousand œons; it is inhabited only for a hundred, being at first too hot and at last too cold; and of this last period human history covers at most a tenth. Mankind as well as men is mortal and short-lived. Man has not time for indefinite progress before the date when he will be called on to contend for mere existence against the adverse influences doomed to extirpate him.'

Merton.—' At any rate, in the course of a thousand or ten thousand generations, humanity may well be ennobled, exalted to an excellence of which we can form no conception at present.'

Cleveland.—' I don't believe it. The noblest men of to-day are not nobler than Socrates, Pericles, or Hannibal, and the average of mankind scarcely improve at all.'

Merton.—' Historic time has been so short compared with that which remains to work out the destinies of Man.'

Cleveland.—' It may be so. But your religion, even if we grant that it might, never will influence men. The existence of your ideal Humanity will always seem at least as dubious as the existence of a personal God; and as many have found a personal God too distant, too indefinite for their worship except as represented by a human and incarnate Divinity, so your ideal Humanity, even if we could believe in it, is too remote to affect our lives, to be the object of devotion or even of interest. What do we, the best of us, practically care for mankind at large? How much does any of us feel the news that a wave has swept away a hundred thousand families in a remote province of India or China? Would any one of us feel the submergence of the Celestial Empire, nearly two-fifths of mankind, as we should feel the destruction of half our own parish, kinsmen and neighbours, by a pestilence?'

Merton.—' We ought; and it is only the imperfect cultivation of our sympathies and our imagination that prevents us from so feeling.'

Cleveland.—' Are you sure of that from thought, or for want of thought? You take it for granted? Exactly; so every man does till he is led to think it out. Now—is it not possible, is it not eminently probable, that the limitation of our imagination and consequently of our sympathy is a necessity of our finite nature? May it not be that our feelings are strong only when concentrated, and would be weakened by diffusion? that we have but a certain stock of sympathy, a certain capacity of feeling, and if we spread it over a vast surface it would become shallow and dilute? We feel for our own household more than for the whole population of China; if we felt alike for all, should we feel for each of four hundred million Chinese as for our own children—or, that being obviously impossible, would not the result be that we should care no more for our children than for Chinamen?'

Lestrange.—' As matter of calculation, obviously the latter. The affection that really warms a single hearth would be utterly imperceptible if divided among millions.'

Cleveland.—' Positivism should take that danger into account. If distinction of faith, race, and speech are to be swept away as narrowing—if Cosmopolitan Humanity is to supersede patriotism, and the Commune to absorb the family—will not the result be that our sympathy will be too dilute to have any effect at all?—shall we not combine absolute practical selfishness with a decorous pity, an ephemeral show of black gloves and hat-bands, for all the griefs of others? If we are not to feel the destruction of ten of our own familiar friends more than that of ten thousand Hindoos or Chinese, a thousand Frenchmen or Germans, shall we not sink into contented indifference to all three? Such seems to me a probable result of all attempts to set up universal Humanity as an object of professed devotion; and sure am I that such philosophic hardening would do more to render us egotistic and unsympathising than the Religion of Humanity could do to soften and humanise us.'

Sterne.—' But Christianity itself aims at merging patriotism and local narrowness in care for Christians at large.'

Cleveland.—' Yes: and in proportion as Christendom has extended Christian sympathy has grown feeble and vague. While the Church was a limited, close, mutually dependent body, a minority in the midst of a hostile majority, common Christianity was the strongest of all ties. As Christianity became the common profession of distant nations it gradually ceased to be a tie between man and man. And since Christianity has ceased to be opposed to any formidable rival religion, since there has been no great Mahometan or Heathen power capable of threatening Christendom, even such common Christian sentiment as existed in the Middle Ages has ceased to be felt. Even the vulgar parlance distinguishes not between Christian and Heathen but between Christian and brute. Humanity is too big to be an object of intense sympathy or passionate devotion.'

Sterne.—' God is much greater.'

Vere.—' Aye; but God can come near to each individual, can be realised by each soul as a sympathising Person as close as a brother. Humanity can by no possibility be nearer to us than the average man, remote from us as that average man must ever be.'

Lestrange.—' And contemptible. I cannot care, and I don't believe that any one will or practically does care, for a future humanity which neither he nor any one he now loves will ever see. What interest we have in the future of mankind depends on a sort of instinct by which we fancy ourselves as members, or at least spectators, of a future generation happier than our own. As we realise the certainty of our personal extinction within a few years, the extinction of our children, grand-children, all in whom we are personally and immediately interested, within a few more, we shall cease to carry our interest further.'

Sterne.—'Cleveland said once that infidels were as bigoted and intolerant as believers. Let me say in return that believers should not imitate the vice they impute to Agnostics—disbelieve in the sincerity of feelings they do not share. If our argument is to be worth anything, you must give Agnostics credit for thorough earnestness in that devotion to the future of Humanity which they profess, even if you cannot share or understand it.'

Cleveland.—' Granted. But it is an artificial

enthusiasm got up to compensate themselves for the loss of that religious feeling which, while they have renounced its object, they dare not dispense with. You see this in every line of their writings, in their systematic efforts to adapt the language of Theism to an Atheistic creed, in those parodies of Christian and Theistic phraseology, which are only not blasphemous because they bear such strong reluctant testimony to the value of the truth they deny, to the barrenness of the desert they adorn with flowers plucked, but without their roots, from the Christian Paradise. Agnostics cannot spare even the commonplaces, the terminology of the faith they have forsworn. They must talk of immortality, though they believe in annihilation; they must deify man, because they have dethroned God; they must invent a Paradise on earth, because they have abolished Heaven and yet cannot do without it. In all this, the utter artificiality of the "Religion of Humanity" is unmistakably evident. Such a religion will never restrain the passions, curb the selfishness, inspire the persistent labour of men when once the stimulus of antagonism is withdrawn. Agnosticism is passionate only because it is as yet merely propagandist; it is partisanship, not natural care for your idol itself, that gives zest to your idolatry. Yours is the passion of conflict, not of love. Agnostic hope, Positivist zeal is for victory in the present controversy, not for the accomplishment of a remote and perhaps impracticable purpose; one, at any rate, too remote, too uncertain to affect the generality of men at all when once the heat of controversy has cooled, and Positivism taken its place among recognised creeds.'

Merton.—' You forget that whatever the ultimate future of humanity may be, whatever limit may cut short its indefinite progress, there is always a present immediate progress to work for and to witness.'

Cleveland.—' Aye; but it is too small, too slow to satisfy those who are, once more, impatient because mortal.'

Lestrange.—' And why should we care for it? A religion should inspire, a morality worth the name should coerce. Positivism is a creed to fight for, not to live by; its vitality lies not even in its youth, but in its venom. Its strength is that of hatred, not of sympathy. What has it to offer to those who think humanity at best a somewhat contemptible thing? What sanction has your moral code, or what authority can give it a foundation or draw out its precepts? What is left of it when there is no longer a God to abolish or a Bible to pilfer from?'

Merton.—' Conscience and the interests of humanity.'

Lestrange.—'" What has posterity ever done for me that I should do anything for posterity?" I care something for my country; but I care for my country as limited and distinguished from others. Extend, dilute England into an European federation, and I should no longer feel any pride in the name of Englishman.'

Cleveland.—' Preference for her, not necessarily hatred for others. It is because England is not France, or Europe, or China, that Englishmen feel a strong attachment for her. She is their home because they would not be at home elsewhere. If all the world were alike to us, home and country would be meaningless words; and Humanity, having nothing antagonistic to or outside it, could never replace them.'

Merton.—' It ought.'

Lestrange.—' You have no right to that word. Ought means something owed; the debt can be claimed no longer now that you have blotted out the name of your creditor from the universe. Duty is immediately dependent on conscience, and conscience has no meaning for an Agnostic.'

Merton.—' You know that no Agnostic will allow that.'

Cleveland.—' But what is your conscience? For

us it is the voice of God; for you, what? How came it into being?'

Merton.—' You know its history, as one of the ablest of Agnostics has written it in full. Unselfishness, self-devotion, self-denial for the benefit of the tribe were the virtues that gave the tribe ascendancy, that preserved it. The tribe which most successfully encouraged these virtues prevailed in the struggle for existence. Natural Selection preserved the conscientious races, those in whom the tribal conscience overpowered the selfish instincts; and thus, each generation improving on the preceding, the habit strengthening by inheritance, conscience has come to be what it is, an instinct whose natural direction, whose very reason to be, is the welfare of the species through the suppression of all individual desires hostile to the general interest.'

Cleveland.—' That is, conscience is the habit of obedience to the will of the Many.'

Merton.—' I suppose it comes to that.'

Cleveland.—' Well, and the Many for their interest have compelled, enforced this habit or instinct on the individual; the selfishness of the race is reflected in the conscience, taught age after age by the Many for the benefit of the Many. Do you not see that, this once admitted, conscience has no force? It becomes a superstition, a tyranny, a deception of which a wise man will rid himself as soon as possible.'

Merton.—' Not at all. It is right that the individual should subordinate his interests to those of the race.'

Lestrange.—' Why ?'

Merton looked somewhat puzzled.

'Does any one doubt it?' he said at last.

Cleveland.—' If not, it is only because this tribal instinct has been by *force majeure* so deeply stamped upon every mind. Don't you see that you are arguing in a circle ? You tell us to suppress our own desires for the interest of the race. We ask why ? Conscience commands it. What is conscience ? The hereditary habit of subordinating ourselves to the race. How do we come by that habit ? Because the race, for its own purposes, has forced us to do so—has extirpated those who did not. What authority can conscience so explained possess ? And what satisfaction do you offer after all to this superstition, this illusory instinct impressed on us for the advantage of the Many by the Many ? Not even the permanent, eternal welfare of this race for which we ' ought ' to care—because, as it happens, we have been taught to care ! You know that the race itself must end. All that our utmost self-sacrifice can possibly effect is that the mass should at the end have risen a step or two higher, that the history should end a chapter or two later, than if we all of us had cared simply for our own happiness. What can such a reward be to us? What authority can such an inward law possess over our reason? We see that it is unreasonable, we see that it is a superstition, a lie told us for the benefit of those who told it, and a lie none the more authoritative, none the less impudent because it has been so long and so unceasingly repeated.'

Merton.—'But why a lie?'

Cleveland.—'Because it was essentially arbitrary. Right meant simply the interest of those who had the power of moulding the thought of the individual through education, personal and hereditary. By what right did the majority so mould the individual? By none which would not have equally applied to an exactly opposite teaching.'

Lestrange.—'Thank you, Cleveland. You and Merton between you have worked out a fuller justification of the cynic philosophy than I had thought possible. It is not merely that, when I have renounced fealty to a Divine Sovereign, the democracy of mankind is too contemptible to claim any allegiance from me; it seems that conscience, compassion, sympathy, all instinctive checks on pure selfishness, are as mere inventions as priest-craft itself; merely the teaching of those who were able to mould in their own interest the minds of my remote ancestors. I don't care for mankind; I certainly would not work or suffer in order that a thousand or ten thousand years hence somebody, I don't know who, might be wiser or better for what I have done, and utterly ungrateful to me for doing it. And very sure I am that when this is once recognized by the generality of mankind, when it is seen that morality is a matter of force exercised long ago, as law of force exercised now, neither one nor the other will have one whit more power than force can give them. But the consequences are certainly such as Agnostics will hardly like to contemplate; such as if seen would, I think, silence them.'

Sterne.—' I think not. Truth is truth, irrespective of consequences.'

Cleveland.—' Truth is truth; but *you* cannot call anything good "irrespective of consequences." In your creed and Merton's, consequences *make* good or evil: that is good which tends to the weal of mankind. With us, that which is good will tend to the weal of mankind—a totally different doctrine. Why?—because God has so willed.

And we do not care whether it be so or not; our business is to obey God, not to benefit men. We whom He has commanded to be true, have a right to believe that truth will always be good. You have no such right; you can prove no natural, necessary relation between the truth of a given dogma or opinion or theory and its utility to mankind. You are—what we are not—responsible for the consequences, and must seek them in each case by a calculation of probabilities. Now, so far as human foresight can go, it is often eminently probable that what looks like truth would work what we could hardly doubt to be evil.'

Merton.—'I should like to see what evil consequences are to be apprehended from the truth that we know nothing of a Divine Creator or Governor of the world!'

Cleveland.—'That there will be then no authority for the moral code, no sanction for morals except such as the law can apply.'

Merton.—'And social opinion, to which more and more the minds of individuals tend to defer.'

Cleveland.—'Of the weaker, meaner individuals. But even these would hardly be restrained by opinion alone, when it was backed by no conscience, or by a conscience confessedly originating only in the social opinion of a more ignorant past.

What evil consequences will follow? Well'—he looked round and observed that his wife was no longer present—' the first, that marriage cannot stand for a generation after its divine origin is recognised as a fable. Obviously, men and women have a right—apart from any supernatural law—to live together on such terms as they mutually arrange. Society has no sort of right to impose either permanence or unity upon a purely secular and personal partnership. Of course provision must be made for children, if children are brought into the world—which under a thoroughly Agnostic system might or might not be. But there the right of interference ends.'

Merton.—' But, if such license were clearly injurious to social interests, Society would have a right to forbid it.'

Cleveland.—'It neither would have the right nor could exercise it. The social consequences are far too remote to overbear the immediate, obvious, passionate claim of the individual to do as he will, not merely with his own but with himself. You might as well forbid men to eat and drink what is not good for them, on the ground that it impairs in the long-run their efficiency as members of the community. And we see that this consequence of Atheism—or Agnosticism, which comes to the same thing—is real, not merely theoretical; though the logical necessity is so obvious that practical evidence is hardly needed to support it. Where no religion, there no marriage. There is one European country in which a large proportion both of men and women have no religion, and in which the religion of a larger part of the population hardly pretends to authority over marriage. The consequence is that among German Protestants, or rather non-Catholics, marriage is rapidly losing all sanctity and almost all sanction. The proportion of purely secular marriages in those great towns and other districts which have a great non-Catholic population is so large that, except for Catholics, it is hardly too much to say that the religious idea of marriage has disappeared. The consequence is, first, that divorce has ceased to be disgraceful, and has become matter of mutual arrangement—apparently that it is often contemplated and almost arranged for before marriage; next, that the proportion of illegitimate children among Protestants rises to one-fifth or one-fourth, while in Catholic districts it hardly exceeds two or three per cent. Now the significance of illegitimate births is much greater than appears in a statistical table; it means much more than the same proportion of illicit unions, marriage being at least threefold as prolific as unlicensed intercourse. Here then you have the first consequence of Agnostic ethics, that the relation of the sexes ceases to be a subject of morality. It is not merely that there is much vice, but that there ceases to be anything which can be called virtue.'

Merton.—' It is not fair to ascribe that consequence to Agnostic ethics. Positivism is as strict on that subject as Christianity.'

Cleveland.—' Positivists are, or wish to be so. But Positivism, Agnosticism, cannot give either a reason or a sanction to the law its votaries would fain lay down.'

Sterne.—' Grant that a great change in religious thought would lead to a considerable change in the relation of the sexes; need that necessarily be evil ?'

Cleveland.—' Wherever those relations have become very lax, society has become otherwise demoralized. A nation that does not respect the purity of maidenhood, the sacredness of marriage, loses very soon even the strength, pith, courage of manhood; sinks into utter political and social rottenness, and, under the rough rule that has hitherto formed the law of nations, is presently destroyed to make room for a healthier if ruder civilization. But I am content to let the consequence stand by itself; content to lay down that the decay of religion involves both theoretically and practically the utter relaxation of marriage. We see something of this among ourselves. As the old strict religious doctrine loses hold on our women, as they cease to accept the subordinate position assigned to their sex by Christianity as by almost every other religion worthy of the name, marriage becomes more and more rare, especially among the educated classes. Look round upon the families each of us knows in these classes which the relaxation of religion has affected. Take the number of women belonging to the last generation, of women now over forty, who are married—were married before they were five and twenty. Take now the women of the rising generation, from eighteen to twenty-five. The proportion of marriages among them is very, very much smaller. And naturally so. Only a fool will enter into a partnership absolutely unlimited, practically interminable, with no distinct decisive power of control, no certain swift settlement of disputes, no easy means, no acknowledged right of checking extravagance or maintaining peace and order. Our daughters may depend upon it that subordination, subjection if they prefer so to call it, is an indispensable condition of marriage as we and they equally desire to have it, indissoluble; and that in proportion as the yoke is relaxed for them, and consequently rendered heavier for the men, fewer and fewer of the latter will hurry to place their necks under it.'

Sterne.—' I think reluctance to marry would be little affected by feminine insubordination, if the alternative were not made so easy to men.'

Cleveland.—' Possibly. But observe, the one evil tends to aggravate the other. The more difficult women find it to get married, the easier men find it to dispense with marriage, to obtain the society of women on cheaper terms.'

Sterne.—' But after all, important as is this branch of ethics, it is not the whole. It is even conceivable that society might exist though the relations between men and women settled themselves on an entirely different footing; though society abdicated its pretension to regulate them.'

Vere.—' I don't think so. After all, social euphemisms have generally a sound sense at bottom. It is absurd, of course, to speak as if illicit indulgence of one particular passion were the sole "immorality." But practical morals, as apart from the domain of law, are concerned with three principal topics, the family, property, citizenship; and of these the first is certainly the most fundamental and vital. Property moreover is to a much greater extent protected and governed by the law, is comparatively independent of individual consciences. Abolish the family, and the present structure of society, at least—nay, I might say every form of society the world has ever seen—falls to pieces at once.'

Cleveland.—' Nevertheless, we shall best see the effect of irreligion—using the word to signify the general negation of religion—upon morals by looking at the latter as a whole, not on one side only, though that be its most important side. Now what will be the basis, what the sanction of morality—how prove that men have duties, how induce them to perform those duties—when everyone is convinced that there is no God and no future, no censure to be apprehended but that of public opinion, no penalties but those of the law?'

Sterne.—' Selfishness is the basis, the radical immorality, the root of sin in domestic, in social, in civil relations. Religions have always been successful in proportion as they have appealed to the enthusiasm of self-devotion; and of that self-devotion Man must be the real and ultimate if not the immediate object, since man can in fact do nothing for God, render Him no real service.'

Vere.—' More properly, since God has no need of man.'

Sterne.—'Yes; then the religion that appeals most distinctly and directly to the enthusiasm of self-devotion, or what Positivists call the enthusiasm of humanity, is surely the most rational, and therefore probably the religion of the future?'

Lestrange.—'If man were not essentially selfish. He is drawn out of his selfishness chiefly and most effectually by the nearest and strongest ties. He is driven out of it by examples and menaces that appeal to it, that are in fact the sanction, if the unselfish influences are the base, of human morality. What will you say to men like myself, who fear not God neither regard man? In proportion to our knowledge, to the development of practical education which will render the experience of age available to youth, we shall shrink from the weight of family cares, responsibilities, labours and squabbles: we shall know that love the purest and strongest is after all a matter of a few years, that to those years it would be madness to sacrifice the whole of life.'

Merton.—'That is going back to the subject that Cleveland asked us to drop.'

Lestrange.—'Very well. Now, not believing Him to exist, I don't fear God any more than you; but, unlike you, I neither care for the welfare of mankind nor trouble myself about their opinion. Why should I not do just what pleases me, within that very wide sphere in which the law must leave me at liberty?'

Merton.—'Social opinion has its own way of enforcing its sentences, of making its censures effective.'

Lestrange.—'No; the world may think as ill of me as it pleases. What can it do to me? So long as my employers know that I am loyal to their interests and can serve them better than any one else they can lay hold of for the time being, their disapproval of my opinions or my conduct in other respects won't prevent their employing me and paying me. So long as my society is agreeable to them my acquaintances will give me theirs. Their selfishness is my guarantee. So far as I need them, society at large will sell me its services. I have not to pay higher rent, higher wages, higher prices because I am unpopular. Why should I abstain from anything that gratifies me during the short time I have to live, because it may injure a posterity which cannot revenge itself on me?'

Merton.—'And which you have no right to injure.'

Lestrange.—'I have a right to do as I will with my own. The rights of posterity against me amount at most to these. I have no right to destroy what it cannot replace—for example, to burn an art antique, demolish a monument or drown arable land. I have no right to inflict on it the permanent inheritance of disease or incapacity in my children. But if I bring no children into the world, and consume no more than I earn—that is, than what in one sense or another I produce—posterity has no claim on me. And if it had, I repeat, as it cannot punish me, why should I care if I do infringe its rights?'

Sterne.—' Because you know them to be rights; you know their violation to be iniquitous.'

Lestrange.—' Aye; there you appeal to conscience. But you have taught me that conscience is a silly superstition which has no right to influence my conduct, that it is in short simply the hereditary selfishness of the race at large enforced upon my mind before I was born by the bullying of generations.'

Merton.—' There are always some men whom any religion fails to influence. Will there be more men like you, insensible to conscience and to opinion, indifferent to the welfare of the race, hardened against human charity, under the sway of the Religion of Humanity than under that of Christianity or Theism? I don't think so.'

Cleveland.—' You miss the point altogether. A man who believes the truth of Christianity is restrained from what he recognizes as open glaring unbounded selfishness by that fear of God which you have abolished, by that regard for man which God enjoins.'

Sterne.—'But your fear of God is limited in its influence at any rate to Christians, and to those Christians who believe in direct Providential Government or in direct retribution hereafter.'

Cleveland.—'No. To a true Theist, to one for whom God is not merely the Creator but an ever-living universal Presence in relation with the individual soul, the fear of estranging one's own soul from Him is the most effective of all deterrent influences. To be damned, after all, is to "depart from Him into outer darkness;" and that is a sentence which may be passed and executed in this life.'

Merton.—'That view, that feeling is confined to a small minority.'

Cleveland.—'The highest form, the highest influences of all religions are necessarily confined to such a minority. The most of us will always need some direct penalty appealing to our lower nature to keep that nature from breaking loose under strong temptation. Now both Christianity and Theism have such penalties, do make such an appeal to the fears and consciences of the multitude.'

Sterne.—' Theism ?'

Cleveland.—' No man who really believes in God but fears Him in one way or another; unless indeed he regard Him as " sitting outside His machine and seeing it go." It may be true that the multitude do not consciously feel afraid of estrangement from Him, that for them there is no terror in that which seems to me the most awful of all judgments :—

> " Our fathers would not know Thy ways
> And Thou hast left them to their own."

But then their lower conceptions of God make them afraid of His direct physical vengeance. Your Religion of Humanity appeals only to the highest, or rather the wholly unselfish, motives; and tends to render these vague and weak in the extreme. It has nothing whatever to frighten those who are not ashamed to be selfish; nothing to restrain hypocrisy, nothing to deter from rebellion. And even for those who do accept it to the full, who feel in their higher moments all the enthusiasm at present generated by artificial incidental conditions, it is not a restraining but simply an elevating influence. When strong temptation comes, when we are disgusted or weary or disappointed, and see before us pleasure, peace, comfort, repose in the violation of ethics directed to the ultimate benefit of a possible shadowy future humanity, what can it do to keep us straight? Shall we be content, be able to suffer, to restrain ourselves, lest our self-indulgence should exercise some hardly conceivable or intelligible influence for the worse ten thousand years hence?'

Merton.—' No; *for* ten thousand years, I might say for ever.'

Cleveland.—' Not for ever, because the total future of the human race is narrowly limited.'

Merton.—' But, as you know, every action leaves its impress on the Universe for ever.'

Cleveland.—' Practically that is a phrase and not a fact. The circle grows fainter as it widens; the eternal influence is an Infinite series of infinitesimals, and its sum is very small indeed. Nor can we tell whether the impression of our acts on the Infinite will resemble them in quality. Granting that human sin must always be injurious to humanity—which *you* have no right to assume—the mischief of each individual sin, even of an individual life of sin, is too small—I don't say to be worth considering but—to be considered when the temptation is strong and the enthusiasm of humanity is weak, as it will generally be. As to the influence of sin on the Universe, we know nothing. It may be good for aught we can tell.'

Sterne.—' I am not sure that we do not greatly

overrate the importance of domestic and underrate that of civil duty and morality. Will not the Religion of Humanity, as Merton calls it—Utilitarianism, as I should prefer to name it, giving the credit of its authorship where it is really due—produce a higher civil morality, a stronger sense of duty to the State and to society than Christianity or Theism have ever done?'

Vere.—'I should say not. Disbelief in immortality must tend to render death much more terrible. After all, what most men dread is not death but annihilation; death, because it looks so like annihilation, because it is so difficult to realize immortality. It is to a great extent their real if vague belief that death is not annihilation which assists men to face it calmly in the cause of duty.'

Sterne.—'I don't agree with you. The races most ready to die are generally very indifferent to if not incredulous of immortality; and some of the bravest races have never really believed in it, or have believed in a future more dreary than annihilation itself.'

Vere.—' But the one class of races are of low vitality, the other brutal and insensible. Your religion is meant for, is applicable only to a race of intense vitality, intense mental activity and energy, and therefore of intensified sensibility.

Your future ideal men, and all whom you can influence in the present, will be men who can neither forget death as the ultimate fact, the most terrible and incurable evil of our human condition, nor endure contentedly the horror of parting with the life which their very elevation in the scale of existence renders so intense and so precious.'

Merton.—' But death is inevitable; and whether it come at thirty or at seventy will not be such a very vital matter. And, if men become a little less disposed to die for their country, they will at any rate be more eager to live for it.'

Cleveland.—' Why ?'

Merton.—' You have under-rated throughout the influences which our religion retains, and exaggerated greatly those with which it dispenses. It is not true that people's conduct is, as a rule, greatly affected by the fear of being damned or the hope of Heaven. First, nobody, while he has as yet much power over his conduct, thinks that he will be damned for anything that he does. He always means to repent, and thinks he will have time. We do hear of men firmly convinced that they will be damned; but they are men past the power of changing their conduct materially, who—as you implied just now—feel that they are damned already. Men do contrive, on the whole, to keep tolerably straight, outside the mere terror of the law. If they are not very good, yet they certainly abstain from that life of utter selfishness which Lestrange commends. Their motives are very mixed, very various, and very imperfectly known to themselves. But the consequences after death are the smallest part of the controlling force; respect for the standard of their class, and for the opinion of those among whom they live— two different things, by the way—the example of those around and above them, education, the love of approbation, keep them in a path which, if not that of moral rectitude, does not depart very far from it. Setting the criminal classes aside, the principal vices of any class are those which its opinion does not condemn. If men go very far astray, it is in the directions to which their special profession, or the society to which they belong, gives a liberal license. Stock-speculators, for example, go further towards downright cheatery than almost any other respectable men; the lower class of artisans and labourers get drunk and beat their wives; the youth at least of the higher ranks, especially of the idle classes, are unscrupulous in their relations with women; journalists and politicians are shameless in slander; clergymen are apt to be lax in that finer morality which we call honour; and so on. In every case, the standard of right and wrong is given by class opinion; and that opinion is gradually modified by the wider, and on each particular point stricter opinion of the public at large, whence comes the gradual improvement in the special morality of each class from generation to generation. After such punishment as the law can inflict, infamy is the thing men most dread, fame that they most desire. The religion of humanity intensifies both these influences, and we may surely believe that, as they do three parts of the work that is done now, they will in time accomplish all that will be needed; especially as men become tamer, more easily controlled and governed, with the progress of civilization.'

Lestrange.—'In so arguing, you abandon the pretension of your creed to be nobler than others. The motives you rely on are quite as selfish as the Christian, much weaker and much lower. Infamy—offending public opinion! fame—winning popular applause! Fools and cowards will fear the one, fools and fops will desire the other. As men become cooler and wiser, they will see how little popular contempt or dislike hurts them, how utterly worthless is popular applause, and how little of either they are likely to get. Practically, a man may prove himself a scoundrel without being pelted, a hero without being cheered, and in either case find his conduct forgotten a month afterwards by nearly all his acquaintance. Even now we despise a man who avows himself in fear of opinion. We do not condemn, we may admire, the man who toils, makes sacrifices, perhaps dies for fame; but it is because of the sacrifices, not of the motive. If he sacrifices fame itself to practical utility, to domestic charities, even to personal tastes and convictions, we admire him more. You assume that men are to become more practical, less imaginative; and that sweeping away the world where imagination had free play, the so-called spiritual Universe, must tend to render them so. Practical men soon learn, first that fame is hardly worth having, next that such fame as they could care for is hardly to be had, finally that it is far too costly. Posthumous fame, posthumous immortality as you call it, is the most ridiculous of all things. Only an utterly fuddled imagination can care for it, except while the man fancies himself immortal and able to enjoy, whether in Heaven or elsewhere, his reputation on Earth. Who will work for a reward which he can never receive? Who will be fool enough to care for that which he will never know, which for him will never exist? The strongest minds will see this the first, will be the first to dismiss all regard for human praise or blame. They will probe to the foundation that moral code which you propose to enforce after you have abolished the God who gave, the future life that sanctioned it. What foundation will they find? What distinguishes between right and wrong?'

Merton.—'The common moral sense of mankind.'

Lestrange.—'As if mankind had a common moral sense; as if on every point of morals they did not directly contradict one another!'

Merton.—'No; all admit beneficence to be right; all allow, affirm that to benefit your fellow-creatures and abstain from injuring them is a duty.'

Lestrange.—'Pardon me, no such thing. They hold pretty universally that to injure your country's enemies is a duty; that to prefer the welfare of your family to public interest is, within certain limits, a duty also. Most people censure any man who neglects to earn luxury for his wife, a first-rate education for his children, in order to devote himself to the highest interests of the public. And on all the details of ethics the contradictions are flagrant and fundamental. But admit that mankind agree that he who benefits them does well. Of course when they are conscious of the benefit they own the merit, they approve the benefactor—*because* they are selfish. Is selfishness then a virtue in the Many? The approbation of their common moral sense is, when you test it, merely a payment for value received. Suppose I don't want that payment, why should I give the value? And men of sense will, as I have said, become more and more indifferent to the payment, as already you find them. Proud men, strong men tend more and more to say, "I don't care what men think of me, I do what I think right, or what I will."'

Sterne.—' They prefer the approbation of their own conscience to that of mankind.'

Cleveland.—' Mostly ; because either they believe that conscience is the voice of God, or fancy it something peculiar to themselves. But when you have taught them that conscience means only the past opinion of mankind, their pride, which now supports, will be in arms against it. They will resent the inherited bullying of former ages as they defy the actual bullying of their contemporaries.'

Merton.—' Why should we not be swine?'

Lestrange.—' Why not, if we like it? Some of us do, and swine accordingly they are. I don't happen to like straw and pigwash. A cultivated intellect, interesting intellectual occupations, the excitement of controversy, the egotistic pleasure of triumphing over adversaries, the combative instinct inherited from the days when your "tribal conscience" was in course of formation, give me a satisfaction I could not find in getting drunk every Sunday. Cleveland here finds a pleasure in his books, his flowers, his home, such as I find, or probably much greater than I find, in the excitement of journalism and politics. But it is all a matter of taste, and each man is free to indulge his own; since there is no God to whom he must answer for the talents bestowed on him, and no future in which he can have cause to repent their misuse.'

Sterne.—' Then by what right do you look down upon the human swine ?'

Lestrange.—' By no right, but by necessity, because I stand on a higher level. I don't look down on Cleveland because I work, take part in the active fighting of politics, the strife by which more or less the welfare of my countrymen may be affected, and he does not; nor should I look down upon him, even if at the end of his life he had the sense to put all his manuscripts in the fire—always supposing that his children could derive no satisfaction from the fame they may bring.'

Sterne.—' Nevertheless men will always wish to

stand on a higher level, to look down rather than up.'

Lestrange.—' If it do not give them too much trouble. Therefore the swine, when they find it too hard to climb, want always to pull down those who have risen. But when the level is recognised as being mere matter of taste, people will climb or not according to their humour. Some rich men will fight for the sake of fighting, and politics will degenerate into a mere squabble of factions without principles. Other rich men will amuse themselves, whether with books, with art, with gardening, or with women; not with wine or gluttony, because those entail certain and speedy if not immediate diminution of the power of enjoyment—but selfishly. Each nobler, more independent man, whether his independence be a matter of fortune or character, will show himself more and more contemptuous of popular prejudice, whether in the form of moral sense or political passion; and such example will tell on inferior natures, till, by the time all nations are at peace in the "federation of the world," society will have grown as utterly selfish and corrupt as was that of the civilized world when, some eighteen hundred years ago, it subsided in the Roman peace and rotted into the Lower Empire.'

Vere.—' Lestrange, don't you know you are

talking paradox? Honestly, do you believe a word of what you say, or rather, do you feel it?'

Lestrange.—' Honestly, Vere, I believe every word of it. I cannot feel it because I have not yet—as mankind will not for a while—got rid of the conscience which is now pronounced to be an inherited relic of primitive savagery.'

Merton.—' No, no! Founded perhaps by primitive savagery, but improved by the collective influence of each successive generation as it improved in intelligence and civilization.'

Lestrange.—' But the product in any case of collective selfishness, against which each man is perfectly entitled to set his own individual selfishness.'

Vere.—' But can you believe that there is no right or wrong, no distinction between yourself and the human swine of which you speak—that you are in no sense nobler or better than he?'

Lestrange.—' Nobler, higher, a finer species of animal—yes. But there is no more merit in my being so than in his being a man, and not an actual pig.'

Vere.—' Not, of course, if you both are as God made you, if neither have done anything to raise or lower himself.'

Lestrange.—' Nay; but more than that. There is no merit in rising or falling, if there be no ultimate height to which we should draw nearer, where we shall find better company; if there be no future in which we may gain indefinitely, improve indefinitely in consequence of what we have done here. If we are to come to an end, as we shall, in ten, fifteen, or twenty years, what matters it what we have done with that time? All we need care for is to enjoy it as much as we can on that level of culture, in that form of enjoyment, which suits our own characters.'

Merton.—' A much nobler thing to say " if the life be so short, let us make the most of it for others." '

Lestrange.—' Once more, why? For me, so far as I am concerned, the world ends when I am dead. What have I got to do with that which is for me a nonentity? It would be the height of folly to sacrifice one hour's enjoyment of the little life I have for the benefit of a world which was to be destroyed at my death; and if death be annihilation, then for all practical purposes affecting my life or my conduct the world does end when I die. *De non apparentibus*—for me that is not of which I can never be conscious.'

Cleveland.—' Well, I doubt whether you are quite right, even if there were neither God nor future; but I am sure of one thing. The poorest, flimsiest, sandiest foundation on which to

build a religion or a morality is the opinion of
mankind at large, or the common moral sense
which is after all but the popular prejudice on
moral questions, biassed more largely than even
on others by the self-interest of mankind. The
shadowy Hades of Homer is substantial, satisfactory compared with the posthumous immortality of
the Positivist—an immortality, like the Homeric
Elysium, to be attained by very few, and on very
arbitrary conditions. And of all idols our Father
Man—or our child Posterity—is the most contemptible; of all Eidola the emptiest and most
delusive.'

CHAPTER V.

MORALS OF PROBABILITY.

STERNE, Cleveland, and myself took advantage of a fine interval, when a sharp frost had given solidity to the ground, soaked with a winter month's share of the sixty inches of rain that falls yearly at Ferndale Holm, to cross a mountain-pass that affords more than one splendid view. The higher hills were all snow-capped, the grass, wherever the sun had not directly reached it, white with hoar-frost; and more than one bog that would have been impassable even in the drier months of summer was now hard frozen, which shortened our route considerably. Lestrange was sorely tempted to join us, but this Mrs. Cleveland would not allow, asking him to drive her in the phaeton by a somewhat circuitous route to a point at which they might meet us. The crisp, cold air unusually calm, the bright sky, and the signally altered scene so familiar to us in its summer dress, made the excursion a very pleasant one, and it was some time before we reverted to those topics which alone gave our conversation weight enough to impress it on my memory.

'Cleveland,' said Sterne at last, somewhat abruptly, 'do you seriously believe that truth can ever be injurious; or, to put it in another form, can it ever be right to lie systematically and persistently to the multitude for their own good?'

Cleveland.—' The questions are not the same, as you seem to think.'

Sterne.—' No ?'

Cleveland.—' Certainly not. It might conceivably be our duty to speak the truth, though we knew that it would do pure unmitigated harm.'

Sterne.—' Surely not; except, of course, on the general principle that the example of lying in one case would do more harm to the weal of mankind at large than the truth in that one case could do? But that implies that truth is essentially beneficial.'

Cleveland.—' Who ever doubted it? Truth between man and man, truthfulness in the practical relations of life, is a necessity of social order and human co-operation. But you are thinking of speculative, not narrative truth; frank avowal of opinion, not veracity in matters of fact. Well, the question is not an easy one. I grant that it would hardly do for any man systematically to preach, even on subjects of ethical or theological speculation, what he disbelieved; above all, it would not be well that he should say one thing in public and another in private, have one doctrine for the profane many, another and opposite esoteric truth for the educated few. But, though speculative truth be ever so injurious, it would not necessarily be the duty of those who believe it, who have, or think they have hold of it, to lie.'

Sterne.—' Surely it is their duty not to do what they believe injurious to the welfare of humanity?'

Cleveland.—' There may be higher obligations. You are too apt to take the utilitarian theory for granted. But, even on utilitarian grounds, it does not follow that, because truth is injurious, lying is a duty. It is enough that those who hold injurious truth should keep it to themselves. There will always be a sufficiency of honestly mistaken men to propagate and maintain beneficial falsehoods.'

Sterne.—' I should doubt that. With the spread of enlightenment, the number of competent teachers who hold speculative falsehoods must rapidly diminish.'

Cleveland.—' Ay, if the falsehood were not

prima facie beneficial. But there will always be numbers of thoughtful people who cannot practically believe that what is beneficial is false, that what is palpably noxious can be true.'

Sterne.—'That is turning the matter wrong side out, inverting the relation between truth and profit.'

Cleveland.—'Possibly; but, if a rare argument, it is a common creed.'

'Is it a rare argument?' I asked. 'One finds Christian preachers constantly resting the real force, laying the practical stress of their case on the service Christianity has rendered to mankind, on the impossibility of doing without it.'

Cleveland.—'True. But if you put the matter to them clearly, make them see the meaning of their own reasonings, they will repudiate them. Nobody, or hardly anybody, will *say* "this must be true because the belief in it is wholesome;" but multitudes even of thinking men practically think or feel so. Those who can let go a belief they feel to be essential to their own happiness and virtue are few. Those who would like to see the general decay of a creed they think necessary to keep the multitude in order are perhaps fewer still.'

Sterne.—'Then are they right? Do you believe that truth can ever do harm?'

Cleveland.—'Do you deny that falsehood has done infinite good?'

Sterne.—'Absolutely. I know what you mean; but what good Christianity has accomplished has been due to its comparative truth, not to its absolute falsehood. And it has done enormous harm. Clifford hardly exaggerated its power for evil, strongly as he has stated it.'

Cleveland.—'Look what decaying Paganism was. Compare the latter state of Pagan Rome with Mediæval Christianity, or again with primitive Protestantism, and you can hardly doubt that, frightful as have been the crimes committed in the name of religion, the balance to its credit is stupendous.'

Sterne.—'I don't know. Marcus Antoninus was equal to any Christian saint.'

Cleveland.—'Perhaps; but the Stoics persuaded a few thoughtful men to believe their creed, of whom a very small minority practised it. Christianity persuaded millions to believe and thousands to practise, not perhaps what Christ would have recognized as His teaching, but something far better than the world had known before.'

Sterne.—'But that was in virtue, as I said, of its comparative truth, not of its absolute falsehood.'

Cleveland.—'No. The best thing the author

of the "*Enigmas of Life*" has ever said is that the one falsehood common to all creeds is the very principle of their life, the very basis of their power. They all assume *certainty*, all affect a Divine origin, and on this point *they all lie*. But it is precisely this affectation of certainty that gives them their hold on men. Probability may be the guide of life, but it guides because it is not recognized as probability but taken for certainty. Seriously persuade men that there is one chance in fifty that the sun will not rise to-morrow, and you will—disturb their sleep. Convince them that summer may possibly fail to return, and though you may prove to them that the chances in favour of its advent are a hundred to one you will produce a visible effect upon the harvest.'

Sterne.—' Only with fools.'

Cleveland.—' Perhaps; but on this point most men are fools by instinct. It is just because a vast probability is to us an apparent certainty that we do act on it so confidently. If Christian preachers could make us feel that life is practically, immediately uncertain, uncertain for each of us each hour—if most of us believed, as one or two women I know do seem to believe, that it was doubtful whether going to sleep in health we should live to wake again—the idea would make us seriously uncomfortable, if it did not materially improve our conduct. We run risks, we do not incur certain and heavy sacrifices, on a chance, unless in the spirit of the gambler. No man was ever a martyr for a creed that he thought probably true.'

Sterne.—' I suppose not.'

Cleveland.—' And no such creed would ever make converts or control conduct. No man would forego an immediate deeply-desired pleasure, resist a strong present temptation, curb a passion he could certainly and instantly gratify because the chances were three to one that he had a soul, and six to one that his soul would be damned for yielding.'

Sterne.—' And that is just the weakness of all your theologies. Punishment and reward are alike probabilities to all but the most devout, and therefore they are so ineffective.'

Cleveland.—' Well, but observe, you say falsehood must be injurious; that religion has benefited mankind in virtue of its truth, not of the attendant fiction. Now, mark: the one thing common to all religions, without which none of them could have gained a hearing, much less held its ground, controlled and governed multitudes, inspired champions and martyrs, is the one thing certainly false. A God is at any rate *prima facie* probable; Heaven and Hell are almost necessary consequences of immortality, and immortality at least seems to human instinct and human thought very possible. Buddha's teaching of perpetual re-incarnations till purification accomplished by trial is rewarded by absorption into the primary Life, strangely as it conflicts with other more popular doctrines, is consistent enough, and certainly no one can say that it may not be true. But Buddha, Moses, Christ, Mahomet, all tell us that they know these things; that they received their information supernaturally, and directly or indirectly from the Deity Himself. As they contradict each other, and every one contradicts *every* other on some important point, it is plain that in this statement three of the four must have been, and none of us now doubts that all were, mistaken. But, as the *Enigmas of Life* reminds us, it was this essential untruth, this false allegation that gave strength to every one of these teachers. It was the falsehood that won a hearing for the truth. Even the peculiar personal character of Christ, his attractive influence, magnetising all who came into contact with Him—exercising over all a power, attractive or repulsive, the strongest ever wielded by man—would not have sufficed to make Him more than a Jewish Rabbi of unusual reasonableness and popularity, whose teaching probably would have been sooner forgotten than that of any other in proportion to its simplicity and excellence. Another radical falsehood, if it has done much harm, has been perhaps almost equally necessary. I doubt whether any religion would have made way which had not made belief in itself a paramount if not the paramount merit, which had not promised Heaven to the true believers.'

'Are you not proving too much, Cleveland?' I said. 'You prove not only that if there is no God falsehood might well be more beneficial in particular cases than truth, but also that God has made falsehood a principal instrument in working out His design.'

Cleveland.—'Certainly. But the whole Providential scheme whether of nature or of human progress consists in bringing good out of evil, or the better out of the worse. Your criticism as you put it is startling, no doubt; but that is due to a verbal ambiguity. Providence neither lies nor employs liars as His favourite servants. Moses and Buddha, Christ and Mahomet doubtless believed all they taught, and believed nothing more confidently than their own inspiration. Mankind being so constituted that truth pure and simple would not have found acceptance with them, their prophets—those who have been the instruments of Providence to give them a morality and a religion—have, not consciously but necessarily, mixed with their truth the requisite falsehood, not because they were prophets but because they were men. The same human weakness which rendered it certain that mankind would not accept a religion of probability, rendered it impossible for any prophet to offer such a creed.'

Sterne.—' You mean, they thought it right to do evil that good might come; confident in the truth of their doctrine, believing or knowing that it would not be accepted on their authority, they conceived themselves entitled to forge the Divine signature to a message they believed Divine in essence?'

Cleveland.—' No. The same human infirmity, the same peculiarity of our nature, which in the average man takes the form of demanding certainty, assumes in the Prophet the form of absolute assurance. Having grasped what he sees to be a sublime magnificent truth, feeling his soul suddenly overflowed with light, he feels a certainty absolute and unquestioning that he has received instruction, and therewith authority, directly and immediately from the Source of Light.'

Sterne.—' But if the prophets believed the stories they told of the means by which they received their inspiration, they must have been mad. And it is difficult to believe that they were mad on this point, and yet sane, as we see them often to have been, on all others.'

Cleveland.—' A few of the Jewish prophets would certainly in these days have been consigned to an asylum, quite apart from their prophetic teaching. They connected their insane proceedings with their prophetic inspiration; at least, they interpreted their insane impulses as symbolizing some moral or practical truth. But, if not mad, they had a taint of mental unsoundness about them; yet I see no taint of insanity in any of the four great teachers, except the epilepsy of Mahomet.'

Sterne.—' But you think—nay, you are sure—that their supposed direct communication with the Deity was an illusion?'

Cleveland.—' Or a mistake?—yes. They misconceived a vast, a signal, and probably a sudden illumination, given naturally or supernaturally; perhaps the result of long, deep thought, reflection, or reverie, perhaps rushing into their consciences in the strange way in which thoughts whereof we have been previously wholly unconscious do sometimes strike all of us. The light was so brilliant, so clear, so superior to anything that existed around or in themselves, that they necessarily imputed it to the direct immediate gift of God.'

Sterne.—' All very well; but if they believed that they heard a voice from Heaven or from the clouds, or that an angel came and spoke to them, or that they went up to Heaven on a donkey, they were *pro tanto* mad; and if they did not they lied. Do you suppose that Moses believed himself to have seen the back but not the face of Jehovah? And, if he did, was he not clearly insane ?'

Cleveland.—' I don't believe he ever talked such nonsense. We have his teaching recorded only in a much later age; we have no reason to think that a word of it, except perhaps the Ten Commandments, was written down for generations after his death. We may believe that he went up to the top of Sinai, there to seek in trance or reverie full enlightenment, as he thought from Jehovah, in reality from his own mind. But I no more suppose that he saw the earthquake, the tempest, followed by the " still small voice," than I suppose that he actually lived without food or sleep for forty days and nights. The very number is conclusive as to the poetic or traditional character of the story. Neither Christ nor Buddha told us how he spoke with God; Mahomet, the only one of the four who did give a distinct account of the method of his inspiration, gives the most absurd, but at the same time the most modest version. He was merely the scribe who wrote down what not God but an angel dictated. And Mahomet claimed neither infallibility nor impeccability. It is noteworthy that by his own confession he once mistook the dictation of Satan for that of Gabriel. It is touching, interesting, and a very strong proof of his sincerity that he recorded the rebukes he received for personal faults and errors; for that pride and impatience which, of all errors, a Prophet who was also the leader of a half-savage warrior band would have shrunk, save under strong conscientious conviction, from acknowledging as faults. It seems to me probable that as he grew older, as he was more deeply involved in war and politics, perhaps as the excitement of his life impaired more and more the balance of a brain never perfectly sound, he allowed himself to deceive himself—allowed his passions to usurp the place of conscience, and to speak with the voice of Gabriel. For the rest, his visions appear to me quite consistent with absolute sincerity in an ignorant Arabian enthusiast, who was unquestionably liable to attacks of a disease closely related to insanity, though at other times nobly and vigorously sane. But Christ never spoke of any outward personal vision, never told His followers how He learnt what He taught them; and the authority with which He spoke was as distinct from that of the ordinary Jewish prophets as from that of the Scribes and Pharisees. He spoke as one who shared too intimately the counsels of the Father to ask or be asked how He came to know the Father's mind on any particular point; and such was evidently the feeling of those who surrounded Him, who heard and recorded His teaching. Even St. Paul, logician as he was, never seems to have asked himself the question. He tells us sometimes how he knew the mind of Christ; it never occurs to him to ask, never occurred to him that any one would ask, how Christ knew the thoughts of the Deity. It was just this absolute confidence that gave to the arch-teachers of the world the extraordinary courage and security, the peace and self-reliance in the midst of outward peril, that their position demanded; gave them, too, that ascendancy over others that made them prophets and founders. And yet this confidence was unquestionably mistaken.'

We walked on for awhile in silence, Sterne I believe pondering, as I was pondering, over Cleveland's latter sentences; our thoughts now and then interrupted as we reached one point after another from which a new aspect of the striking winter scene below and around us came into view. As we paused at the top of the pass, Sterne observed:

'If uncertainty be fatal to the influence of a religion, all religions must be in imminent and irreparable peril just now; for uncertainty is the characteristic of the thought of the present age.'

'Yes,' said Cleveland; 'no one is sure now except those who have never thought things out; and, with certain exceptions, those are surest who have never thought at all. The only cultivated, intelligent thinkers who venture to be positive are positive only in negation. The Agnostics alone think that they know anything.'

Sterne.—' And that is the strength of the new religion that Merton preaches. We cannot know, we can at best conjecture, the mind and the will of God; we can know mankind and what is good for them. Faith, the claim alike of Moses, Christ, and Mahomet, is in itself a confession of uncertainty. The believer trusts to the character, the truth, and the knowledge of his Prophet; and, after all, he cannot know that the Prophet is neither deceived nor deceiving. Positivism has at any rate the advantage of certainty.'

Cleveland.—'No, indeed. The fatal weakness of your creed is that there is and can be no certainty about it, and that the uncertainty will be, what that of supernatural religion is not, obvious to all.'

Sterne.—'We know more of man than we can ever know of God, and more of what will benefit mankind than of the scheme of Providence, even if we could seriously co-operate with the latter.'

Cleveland.—'Practically the religious know or think they know all they need; the will of God in so far as they have to obey it, His purpose as to the reward of their conduct. Your faith is political, and the uncertainty characteristic of politics inheres in its very foundations. You will never know, and never agree among yourselves, either what is the ultimate end or how to attain it.'

Sterne.—'The ultimate end is of course the happiness of mankind, improving in quality and in amount with each successive generation.'

Cleveland.—'Aye; but you don't know what will make them happy. Take that which is perhaps the fundamental question—are you to aim at equality or aristocracy? Mind, this is a real problem, even from your own point of view. You, I suppose, desire a perfect democracy. Merton, if he knows his own mind, probably wants the awful intellectual despotism of Comte, the most frightful tyranny that it ever entered into the mind of philosopher to conceive; something infinitely worse, more intolerable in its searching mind-crushing oppression, than any autocracy the world has actually seen.'

Sterne.—' In any case, we desire and must desire a constant approach to material equality, equality of rank, of fortune, of comfort, whether intellectual equality be a practicable and desirable thing or not; and I should say its desirability must depend simply on its possibility.'

Cleveland.—' It might be easy to show that material equality would be a very doubtful blessing. You want a certainty more than any other religion, because your object appeals so little, so feebly, to the imagination and interests of men as compared with supernatural religions. You have no Infinite Wisdom to lay down your code, no personal immortality to give it a sanction. Yet you have to contend with the same passions, the same temptations, the same innate weaknesses and selfishness of human nature that have proved so often too strong for the promises and the terrors of Christianity and Mahometanism. A man might well be restrained by the fear of Hell, even though he be not absolutely sure that there is a Hell at all. He might prefer a great probability of Heaven to secure self-indulgence for a few years on earth; yet practically we find that doubt is fatal even to such threats and promises. But an uncertain progress towards an uncertain goal for humanity in an indefinite future will never inspire or restrain anybody. No man will deny himself repose or luxury, forego the charms of woman or the indulgence of revenge or ambition, in order to render a possible but uncertain service to a cause which may probably benefit and possibly injure mankind in the future. The first step to founding such a religion as Merton dreams of must be the definition of your material terrestrial Paradise of ten thousand years hence. The next must be to lay down certainly and clearly the way thereto; and you can do neither the one nor the other.'

Sterne.—' I think I should find no great difficulty in laying down the outlines of both.'

Cleveland.—' And Merton would lay down quite different ones. Nor could any dispassionate man unbiassed, uninfluenced by the prejudices or conflicts of the present, undertake confidently to say which of you was right. Take what is, as I say, perhaps the fundamental question. Do you want even material equality? Will it tend to the benefit of the future race?'

Sterne.—' Surely.'

Cleveland.—' I doubt it exceedingly. I doubt whether material equality does not necessarily mean material stagnation. Suppose all men equally well-off, every one obliged to work eight hours a day, and laws carefully providing that no great inequality of benefit shall result to any one from his individual exertions or those of his fathers. What motive will there be to progress? Lord Lytton in *The Coming Race* has missed this point ; but he has shown more clearly than he saw that equality would destroy all the motives to individual exertion. At present a man invents from one of three motives; interest in his subject, the hope of profit, and the hope of fame. You leave him the first of these and that alone ; for if fame once becomes a great and real satisfaction, a powerful motive in a society in which the hope of wealth is destroyed, all the evils of inequality would be restored ; you would have again a higher class possessing that which others covet, and envied by a discontented majority. Now, mere interest in the subject would hardly impel a man to overcome all the difficulties in the way of invention in a society where the law practically exacts eight hours' work from all and forbids alike leisure and wealth. In order to invent, the man must deny himself repose, must work sixteen hours a day instead of eight, and that for years, without hope of reward in future leisure and future enjoyment. Or—*I* should say, and—he must sacrifice the whole or a large part of the working time demanded by society directly or indirectly; that is he must break a positive law, or, if the only penalty enforcing regular work be as now the loss of remuneration, he must be content to half starve himself, to live a great deal worse than his neighbours, for years, with no hope that he or his children will hereafter be the better. Here is a check on invention which would of itself suffice to extinguish four-fifths of the inventive genius of the present day. If the family still exist in that age, there will be a heavier and almost insuperable clog on such self-sacrifice. The man will be starving, denying, inconveniencing his wife and daughters for something in which they probably don't believe. When he has reached a certain stage he wants assistance. How will he obtain it when those who assist him cannot hope to make profit out of their sacrifice? You, who are acquainted with Gerard, know that invention is not the simple easy thing that the public and the political opponents of patents suppose. No invention worth anything but has cost years of labour and generally large outlay. I have shown how difficult it would be to get the first under your ideal state of equality; how will you possibly get the second?'

Sterne.—' From the State.'

Cleveland.—' Would any invention ever have been taken up by the State if the inventor had

EQUALITY MEANS STAGNATION. 143

been left to himself, had had no resources beyond those of an average citizen, and no help from without? He would never—at least, not in one case out of fifty—be able to bring his invention to that point, or to present it with that clearness which would justify the State in taking it up. For such a purpose the State means a body of officials necessarily ignorant of the special details of each kind of business, incapable of judging what inventions are and what are not worth State support. Their one bias must be in favour of saving the public money; and since they will not be much wiser than inventors at large, we must assume that two-thirds of the inventions they do take up, probably nine-tenths, will be blunders. You see that equality has at least a strong tendency to put an end to the greater inventions, those that require the devotion of men's minds for years. But even the smaller ones, devised by the ingenuity of men engaged in a special craft to make their work a little easier or a little more efficient, will be terribly discouraged when by no invention can a man improve his own position, when nothing is to make him or his family any richer. In fact, anything approaching to permanent equality means the denial, or the reduction to the minimum, of the reward of energy. It means a very strong tendency; to say the least of it, to reduce industry, and still more that exertion which is more than mere industry, to a dead level. Few men will work harder, more thoughtfully, more earnestly than the average when they are not to be in some palpable way better paid; and better payment means of course inequality. There is, at least, very much reason to suppose that equality *may* mean stagnation, may be an evil. Look at the practical working of this uncertainty when you come to make converts to your creed. When you have swept away supernatural hopes, fears, and sanctions—when your moral law rests upon its tendency to benefit mankind, and benefit them in a particular way—you tell a man who has the choice between a life of selfish enjoyment and one of earnest exertion, between self-indulgence and self-sacrifice—"Forego pleasure, resist temptation in order that you may help a little to establish centuries hence a state of things of which the primary characteristic shall be equality of material wealth." It is absolutely fatal to any idea of influence over the man's conduct—it is a full licence to reject your code and defy your censures—when he can say, "I doubt very much whether, if I could give you your object at once, I should not have done more harm than good." And this he will always be able to say. You may satisfy *yourselves* that the balance of argument is on your side; but so long as the very foundation of your ethical system is arguable, so long as men *can* honestly doubt whether the whole is not a delusion, they *will* doubt, and act on the doubt, precisely where your code, if it is to be good for anything, should coerce their consciences. Remember, your moral law must be founded on the tendency of certain rules to produce a certain future state of society. You can give but one reason for obedience—that obedience will tend to produce this ultimate social Paradise. Obedience must necessarily be often a hard and disagreeable thing; men will always have strong reason to wish to disobey. I allow that conscience is to remain as powerful as now, or even to gain strength; I set aside for the nonce what seemed to me Lestrange's unanswerable argument, that a conscience ascribed to the evolution of a tribal instinct will be for nine men in ten a superstition to be dismissed as quickly as possible. Suppose your creed or Merton's accepted—suppose men convinced that they ought to do their best for the future of mankind, and ready to do as they ought—still they are necessarily biassed against each claim made upon them; and when they can honestly doubt whether each and every claim be not founded on a blunder, the bias and the doubt together will almost always preponderate.'

Sterne.—'They should not, and as men grow more rational, I think they will not. We shall be able to show on every point a strong balance of argument in our favour, to show that our object is beneficial to mankind, and that our method is the right one. Of course we may make mistakes; but those mistakes thought and experience will gradually correct.'

Cleveland.—'But after all the obligation remains uncertain, *arguable*. It is a question of the comparative weight of conflicting probabilities; and remember, the scales are always loaded against you. The temptation is present, the gratification certain, the sin very questionable; the penalty falls on others, is very remote and admits of utter scepticism. You can but threaten, " If *you* sin or refuse to suffer now, *my* great grandchildren will probably spend some years in Purgatory," and this to men who are warned in vain, " You will go to Hell yourself, certainly and for ever!" If the penalty were to fall on the man himself or his children, its probability might affect him more or less; but the probability of future evil to others, a thousand years after his death, will never induce any man to accept a present pang or forego a present pleasure.'

Sterne.—'Has the uncertainty much to do with the matter?'

Cleveland.—'This much: it affords a complete salve to the man's conscience. He has only to disbelieve in the desirability of your object, to satisfy himself that your future Paradise might be a Purgatory, and he is released from *all* moral restraint. The very foundation of your code—which, remember, is then to be the only one—has given way. A religion whose Heaven is impersonal, whose Deity is a personification, must be feeble at best. But when the Heaven may be Hell and the Deity may lie, it can have no hold whatever upon the conscience which can reject its sanction or the intellect which can challenge its authority.'

A.—'I am not quite clear that I fully understand your meaning. No religion binds the unbeliever, no moral code coerces him who does not fear its penalties, for whom its sanctions have no force.'

Cleveland.—'Of course not. But men may accept the two fundamental tenets of Positivism, and reject all the practical inferences on which its moral code must rest. They may admit the possibility of a terrestrial Paradise, admit that man may find the way to it, and yet reject both the kind of happiness proposed and the guidance offered. They may hold, on strictly Agnostic grounds, that the Paradise is not worth having, and that it is not to be attained by the road in question. They can hardly help *doubting* both, in proportion as they are thoroughly logical, and a doubtful religion can never control or inspire. Suppose it laid down by the Positivist Church that material equality and scientific despotism are the primary conditions of general happiness; suppose it further laid down that men individually will promote this state by maintaining the family system in all Christian strictness; suppose a man accepting the first principles to be, as men always will be, strongly tempted to prefer a life of license to marriage. If it were *certain* that by so doing he would injure so far as in him lay the progress of mankind towards the Positivist ideal, and that that ideal was really desirable, then, though he might yield to temptation, though the sanction that would restrain him would be comparatively feeble, still his conscience would exert the full force of whatever power it possessed in favour of obedience. But he never will or can be certain. It can at best be but a probability that the ideal is worth attainment. It can but be a somewhat stronger probability that the right way of attaining it has been chosen. Conscience then will be perplexed or silent, for the intellect will always be able to lull or bewilder it. If, or where, Christians can doubt what Christ really taught, they always find reasons for supposing that He taught what they wish to think. If a man doubt whether Christ taught truth or falsehood, he will always reject Christ's teaching where it comes into conflict with his own strong and immediate desires. Now the uncertainty which occurs to some men as regards the authority of Christ, the perplexity which on a few points is felt as to His actual teaching, inheres in the whole scheme of Positivism. Admit the basis of its ethics, the inference must always be arguable, and passion will always throw its sword into the scale of argument.'

Sterne.—' So it does with religion.'

Cleveland.—' When it can. For example, Christians have contrived to convince themselves that Christianity permits war; but no one can persuade himself that Christianity permits revenge, or sensual indulgence, or divorce at will. On ninety-nine practical questions of human conduct in a hundred we cannot doubt what, as Christians or Mahometans, is our duty. On every point we must always doubt more or less what is our duty as Agnostics, because the Agnostic code— be it Comtist or Benthamite—is a matter of deduction from questionable premisses. The probability will never be mathematically calculable; and if it were, the sacrifice being certain and personal, the reward impersonal and uncertain, the tempted man would always run the risk and justify it to his conscience.'

Sterne.—' Yet probability is the guide of life, and though as you say men do not realize this, that is merely a matter of temporary ignorance. Those who do recognize it act just as those who do not; and when the truth is universally recognized—when education has taught the whole world that, at least outside of mathematics and perhaps of natural science, we can attain nothing beyond probability—will that affect men's practical conduct; will they plough and sow less diligently because the return of the seasons is matter of probability only, though of a probability practically infinite ?'

Cleveland.—' Of course not. In such matters educated men will feel that probability indefinitely strong is practically the equivalent of certainty.'

Sterne.—' Then why not in morals ?'

Cleveland.—' For two reasons. First, the probability will always be much less than overwhelming. It depends on human foresight in that political field in which confessedly human intellect is most liable to err and most misled by prejudice and passion; and again impulse, temptation, passion will always govern men's estimate of the probabilities that should restrain them. Secondly, if we disregard the probabilities of practical life the penalty falls on ourselves; if we disregard or miscalculate those of Agnostic morality, the penalty falls on indefinite multitudes and distant ages. Do you suppose that man will ever incur severe certain suffering and self-denial on a calculation of probable advantages to a remote generation; advantages which, in so far as they depend on his own individual conduct, must after all be infinitesimal?'

Sterne.—' Men do act, do take trouble and make sacrifices to render infinitesimal benefit to a cause in which they are warmly interested. How else would each man vote in a constituency of thousands? He knows the chances to be very great that his vote will make no difference to the result, and yet he takes no little trouble to record it for a favourite candidate. When we have educated men to think and feel as they ought, to care a thousand times more for the future of the race than for the success of a local faction, will they not be at least equally eager to do their little possible for so grand a cause?'

Cleveland.—' There are several objections to that reasoning, specious as it is. First, educated men, who fully appreciate the insignificance of their own individual votes, are even now very apt to stay away from the poll on a wet day. Next, there is much personal satisfaction in the mere act of giving a vote, of expressing one's own devotion to Gladstone or detestation of Bright. Lastly, we know that our vote does help our cause and cannot hurt it; we can never be sure of that in regard to the influence of our conduct on the future of mankind.'

Sterne.—' Is that true? Are there many practical questions of conduct in regard to which we can have serious doubt?'

Cleveland.—' Yes. Take that which is confessedly the *crux* of Agnostic morality, because experience is so strong on one side and logic so peremptory on the other. The Positivists proper insist strongly on the permanence of marriage. The most consistent, the most advanced Agnostics, if they do not denounce marriage altogether, assert a right of divorce, an equality of the sexes which are utterly fatal to marriage. Here on a fundamental point, and a point where temptation and passion will have the strongest influence, your moralists contradict one another, and your code must always speak, if not with a doubtful voice, yet with doubtful authority.'

Sterne.—' So does Christianity. The Founder never pronounced against polygamy.'

Cleveland.—' But the Church has done so, and emphatically. Moreover, between monogamy and polygamy is but a question of degree. Either will work, either affords a solid basis for the family, a practical security for women, a permanent marriage bond. Mahometanism and orthodox Christianity alike make the relation a subject of law, not of license. Agnosticism at present leaves it open, and as I think—and have a right while the controversy continues among yourselves to think—must always leave it open, whether there is to be any moral legislation on the subject; leaves the law and license as yet on an equal footing before the tribunal of conscience. And while this is the case, it is hopeless to imagine that there can be any other practical issue than the triumph of pure licentiousness.'

Sterne.—' But you hold with me—and with almost every man who has any real knowledge of the matter, whether from physiological science, historical study, or practical investigation—that license in that sphere is utterly fatal to the welfare of mankind; and *that* suffices to establish the Positivist or Agnostic doctrine, leaves no doubt as to the rule of duty, no uncertainty to perplex or enfeeble the utterance of conscience.'

Cleveland.—' Each doctrine is part of a whole system of ethics, which Agnosticism repudiates.

The experience on which we rely belongs to an order of things which Agnosticism would sweep away. It will always be open to the advocates of license to say that marriage was a necessity of the past, an institution suited to the old superstitious morality, which the higher morality of the future can dispense with, must shake off as an incubus, as it shakes off a priesthood that may once have been needful, but has done its work and become worse than useless. And, as Lestrange says, marriage is essentially illogical; and no illogical virtue can find a place in a code which is nothing if not strictly logical. Logic is the basis of Agnostic ethics, and no logic can justify the binding together perforce, against their will, of two equal and independent beings in a relation which becomes hateful when it ceases to be willing.'

Sterne.—' But all the logical objections to marriage are independent of Agnosticism. They are just as valid, as forcible in a Christian or Moslem as in an Atheistic community.'

Cleveland.—' Possibly; but they are overridden. Christ and Mahomet have spoken decisively, peremptorily on the subject, and the law they have given is upheld by a force of sentiment and experience against which logic directs its artillery in vain. Prove that a Christian law is illogical, and you have proved nothing. It does not pretend to be based on logic. But prove to an Agnostic that a law is illogical, and you have destroyed its very foundation. His every ethical precept is and must be a logical deduction from his first principles.'

CHAPTER VI.

WOMAN'S FUTURE WITHOUT FAITH.

Mrs. Cleveland had so well timed her drive that when our route brought us out upon the road we saw the phaeton approaching less than a quarter of a mile off. Lestrange got out and joined us, Mrs. Cleveland drove on to the neighbouring village, where she had business, and we strolled homeward by the road on which she was to overtake us.

'We have been arguing,' I said, 'whether the triumph of Agnostic ethics would not necessarily be the abolition of marriage.'

'Free divorce, at any rate,' said Lestrange. 'Most of the female Agnostics go for that; and it is the one merit of their system.'

Cleveland.—'Yet you must know that free divorce means the slavery of woman.'

Lestrange.—'And serve her right. For the last fifty years women have been practically emancipated, and the use they have made of their liberty has reduced married men to servitude. To be tied to a partner you cannot control is obviously intolerable. Now I suppose the equality of the sexes is an established Agnostic tenet, though I cannot see why.'

Sterne.—' Why should they be unequal ?'

Lestrange.—' Because they are. If Agnosticism have a fundamental principle, it should be to accept the laws of Nature; and those laws have made women unfit for independence, and require them to be controlled and guided by men, as plainly as they have made men and women social beings and mutually dependent. But of course you cannot bind two citizens to live together when they are tired of doing so, except on supernatural grounds; and I don't admit your right to do so on any ground whatever.'

I had not courage to apply the *argumentum ad hominem;* but Cleveland's greater tact and fuller knowledge of the man enabled him to state it without personal offence.

' Yet, Lestrange, you would not allow that anything, short of that breach of the contract which perforce forfeits its benefits, would justify a husband in repudiating a wife ?'

Lestrange.—' No, not as things stand. He has bound himself, however foolishly, however ignorantly; he has received part at any rate of the consideration, and he must stand by his promise. I am speaking of a time when the law will render such engagements terminable at will.'

Sterne.—'And you think it ought to do so?'

Lestrange.—'Certainly. I can see no principle that can give the State a right to rule the terms of domestic any more than of commercial partnership.'

Cleveland.—'Nor does it.'

Lestrange.—'Yes, it does; for if you do not enter into a permanent perpetual partnership, such as it will allow in no other case, it stigmatizes your children and deprives them of the right of inheritance. More than that, it treats all other forms of union as, if not criminal, yet immoral and contrary to public policy: it invalidates all contracts based thereon. Short of actual penal enactments, it could not persecute more cruelly those who object on principle to the permanence of marriage.'

Cleveland.—'I might repeat your remark—" Serve them right." But I grant that marriage is illogical and indefensible when once you abolish the religious ground. I am not sure that I think so: but I am not prepared to say that the State could, and we may be sure that it will not, enforce real permanence on any other ground. Do you seriously think that the consequent state of things will be endurable?'

Sterne.—' Why not? Free divorce seems to exist in the Western States of the Union.'

Cleveland.—' Not theoretically; and social opinion does not sanction it. It is still disreputable.'

Sterne.—' Apparently not in California, if I may trust an article I read lately on the Society of the Golden State.'

Cleveland.—' I think that must be considerably exaggerated. At any rate Californian society inherits the traditions of the older States, and most of its citizens have been brought up to believe in the permanence of the marriage tie.'

Lestrange.—' Still free divorce exists, and it don't seem to work so badly. Certainly it has not made women slaves.'

Cleveland.—' No; and for the most obvious of all reasons. They are there in a very decided minority. The demand greatly exceeds the supply. In old countries the case is and always must be the reverse.'

Lestrange.—' I don't know. There are two conditions that well may redress the balance. It is becoming increasingly possible for women to earn their own maintenance; and secondly, freedom implies the possibility of polygamy, and polygamy would soon absorb the small excess.'

Cleveland.—' Polygamy means female slavery, if anything does.'

Lestrange.—'I don't know. You cannot call it slavery where the slave can leave her master at pleasure.'

Cleveland.—'Not if she can do so practically. But when the penalty is starvation, it might as well be the lash. Slavery existed when only the Ohio, or an imaginary line, lay between the fugitive and a free State. It was not the Fugitive Slave Law—which never was observed—but the peril of starvation in the North, that prevented the slaves of Maryland and Kentucky from running away *en masse.*'

A.—'Nonsense, Cleveland! If they had been discontented, if slavery had really been in those States a cruel hardship, the negroes would have taken their chance of finding work on the prairies of Illinois or in the mines of Pennsylvania.'

Cleveland.—'Possibly. It was slavery nevertheless.'

Sterne.—'But even now the penalty of starvation is hardly real. Our female servants would not be so very ready to throw up their places if it were. A woman can always earn a living, though it may be at a total sacrifice of everything but independence and bread.'

Cleveland.—'That is not much to the point. A woman brought up to domestic service, who has any sort of character, can always earn a living till she is past work. How after that? And on women not brought up to domestic service, not qualified for it, to whom it would be an intolerable degradation, the penalty remains effective, and will remain. Their choice will lie between submission to the master's will and an intolerable condition. It will be slavery with just this mitigation, that the slavery cannot be worse than the workhouse without driving the slaves to revolt.'

Lestrange.—' There will always be a sufficient demand to give a woman a choice of masters, when the present morality is so done away or altered that she can change masters at will.'

Cleveland.—' Perhaps; though there might be a kind of Trades-Union feeling among the men, a disposition to proscribe a fugitive slave and to Boycott any man that received her. But say there is not—grant that while the fugitive is young and attractive she will always find a refuge. How when she has ceased to be so? What will become of women past middle age?'

Lestrange.—' I think it will always be their own fault if after twenty years of wedded life their husbands wish to part with them.'

Cleveland.—' To part with them absolutely, perhaps; to choose another partner, no. There is one physiological consideration which will always render free divorce intolerable; the fact that men are much younger than women at the same age.'

Sterne.—' Don't you see, Cleveland, that, in proving free divorce to be iniquitous and intolerably cruel to women, you prove that in a society where women are equal with men it will never be allowed?'

A.—' How is it then that so many women are clamouring for it now?'

Lestrange.—' Because they are fools; they don't know what's good for them.'

Cleveland.—' That is not the whole answer. Those who clamour for it in this country are very few, and scarcely one of them would be affected by any marriage law whatever. No man would have them on any terms. The Americans see only the American situation, where from local conditions there is a demand for women's services in every department of life far exceeding the supply.'

Sterne.—' You have not answered my question.'

Lestrange.—' You cannot rule out the liberty of equals to make their own terms with one another, to regulate their life as they please.'

Cleveland.—' Not under the present economic regimen, not while liberty is the paramount idea of mankind at large—at least of civilized mankind—and the watchword of Revolution. But observe that Positivism is the absolute denial of individual liberty; its theory is neither the rule of the majority nor the freedom of the individual, but the despotism of an intellectual priesthood. The Positivists proper—the Comtists—might, like the Puritans, prohibit under heavy penalties every form of marriage but that which approved itself to their judgment.'

Lestrange.—' Possibly; but the one thing we shall not see is a Positivist Commonwealth. The choice of the future lies between a gradual development of the present system based on religions in which men have ceased to believe—a thing which cannot long endure, as you cannot repair a building whose foundation is rotten—and a political democracy with an Agnostic theory of life, with no law that cannot commend itself to the multitude on logical grounds, and no moral code that cannot enforce itself on the intellect of the individual.'

Cleveland.—' Agnosticism, being a mere negation, will never coerce the conscience of the democracy. Religion might conceivably extort, as it has extorted in the past, freedom for the individual conscience. Agnosticism can never do so; and a democracy is always not merely despotic but arbitrary in temper. As polygamy must always be the indulgence of the few, the many may take a fancy to put it down.'

Lestrange.—'I don't see how they can. You cannot possibly justify interference with the freedom of the individual, with his or her right to make what terms he or she may please. You cannot force men and women to enter into perpetual partnerships if they prefer limited ones; you cannot abolish freedom of contract in the domestic sphere.'

Cleveland.—'Can't you? You are going to abolish it in every sphere where it seems to tend to the advantage of the Few rather than of the Many. You have abolished it to a great extent in Ireland by law, and the chief effort of the Trades Unions, which after all represent the tendency and the ruling thought of the democracy, is to suppress freedom of contract altogether.'

Sterne.—'That is a remnant of mediæval ignorance which cannot survive enlightenment.'

Cleveland.—'No democracy will ever be enlightened. You might instruct its intellect, you cannot educate its passions.'

Sterne.—'Look at the question practically. The men will always wish to be free to make their own terms with women, if, as you say, that freedom will make them masters. A certain proportion of the younger women will see that freedom offers them immediate advantages, at which they will snatch; and thus you will have a majority in favour of license, apart from the strong conviction of a large minority that the State has no right to interfere with perfect freedom in individual life. But will not the power of self-maintenance secure the freedom of the weaker sex?'

Lestrange.—' I think not. The situation will be this: it will always be harder for a woman to earn her living than for a man. She will always earn less; there will always, while property exists, be men ready to offer her present comfort, ease, idleness, a certain instead of a precarious maintenance, on terms that, when once the religious idea of chastity is renounced as a superstition, will seem to her exceedingly easy. She will feel that she is always free to revert to her independence; she will not realise how very difficult, how practically impossible, such return will have become after ten or fifteen years. I say that if men could so easily renounce the hardships and difficulties of independence, most of them would do so. I say that women will do the same, because that which is never open to men will always be a possible alternative to them. You may have a number, and an increasing number, of women who will perceive the folly of such a bargain and struggle up-hill to maintain themselves; but these will be a minority. The majority will accept the terminable partnerships offered them in early youth; and this majority will always supply a multitude of women from thirty years upwards weary, sick to death of their domestic slavery, and not knowing how otherwise to obtain a living—numbers too who have been repudiated and can hardly find another home, while they have lost the habit and perhaps the capacity of industry.'

No one answered, and after a minute's pause I said:

'For once, Cleveland, let us have the discussion summed up and judgment passed. What is your conclusion upon the whole argument?'

Cleveland.—'Free divorce is a logical inevitable deduction from Agnostic morality, or rather from the abolition of the religious dogma which alone can prohibit such freedom; and free divorce means the degradation, moral ruin, and material misery of woman, and consequently the rapid deterioration of social life, a relapse into moral barbarism and domestic anarchy.'

Lestrange.—'We have the last already, since women have utterly repudiated one fundamental doctrine of Christianity—their own subordination. A disobedient wife, a woman who meddles in public affairs, cannot be a Christian; for each sets at defiance a dogma as distinctly and positively enunciated by the Christian Scriptures as any one of the Ten Commandments; and to repudiate a single dogma is to repudiate the authority of all.'

'After all,' said Sterne, presently, 'is there any reason practically to believe any of these hideous nightmares of your fancy? Religion is certainly losing its hold, people are feeling less and less confident; even those who do believe are becoming aware that the leading intellects of the day believe less and less. We live in an atmosphere of doubt if not yet of disbelief. Is there a corresponding relaxation of morality? Is there not, on the contrary, an amount of moral enthusiasm such as was never witnessed in any previous age?'

Lestrange.—'More whine and cant, certainly. The anti-vivisection agitation — half a dozen religious fanatics apart—is a fair specimen of "enthusiastic" morality. A lady who is passionately fond of pets, and cares as little for scientific truth as for fair play, represents the best half of it—that which consists of ignorant women and sentimental men. For the other side—anglers, sportsmen, fox-hunters, and fools at large—they merely

> "Make up for sins they are inclined to
> By damning those they have no mind to"

—would atone the carnivorous cruelty of their favourite sports by reviling the philanthropic severity of experiments which in a whole year inflict less suffering than a single battue.'

Sterne.—'I don't see that that declamation, however true it may be, is much to the point.'

Cleveland.—'Yes; it illustrates what Lestrange means by talking of whine and cant. The virtue of to-day is what you call moral enthusiasm: much talk of self-sacrifice, very little of it in act; a general laxity of principle and vehemence of sympathy.'

Lestrange.—'Or of passion. Half the philanthropy of to-day is almost undisguised envy, hatred and malice. The Radical professors from whom Sterne derives his notion of latter-day moral enthusiasm really hate the rich much more than they love the poor. They envy the wealth which is always before their eyes, of which and of its enjoyments they have a much keener idea, a much closer view than the average demagogue; and they hate the aristocracy that keeps them down, they think that in a pure democracy with distributed wealth they would be the foremost members of society. They would, as in France and America, be ministers, ambassadors, representatives—and God help the country then.'

Sterne.—' Well, well; where are the signs of immorality or relaxed virtue consequent on the growth of Scepticism ?'

Cleveland.—' Not among these hills, of course. Go into a London club, listen to the talk of men of the world on moral questions, and see how little of earnest faith in any moral law is left among them. Compare the talk with what it was twenty-five years ago. Then it was an offence to affect doubt of any fundamental principle of orthodoxy. To express unbelief was to invite insult; to assume that your neighbour could be anything but an orthodox Christian was to affront him. Now-a-days even Conservative society rather patronises religion than believes in it, and a similar scepticism prevails on points of morality. A man may to-day affirm that marriage is an absurdity, may challenge the first principles of social order, might have defended murder till the assassinations committed by Land Leaguers and Nihilists frightened society into a passion on that subject; may argue against any of the Ten Commandments, and will be answered on almost equal terms.'

Sterne.—' But are people less moral in action ?'

Lestrange.—' Yes. You cannot get a scoundrel hanged ; and if he is effectively punished in any way, there is a distinct disposition to look upon him as a hardly-used individual.'

Cleveland.—' Social morality—the morality not of the Stock Exchange, the lecture-room, or the Houses, but of the drawing-room and the home—is feminine. Now the unbelief of men does not much affect their wives or sisters; it does affect their daughters. To see how practical morals are relaxed, you must wait till those girls whose fathers have never professed to believe anything are the matrons of the day. And even now, look at the girls of the period! Look at the tone of Society, the freedom with which subjects once tabooed are discussed, the curiosity manifested respecting certain notorious women by their own sex. Look, above all, at the Society journals and the photographers' shops, the publication of the portraits of women not public characters. When I entered on life no man dared have published the likeness of any lady, not a princess or an actress—no newspaper that did so would have been tolerated. To-day I should be thought a fool, I should be sneered at by every man under forty and many of my own age or older, for objecting to have Ida's photograph exhibited in every window in Regent Street.'

Lestrange.—' I wonder it has not been done.'

A.—' Nonsense, Lestrange! How many of the professional or professed beauties are worth looking at? It is not beauty but notoriety that attracts the photographers. Beauty modest and retiring is still safe; but a lady who has the misfortune, for whatever reason, to be talked about could not, even were her husband to walk Regent Street daily with a stout bamboo, keep her portrait out of the shop-windows.'

Lestrange.—' You know V——? He was offered the editorship of one of the best of these Society journals, and expressed his abhorrence of the whole concern in his usual strong, emphatic fashion. The proprietor replied: "I never published a portrait except with the permission, generally at the request, of the lady." And yet among the portraits that had appeared in that journal were those of ladies not only of high rank and fashion, but of high character and stainless reputation.'

Sterne.—' That is matter after all of taste, not of morality.'

Cleveland.—' When women cease to be modest they are not very far from ceasing to be virtuous. We had the other day a costume so indecent that it was actually prohibited at Court. But for that prohibition it would have become all but universal; it would have needed some courage before a woman could have refused to wear it in society. A woman who will exhibit her person half-dressed for the amusement of half London, and allow herself to be embraced and pulled about in such costume in ball-room after ball-room, is not very far from the final stage of demoralization.'

Sterne.—' If that is the worst, these are matters after all of fashion, and the fashion was nearly as bad in former ages.'

Cleveland.—' It is not the worst. Scepticism has made great and rapid way in England, but the way has been too rapid to have penetrated deep. We still retain Christian practice with Atheistic opinion; but where scepticism has prevailed longer, or where opinion penetrates downwards more quickly, in France, in Germany, in America, look at the state of morality. The aversion of American women to bear children, the license of divorce in the West and in California, are from one point of view as significant of widespread demoralisation as from the other the infamous wholesale corruption which yet does not bring punishment, or exclude men from the highest political positions, or deprive them of the widest popularity. When I was in America,[*] I could have named a dozen men in the highest places who were notorious thieves. I have already called your attention to the statistics of divorce and illegitimacy in Germany. Ask yourself what is meant by the limitation of French families, a limitation almost universal. Consider

[*] 1868-70.

what will happen when the French practice spreads to other countries, when the teaching of certain would-be economists and physiologists comes to form an understood if not an admitted part of our own social practice.'

Sterne.—' There is no chance of it.'

Cleveland.—' Is there not? Then what of the half-million purchasers of a notorious pamphlet; and why is the native American population dying out in the North-Eastern States?'

Sterne.—' After all, except what you say of Republican corruption in America, your statements only touch a single branch of morals.'

Cleveland.—' True, but the most fundamental, the most vital of all, and the one in which it is most obvious that legal coercion cannot effectually supply the place of personal conviction. But look at the anti-rent organization in Ireland, a conspiracy of half a nation to swindle, organized by Members of Parliament and defended on the floor of the House! If I call them by their proper name, I shall shock the feelings of the age more than they have done. Still less must I dare to describe in plain English a recent act to " expropriate "—without compensation—men to whom the English Goverment, the Imperial Parliament, had in the most absolute and positive terms, and within the lifetime of the present possessors, guaranteed the full and absolute ownership of their land. Fifty years ago, the man who had made such a proposal would not merely have been hurled from office but would have been hooted from society.'

Sterne.—' I cannot accept a change in political opinion as a proof of relaxed morality.'

Lestrange.—' Then where will you find one? If immorality sanctioned by Parliament may no longer be cited to prove that the virtue of the country is declining, you will never find any evidence of such decline; since the moment that the relaxation has really taken full effect out of doors it will find Parliamentary support and presently Parliamentary sanction.'

Sterne.—' All the same, you will not frighten anybody, you will not make Agnosticism appear dangerous, by accusing Mr. Gladstone of theft.'

Cleveland.—' No; Mr. Gladstone is in politics what certain favourites of society are called—a privileged man. He may steal the horse where a Radical or a Tory would be hanged for looking over the hedge. But, as *Punch* said of his social antitype, "The deuce take such privileged men!"'

Lestrange.—' Don't let the matter drop there, Cleveland, or Sterne will go away with the idea that there is no connection between moral and theological unbelief. The truth, politics apart, is that which you stated just now. It will take a generation before English Atheism will practically and deeply affect English daily life; but on the Continent and in America we do see the moral consequences of Atheistic logic.'

Sterne.—' You mean in free divorce and the like ?'

Cleveland.—' Yes; and moreover in certain political phases to which your objection will not apply. Atheism has produced Nihilism and the Parisian Commune, two tolerably hideous births for a single generation. If those consequences are not sufficiently appalling, we may regard even free divorce in all its varied aspects with indifference.'

CHAPTER VII.

DESPAIR.

'"The fool hath said in his heart, there is no God,"' I said, when we had sat round the smoking-room fire for some time in meditative silence. 'How much truth is there in the suggestion that the fool says it because he wishes to believe it?'

Lestrange.—'.He must be indeed a fool. That there is no God seems to me a painfully obvious conclusion; that we have not the slightest reason to think there is, an inevitable inference from the natural history of theology. But of one thing I am sure beyond all possibility of doubt; no man of sense and feeling can be glad that the Universe is without a Ruler—Man without a future, and without a spiritual Sovereign and Protector.'

Sterne.—' I can't see of what use God has ever been.'

Cleveland.—' Come, Sterne, that is exaggeration.'

Sterne.—' Perhaps. I suppose Christianity did

something to reform Roman society, though the Lower or Christian Empire seems to have been by all accounts incomparably worse than the Paganism of the Cæsars, Flavii, Antonines; and no doubt Mahometanism has done much good here and there, but chiefly by extirpating worse Gods than the Oriental tyrant whom Mahomet enthroned in Heaven.'

Lestrange.—'After all, what dreadful bullies, what atrocious despots most of your Deities are; and despots whose ruthless tyranny is not even tempered by the possibility of assassination! The most infamous piece of immorality I remember to have seen gravely put forward by a moralist— and it is to moralists that you must look for the concentration of human villainy—is a sentence which lies at the root of Mahometanism and of most forms of Christianity: "Shall the clay say to the potter, why hast thou made me thus?" God, so ninety-nine Christians in a hundred and all Mahometans tell us, has made the great majority of His human creatures with the deliberate intention of burning them for ever. What right had He? If one of us could create sentient beings out of clay or otherwise, and did create them in order to torture them, would he not deserve eternal Hell, if any finite sin could deserve infinite punishment? There is no wretch in any of the Hells—Dante's, or Milton's, or St. John's—who can be said strictly to deserve his fate. But the God of Mahomet and St. John is the one being who does deserve the eternal punishment to which He dooms His creatures.'

Mrs. Cleveland was not present, and none of us were disposed to challenge Lestrange's paradox, extravagant as it might seem. Only, after a pause, Cleveland said:

'Everlasting punishment is, I think, a logical consequence of what we know of human nature coupled with what we conceive of immortality. We do not suppose that God will work a moral miracle upon us, either at death or afterwards; at any rate, we don't expect Him to do so against our own wills. If we choose, as some of us doubtless do, to be eternally bad, it stands to reason—that is, it consorts with the order of Nature—that we shall be eternally punished.'

A.—'I don't know. The only rational conception of the future I ever heard is Swedenborgian, whether or not it be exactly Swedenborg's. The man who is, as you say, eternally bad goes to Hell by preference; and what, looked upon from Heaven, seems punishment is to him the greatest happiness of which his nature is capable.'

'Lestrange's invective,' said Vere, after a pause, 'does not seem to me to touch the point to which it was applied at all. Because men have entertained very erroneous notions about God, it does not follow that they would have been better without the idea of Him.'

Lestrange.—' Surely, better worship nothing at all than worship the Devil?'

Vere.—' You know, Lestrange, as well as I that nobody does worship the Devil.'

Lestrange.—' I know nothing of the kind. Not only savages but a great many Christians do worship an Evil Power, for fear He should hurt them. The savages are the more logical. They believe in a Good Power to which they need not pray or sacrifice, because He will do His best for them in any case. But the Christians attribute all they believe to be good to a Power as tyrannical as any idol savages ever propitiated by the customs of Dahomey.'

Vere.—' Now and then you may find a man or a sect that worships God on that principle. But even these believe Him to be just, though their idea of justice is horribly perverse. They fancy at any rate that He will be just to themselves; the atrocious wickedness they ascribe to Him is after all no part of their real conception of His character. It is only a logical theory devised to answer the inconvenient question—what is to become of those who do not fulfil the only conditions under which the believer feels that he himself can be saved.'

Sterne.—' Historically, those logical solutions have very materially affected men's idea of God; they have led them to cut the throats of all whom they expected Him to damn. If it was right for God to roast them, it could hardly be wrong for His true believers to slaughter them.'

Vere.—' A very false inference. A much truer one, even from their own grounds, would have been that which tradition represents as taught to Abraham: "I have endured him these hundred years, couldst not thou bear with him one night?" After all, you cannot find a more unamiable conception of God than that of the Puritans, or a more unamiable set than the Puritans themselves. Yet no rational student of history can doubt how much the Puritan conception did for England, for Holland, and indeed for the world at large.'

' No one,' I said, ' except Lestrange, has given any answer to my question. Does anybody wish to disbelieve in God? Men may revolt from the God of Mahomet or Moses; but does anyone really wish to believe that there is no Ruler of the Universe and no Father in Heaven?'

Lestrange.—' I must suppose so, considering with what enthusiastic vehemence the Agnostics propagate their denial.'

Cleveland.—' And yet the Agnostics find that they cannot do without Him, and create a mock Deity of their own. No doubt there have been not a few Atheists made by revolt from the very Deities of whom Lestrange speaks; but I think Agnostic enthusiasm is partly self-deception, partly partisanship. They see how powerful an argument with the great majority is the belief that if God did not exist we should have to invent Him; and they affirm that they do not miss Him in order to persuade others that He need not exist.'

Sterne.—' What do you want Him for ?'

Lestrange.—' To make life endurable.'

Sterne.—' I can understand your saying that; I don't think you would have found it much pleasanter if you had Him. Cleveland, why do you want a God ?'

Cleveland.—' To make life possible.'

Sterne turned to me, evidently not a little perplexed by the last answer. ' And you ?'

A.—' That men who think at all may not be driven mad by terror.'

Sterne.—' Well, there are three answers, all emphatic, all I suppose meaning something, and probably something profound and well thought out, to those who utter them. I don't suppose on such a point you would any of you answer idly or answer on the spur of the moment. But I have not the remotest conception what any one of you means.'

Cleveland.—' I believe we all mean very nearly the same thing, though we express it in different terms according to our different temperament. To Lestrange, naturally, the difficulty of enduring a life of suffering without reason or purpose in the suffering is the most obvious consideration. To a man who looks always somewhat forward, and always sees the future somewhat *en noir*, the hideous possibilities of a future left to Chance—a future in which anything may be, and in which the worst is *prima facie* just as likely as anything else—must seem the most striking and appalling of horrors. To me, who have every reason man can have to be contented with life as it is for myself, and who therefore look on it as it were from outside and see how it concerns others, the prime marvel is how men are ever to consent to exist, and to accept the conditions of social existence, if they believe the Universe, at least the moral and spiritual Universe, to be one great anarchy.'

Sterne.—' Well, I am not much wiser. I will probe Lestrange's answer first, because I have some glimmering notion of his meaning. If you find life unendurable, why continue to live ?'

Lestrange.—' Because annihilation is more intolerable still.'

Sterne.—' How can that be? Nothing cannot suffer.'

Lestrange.—' No; but to an intellect keenly conscious of itself—perhaps, I do not know, especially to an intellect which finds in its own exercise the sole pleasure, the sole compensation of life—the idea of ceasing to exist is more horrible than all the suffering with which existence can be attended. When it ceases to be so, men do *not* consent to live.'

Sterne.—' Yet sane suicides are very few.'

Lestrange.—' Which proves that, say what they will, men do regard annihilation with intense horror. There are multitudes who cannot possibly enjoy life. If so few of them put a voluntary end to it, it must be because death means to them something more frightful than all the tortures through which in so many cases it comes. Myriads of us endure unceasing misery of which we know that death is the only termination; yet that termination is so terrible that merely to postpone it we are willing to suffer without hope. What more conclusive, overpowering testimony can there be to the universal horror of annihilation?'

Vere.—' There may be another reason. Probably few of the sufferers in question are Agnostics; most of them have a more or less definite idea that suicide will not terminate existence but introduce them to a new phase of suffering.'

Lestrange.—' Did you ever have a really agonizing tooth-ache or head-ache? Because, if you did, you would find that you cannot realize the possibility of worse suffering: you would terminate *that* at any risk except through suicide, and it is easy to persuade yourself that God might, must pardon suicide committed in intolerable agony.'

Sterne.—' Still I don't see. How does your disbelief in a Deity make life harder to bear?'

Lestrange.—' What made the toil of Sisyphus so specially intolerable? He would have been content doubtless to roll the stone for ten thousand years up, and up, and up, so long as a purpose was served, an end might be attained. To an Atheist suffering is purposeless, and therefore not only intolerable but infuriating. He who supposes it inflicted for some good purpose, under the laws of a Lawgiver who certainly intends the benefit of His creatures at large, and probably the sufferer's personal advantage as well, regards it in a very different light.'

Sterne.—' Well; and why should life be less *possible* because there is no God?'

Cleveland.—'Because there is no guidance, no certainty. There always remains of course that kind of mechanical certainty which leads the seedsman to expect the harvest, which prevents a sane man from springing off a precipice, the fixity of the laws of Nature; but there is no certainty in morals without a God, no assurance what will be the issue of conduct. Any consequence becomes possible. We see crime apparently leading not only to advantage, not only personal but universal. We see virtue standing in the path of progress and crushed under its wheels; we see a thousand motives for breaking the plainest moral law in this case and that, and none for keeping it except that it is the law of God and that He will not allow it to be broken with impunity.'

Sterne.—'Moral laws are the laws of Nature as well as physical.'

Cleveland.—'Aye; but in morals there is no certainty that the penalty will be exacted. In morals you may fling yourself over the precipice and find safety and fortune at the bottom; you may refrain from sowing and yet reap the harvest, or you may plough and sow without any harvest or even any chance or hope of one; and this is only endurable when you have faith in a Power above Nature, and consequences behind those you can see.'

Vere.—' I thought you meant a good deal more than that.'

Cleveland.—'So I did. But the rest of what I meant is better expressed in the saying that life without a God becomes too full of terror to be faced. In that case there is nothing that may not happen; no injustice, no cruelty, no misery, no evil—moral evil as well as physical, evil to mankind as well as to individuals, evil permanent as well as temporary—which may not befal. There is no foundation for courage where there is no faith. Courage without faith means simply capacity, or rather confidence in our own capacity, to endure anything we may have to suffer. Now even physically this is impossible. There are sufferings of the body that the bravest cannot endure; there are calamities that the firmest mind cannot face with calmness because they affect— and if there be no God may affect hopelessly and for their whole existence—others than ourselves. Our friend has described a world where no one believes in a God or a future, and the consequent terror has been generally recognized as a natural inference. But what has not been so generally recognised is the extent and the effect of that terror. The critics see that men who believe in no future will fear to die; they seem to have missed the much uglier inference that men who believe neither in God nor in a future can hardly dare to live. And above all, disbelief in God means utter darkness over all time to come. We may be on the right road, we may be on the wrong; our destiny may be to constant progress, steady amelioration; it may be towards unspeakable physical and moral deterioration and misery. We have no reason to be confident rather that mankind are in the way to general comfort and prosperity than that they are on the road to a state in which they will lead the life of wolves and be driven at last to tear one another to pieces for subsistence. The possibilities of evil ahead are too horrible to be willingly contemplated by any man who does not believe that our future is ordered, controlled. To the Agnostic that future is matter of mere chance. It is not even under the guidance of a few wise human minds, but depends partly upon the incalculable agencies of physical Nature, and partly upon the conflicting influences of millions of human wills all seeking different ends by different roads; and the resultant of such diverse forces is from the Agnostic's point of view the merest, most absolute matter of chance.'

Sterne.—'From the Agnostic's point of view there is no such thing as Chance; all is matter of Law.'

Lestrange.—'Very good; but what will be the result brought out by the working of the various laws involved is matter of absolute uncertainty; what effect any given line of conduct will produce, whether the world is advancing to perfection or going to the dogs is, to put the thing in an intelligible and indisputable form, matter of very even betting.'

Vere.—'And there is a difficulty, a danger in life without God which might well frighten an Atheist into absolute inaction. Obeying God's law, we leave the responsibility to God. If the consequence be evil, our own consciences are clear. But if there be no God, if all moral law be matter of expediency, and expediency to be discovered by human wisdom, then we must look solely to the consequences of our action, and we are responsible for every mistake, whether we do evil that good may come or do good with evil consequences clearly in view.'

Merton.—'I don't see it. We are equally bound to go by general laws, not particular instances, whether those general laws are given by God or discovered by Man.'

Lestrange.—'No such thing. A general law on your principle is only the course of conduct which generally leads to human advantage. Your only reason for following it is that it does so lead.

If then a case occur in which obedience leads to palpable evil, and no palpable evil be likely to follow disobedience, then disobedience becomes a duty.'

Merton.—
> '.... Deep harm to disobey,
> Seeing obedience is the bond of rule.'

Lestrange.—' That is, those who have laid down the general rules are so sure of their own infallibility that they dare affirm the effect of a single infraction, in weakening the force of the rule, to be more evil than any harm that can possibly follow from adherence in a case where infraction is obviously and immediately expedient.'

Sterne.—' Will you give me a case?'

Lestrange.—' Well, the murder of a particular tyrant will in all probability be of exceeding benefit to mankind. It may liberate a whole nation from an intolerable slavery. The probability that one successful murder will render human life seriously, perceptibly more insecure is too small to be worth consideration. Why should not any man who has the chance murder such a tyrant? Is it not his obvious duty, if there be no Divine command, " Thou shalt not kill?" '

Cleveland.—' Every political murder I remember has been a blunder as well as a crime.'

Lestrange.—' No; not from the point of view of

the murderer. I doubt whether the assassination of the first great William of Orange was not a heavy blow to the Protestant cause; I doubt whether, but for the murder of Henry IV., the Edict of Nantes would ever have been repealed. The murder of Prim certainly ruined the fortunes of his party, doomed the incipient monarchy of Amadeo to failure. The theory that political murders are blunders is founded on the English feeling—almost exclusively English—that murder is so atrocious a crime as always to produce a reaction in favour of the murdered man or his party, worth more to them than his life. Now, except in England and America—in nearly all the countries where tyrannicide is probable—party feeling is much stronger than the abhorrence of murder. The assassination of Marat produced no reaction in favour of the Terrorists; the murder of Louis XVI. certainly *paid* from Robespierre's point of view.'

Cleveland.—'I doubt.'

Lestrange.—'But if you doubt, that doubt proves my case. Now, in every human life there frequently occur cases where the infraction of a general moral law appears clearly expedient, probably appears more expedient than it really is. That our individual example will have any perceptible effect in weakening the general force of the rule few of us are conccited enough to suppose; moreover, there are cases in which every law must be set aside. Once take from those laws the Divine sanction, and we shall always find reason, or at least excuse, for considering our own case to be an exception.'

Merton.—' Why don't you ?'

Lestrange.—' For two reasons. Because I was brought up a Christian. Those laws are impressed on my mind not only with all the force of early education but with all the force of hereditary instincts. Secondly, because, in nine cases out of ten, the practical question for me is a question not of morality but of honour. I don't lie, because, however expedient lying would be, it is not the conduct of a gentleman. For the same reason I don't cheat, or commit any of those hundred forms of theft which are not punishable as theft by law. But that this rule will not prove effective, will not supply the place of the Divine sanction, you see in the fact that, wherever such forms of theft are permitted by professional morality or rather professional practice, they are perpetrated wholesale.'

Merton.—' No one can ever think that theft is expedient.'

Lestrange.—' Indeed ! John Smith has six children, and they are starving. He finds a purse belonging to a rich neighbour who can well afford the loss. That purse will save six lives. Will anything but a law branded on Smith's conscience with all the force that supernatural authority can give prevent him stealing it?'

Cleveland.—'And from the Positivist's standpoint, why should he not steal it?'

Merton.—'Because, so long as society rests on private property, it is better that six people should starve than that theft should be considered venial.'

Lestrange.—'That is not the question for John Smith, at any rate. For him the question is only this. Is it better that my six children should starve, or that I should run a very small chance that the truth will be discovered, and that my example will exercise an infinitesimal effect in making other people more willing to steal? Now if I am detected, I shall be punished, and the punishment will deter others; if I am not detected, then my example does no harm. Observe, undetected sin can do no harm, can have no tendency to weaken the general law. Its mischief is confined to the soul of the offender. If that soul have but to live a few years and then cease to be, what harm can a secret sin do that even a philosopher would think worthy of serious consideration, when that sin may save a life or avert serious suffering?'

Sterne.—' Practically, when men are starving they do steal, if they can steal with impunity.'

Cleveland.—' But they think it wrong. Once let them fancy that the wrong is questionable, and the theft excused by starvation will be repeated again and again under less serious temptation, till the man becomes a thief by trade.'

Merton.—' Which consequence alone shows that the original theft is wrong, even as judged simply by its perceptible consequences.'

Cleveland.—' Aye; but the starving man will never believe in those consequences.'

Merton.—' If theft were confined to cases of starvation, would it be a sin ?'

Except Vere, there was not one of us who would have dared to answer the question offhand; and Vere would obviously have answered from a standpoint excluded by the argument. After a few moments' consideration, Cleveland replied :

' I don't know : but I know this—once establish the negative in the popular mind, and property will within a single generation cease to exist.'

A.—' Why, Cleveland ? The only inference is, it seems to me, in favour of a poor law.'

Cleveland.—' If pauperism were not made practically penal, it would be the negation of property. Once allow that every man has a right to subsistence, and is not to be punished in any way for claiming that right at the hands of society—and you get back at once to a state which, within the memory of some men now living, did seem to threaten the total confiscation of all property liable to poor rates.'

Lestrange.—' I doubt whether our conclusions, or rather the conclusions to which we are tending, are not more destructive than we have any idea. Practically, we come nearer and nearer to this doctrine, that all moral laws are arbitrary, are founded on our supposed knowledge of the Creator's will. Now, many of those who believe in a Creator do not believe in a revelation; and if we have no supernatural knowledge of His will the existence of a Creator has little bearing upon moral questions. We are drifting to this result—that, Revelation apart, murder, promiscuous sensuality, theft, are mere questions of expediency.'

Merton.—' Well, that is the Positivist doctrine; but it is not difficult to prove that none of them can ever be expedient.'

Lestrange.—' Pardon me, we have made it plain enough that each and any of them may be expedient in individual cases. Grant that they are inexpedient as a general rule; if you rely on expediency, you have still to balance in each particular case the fractional infinitesimal evil of example against the practical immediate advantage, and the latter will always seem the greater to the person tempted.'

Vere.—' Apart from Revelation, the general rule is evidently the Creator's. It is clear that He meant human morality as well as the operations of Nature to be governed by general laws; and the individual infraction of those laws is an offence against His will, whether that will be declared plainly, definitely by a revealed code, or only by clear unquestionable inference derived from our experience of His government.'

Lestrange.—' I think the inference will always seem too dubious to be very effective against strong temptation.'

Sterne.—' So all inferences would be, all laws would be, if each individual case were argued on its merits in the mind of the individual. But it is not so. The general law, however it originate, is impressed on the mind by education, by habit, by inheritance. It is a matter of course to each of us before the time of trial comes. By whatever means, there is and will be, even after centuries of Positivism, engraven on each man's mind the principle, the law : " Thou shalt do no murder;" "Thou shalt not steal;" "Thou shalt not commit adultery;" and it is by that impression, not by the particular sanction attached to it, that men's conduct is practically governed. The Christian remembers "Thou shalt not steal" a hundred times unconsciously for once that he thinks consciously, "There is such a law delivered in thunder on Sinai." So the Positivist will remember unconsciously the same law impressed on his mind ninety-nine times for once that he has consciously to ask himself, "Why is it the law?"'

Vere.—' Probably; but the hundredth time is the time of danger, and when that danger comes it makes all the difference how the law was passed, by what authority it is enforced.'

Cleveland.—' And every infraction tends to impair the unconscious impression; nay, every struggle that is really doubtful may have that effect.'

Vere.—' I don't think so. It seems to me that that is just the distinction between Christian and Positivist morality. He who under strong temptation refuses to steal because God has forbidden it is less likely ever to think of stealing again. He who decides "On the whole, I had better not steal because stealing is inexpedient," reflects the next time: "I made a great sacrifice once to the general interest of mankind; am I not entitled in this case to prefer my own interest?" The Christian law gains force by every case of obedience;

the Positivist law, resting merely on reason and the balance of convenience, loses it.'

Lestrange.—' It comes to this—human ethics can draw no distinction in favour of general rules: expediency, general or particular, is still mere expediency. The presumption in favour of the general, derived from the width of its application, may be overborne by the intensity of the particular. In practice it always will be overruled when the particular expediency is extremely urgent—is matter of life and death.'

Merton.—' Does not that apply to all general rules ?'

Cleveland.—' Of course not. For Theists the general rule is God's command; the particular exception is His trial of our faith.'

CHAPTER VIII.

INVERTED MORAL ASPECTS.

'Do you not see,' said Merton, 'that all these reasonings go to prove the logical necessity of adhesion to general rules in spite of particular consequences?'

Cleveland.—'Yes, and to show that such adhesion is precisely what Positivism will never obtain, what cannot be obtained under any system that denies a Divine authority as the basis of moral legislation.'

Merton.—'On the contrary, all your reasoning, and much stronger reasoning, would be a part of the Positivist catechism, would be impressed upon the minds of children as the first of moral lessons.'

Lestrange.—'And you think you will get a child to understand it or a man to remember it in time of need? Your general rules and particular instances are the terms of philosophy, of metaphysics, not of morals.'

Merton.—'On the contrary, you will find them in every elementary book of morals.'

Lestrange.—'The morals of the schoolmen! You can make a child understand "God spake these words and said;" and somehow the impression lasts when we cease to believe that He did speak or that there is a God. But you will never so impress upon a child the superiority of abstract over concrete obligations. On the contrary, it is only through the concrete that you can impress children or childish men and women. The one thing they understand is a parable or an instance; the Golden Rule comes home to them at once. But you will get no child, and no simple-minded man to realise the enormous human importance of never lying, so that he shall not think it a duty to lie when happiness or life depend thereon.'

Sterne.—'You don't believe it yourself: you hold that there are cases in which it is obligatory to lie.'

Lestrange.—'No; there is but one exception to the rule in pure morals—the case of war. Those who are engaged in crime—who are waging war on society at large or on the society to which we belong—have no right to truth, and as a matter of fact don't expect it. But as between law-abiding members of the same society, or men of any society in time of peace, veracity is of primary and paramount obligation.'

Sterne.—' Once more, you don't think so.'

Lestrange.—' As a point of morals, yes; the one exception is a point of honour not of morals. The obligation to defend a woman's name at the cost of falsehood, even of falsehood on oath, is essentially a point of honour attaching only to a special caste.'

Sterne.—' Don't you approve the Scotsman, who preferred to trust his soul to God's mercy rather than his master's body to the tender mercies of the Whigs?'

Lestrange.—' Don't you see that that is a case of war? The master and man were alike rebels in intention if not in act. They were preparing to wage war against the Government; they were not bound to betray their side to the enemy in a court of law any more than elsewhere.'

Sterne.—' After all, all these are but exceptional cases; the general rules of morality are plain and obvious, and are the same under any religious system. The rules that govern the daily conduct of men and women are never intricate or difficult to understand, and there are always exceptional cases for which no religion provides.'

Lestrange.—' True, so long as you don't call Positivism a religion. All morals are plain and simple on the assumption common to all religions properly so called; and for the exceptional cases it may not matter so very much how they are solved: *de minimis*. But the fundamental assumption that makes the general principles of ethics clear is that of a Divine law-giver; and next thereto that doctrine of human brotherhood which holds good only while you believe in the Divine Father.'

Merton.—' No; that last is of course the basis of all morals, and it has nothing to do with the supposed supernatural paternity. All men are the descendants of a common ancestor, and so far are all brothers.'

Lestrange laughed heartily. ' All vertebrates, according to Darwin, are the descendants of a common ancestor; it is only a question of degree. Now, do we or do we not owe the same duty to mammals as to men?'

Merton.—' Of course not; a duty, but nothing like the same.'

Lestrange.—' You mean because the relationship is so distant. Rest the human brotherhood on common descent, and that must be the sole distinction.'

Merton.—' Well, what follows?'

Lestrange.—' You hold with Tatnall that blood is thicker than water; that we owe duties to our fellow-creatures not in virtue of duty to a common Creator but as an obligation of a common origin, and of course in proportion to the nearness of the relationship?'

Merton.—' Once more—well, what follows?'

Lestrange.—' Negro slavery. The nigger is not a much nearer relation than the ape; and nobody, I fancy, *feels* the ape so near a relation as the dog or the horse. If you try to establish human brotherhood on a physiological ground, you have to acknowledge that some human races are at most distant relatives; and it is at least arguable that if we have a right to slaughter our fifth cousin the ox, to enslave our first cousin the horse, to consign to lifelong imprisonment in the "Zoo" our third cousin the monkey, we may with a quiet conscience conquer and reduce to a milder slavery our second cousin the nigger?'

Merton was a little angry. 'Léstrange, you know that is a paradox.'

Cleveland.—' Not in the least; the paradox lay in your derivation of human brotherhood from the ancestral ape.'

Lestrange.—'I deny that the nigger is my brother in the same sense in which the Aryan is so. If Englishmen and Americans are my brothers, if Germans and Danes are my half-brothers by the father's, and Frenchmen and Italians by the mother's side, then the negro may be my second cousin, but he is no nearer;

and he is fully as far from me as from the ape.'

Cleveland.—' Don't say that in Ida's hearing, Lestrange.'

Sterne.—' Why not? I should have thought it would have suited Mrs. Cleveland's sympathies.'

Cleveland.—' Ida knows the negro too well. He is man—I should say child—certainly not monkey. His relationship to us is a question of degree, a little more distant than that of the Chinese or the Maori, a little closer than that of the Australian savage, but it is human.'

Sterne.—' Then how did you excuse slavery?'

Cleveland.—' As best for the negro; and therefore I never excused the African slave trade.'

Lestrange.—' I don't mean to admit for a moment that Christian brotherhood is practically closer than that which Merton would derive from Darwinism. Christians as devout as Vere slaughter their Christian brethren with as little compunction as their Darwinian cousins.'

Merton.—' It is worth notice that Agnostics, and especially Positivists, are much less inclined to justify or palliate war than almost any sect of Christians; and it seems by no means improbable that the downfall of Christianity and the cessation of war may be contemporaneous, coincident, if you will not allow that they may be connected.'

Vere.—' I should be very sorry to think so.'

Cleveland.—'There is more of irony in that sentence than I have ever heard from you before, Vere. You mean you do not like to think that war will last as long as Christianity. Well, I think Agnosticism will put an end to it.'

Vere.—'In that case I am afraid Agnosticism will have too much to say for itself. Such a result might convert no small number of Christians, and those whom the Master would be most willing to recognise.'

Lestrange.—'Nothing of the sort, Vere. If Agnosticism puts an end to war, it will be by making men far too abject cowards to risk their lives in battle.'

Sterne.—'As matter of fact, are Atheists more cowardly than Christians?'

Lestrange.—'We haven't had time or opportunity to try. As yet, we have never seen an Atheist whose atheism was not a mere intellectual veneer over a solid foundation of Christian education. To know by experience what Agnosticism will make of men, we must have men who have been Agnostics for two or three generations at least, and have lived in an Agnostic society.'

Vere.—'And that I don't think we shall ever see.'

Cleveland.—'It looks painfully probable just now.'

Vere.—'Possibly; but I do not think that society could survive three generations of pure Atheism.'

Sterne.—'That sounds extravagant even from your standpoint. The Roman Empire survived some centuries of practical Atheism.'

Cleveland.—'No. By the end of the third century Christianity was uppermost, was so much stronger than Paganism as to conquer and establish itself by the sword of Constantine.'

Sterne.—'To be overthrown by that of Julian.'

Cleveland.—'Sterne, just remember this. Julian reigned less than three years, and on his death it was found necessary to restore Christianity. Paganism could not reign, not only because it had lost faith beyond this world but because it had become palpably the weaker power in this world. It was felt by the Generals and Statesmen around Julian himself that nothing less than a second Julian could maintain Paganism on the Imperial throne, much less re-establish an anti-Christian empire. If Christianity were thus dominant in the beginning of the fourth century, it must have permeated very thoroughly for many generations those lower ranks of society in which the destructive tendencies are strong and to which they were necessarily confined.'

Merton.—'Then you mean that we have no

experience of a really Atheistic society, a society of convinced Atheists educated for generations in Atheism?'

Cleveland.—' Not on earth!'

Merton.—' Had I leisure and imagination to depict an Utopia, I could of course represent Atheism as producing the highest kind of courage.'

Lestrange.—' No; you might couple the two, you could never connect them.'

Merton.—' Epicurus did so, I believe. Doesn't Lucretius ground the claims of the Epicurean system to human gratitude on the banishment of those superstitions which made death terrible?'

Cleveland.—' Yes; and a stranger perversion of poetic fancy I never remember to have read. True that the Greek and Roman Hades was dreary, dull, desolate beyond description; true that a few signal sinners suffered terrible torments in Tartarus; but after all the latter were rare exceptions, and no one would wish such offenders not to fear death. Now the peculiar terror of Hades is that its tenants are scarcely alive. They have lost all the reality of life, and retain only its shadow; but the very fact that such shadowy immortality was realized and believed in seems to prove that it was preferred to annihilation. Even the lament of Achilles is not over any positive suffering, but over the negation of reality and life. He would not have been consoled but rather additionally terrified by the offer of annihilation as the alternative.'

Merton.—' How can annihilation be terrible or death frightful to him who does not expect to be conscious after death? While we live we are secure from the evil, whatever it may be, and when it comes we know nothing about it.'

Lestrange.—' That is good logic, but very bad philosophy. However you account for it, annihilation is utterly horrible to men, horrible in proportion to their vital consciousness, their sense of life and intellectual power.'

Sterne.—' Yet it is said that the dying are seldom afraid to die.'

Lestrange.—' Because they are half dead already; because vitality is generally exhausted before death. But try to realize what death actually is; the sudden extinction of ourselves, the coming of utter blackness, utter senselessness over the conscious, active, enjoying, thinking brain—the instant approach of nothingness. Can we conceive anything more hideous; is not even a life of suffering less terrible to our consciousness? The proof that so it is, is that even those to whom life means nothing but suffering so rarely commit suicide.'

'You remember,' said Merton, taking down a well-worn book from the nearest shelf, 'what Clifford says on that subject?'—

'"It is often said that the universal longing for immortality among all kinds and conditions of men is a presumption that there is some future life in which this longing shall be satisfied. Let us endeavour, therefore, to find out in what this longing actually consists; whether the existence of it, when its nature is understood, can be explained on grounds which do not require it to have any objective fulfilment other than the life and the memory of those who come after us; and what relation it bears to the equally widespread dream or vision of a spiritual world peopled by supernatural or monstrous beings, ghosts and Gods and goblins.

'"First, let us observe that all the words used to describe this immortality that is longed for are *negative* words: *im*-mortality, end-*less* life, *in*-finite existence. Endless life is an inconceivable thing, for an endless time would be necessary to form an idea of it. Now, it is only by a stretch of language that we can be said to desire that which is inconceivable. No doubt many persons say that they are smitten with an insatiable longing for the unattainable and ineffable; but this means that they feel generally dissatisfied, and do not at all know what they want. Longing for deathlessness means simply *shrinking from death*. However or whenever we who live endeavour to realise an end to this healthy life of action in ourselves or in our brethren, the effort is a painful one; and the mind, in so far as it is healthy, tries to put it off and avoid it. The state of one who really wishes for death is firmly linked in our thoughts with the extreme of misery and wretchedness and disease, and, in so far as it can be realised, we seem to feel that such a one is fit to die. In those cases of ripe old age not hastened by disease, when the physical structure is actually worn out, having finished its work right honestly and well, when the love of life is worn out also, and the grave appears as a bed of rest to the tired limbs, and death as a mere quiet sleep from thought, there also, in so far as we are able to realise the state of the aged and to put ourselves in his place, death seems to be normal and natural, a thing to be neither sought nor shunned. But such putting of ourselves in the place of one to whom death is no evil, must in all cases be imperfect. I cannot, in my present life and motion, clearly conceive myself in so parlous a state that no hope of better things should make me shrink from the end of all. However vividly I recall the feelings of pain and weakness, it is the life and energy of my present self that pictures them, and this life and energy cannot help raising at the same time combative instincts of resistance to pain and weakness whose very nature it is to demand that the sun shall not go down upon Gibeon until they have slain the Amalekites. Nor can I really and truly put myself in the place of the worn-out old man whose consciousness may some day have a memory of mine. No force of imagination that I can bring to bear will avail to cast out the youth of that very imagination which endeavours to depict its latter days; no thoughts of final and supreme fatigue can help suggesting refreshment and new rising after sleep.

'"If, then, we do not want to die now, nor next year, nor the year after that, nor at any time that we can clearly imagine, what is this but to say that we want to live for ever, in the only meaning of the words that we can at all realise? It is not that there is any positive attraction in the shadowy vistas of eternity, for the effort to contemplate even any very long time is weariness and vexation of spirit; it is that our present life in so far as it is healthy, rebels once for all against its own final and complete destruction. And for as much as so many and so mighty generations have in time past ended in death their noble and brave battle with the elements that we also and our brethren can in nowise hope to escape their fate, therefore we are sorely driven to find some way by which at least the image of that ending shall be avoided and set aside. As the fruit of this search two methods have been found and practised among men. By one method we detach ourselves from the individual body and its actions which accompany our consciousness, to identify ourselves with something wider and greater that shall live when we as units shall have done with living—that shall work on with new hands when we, its worn-out limbs, have entered into rest. The soldier who rushes on death does not know it as extinction; in thought he lives and marches on with the army, and leaves with it his corpse upon the battle-field. The martyr cannot think of his own end because he lives in the truth he has proclaimed; with it and with mankind he grows into greatness, gains ever new victories over falsehood and wrong. But there is another way; since, when men have died, such orderly natural and healthy activity as we have known in them and valued their lives for has plainly ceased, we may fashion another life for them, not orderly, not natural, not healthy, but monstrous or *super*natural, whose cloudy semblance shall be eked out with the dreams of uneasy sleep or the crazes of a mind diseased. And it is to this that the universal shrinking of man from death, which is called a yearning for immortality, is alleged to bear witness.

'"But whence now does it really come, and what is the true lesson of it? Surely it is a necessary condition of life that has desires at all that these desires should be towards life and not away from it; seeing how cheap and easy a thing is destruction on all hands, and how hard it is for race or unit to hold fast in the great struggle for existence. Surely our way is paved with the bones of those who have loved life and movement too little, and lost it before their time. If we could think of death without shrinking, it would only mean that this world was no place for us, and that we should make haste to be gone to leave room for our betters. And therefore that love of action which would put death out of sight is to be counted good, as a holy and healthy thing (one word whose meanings have become unduly severed), necessary to the life of men, serving to knit them together and to advance them in the right. Not only is it right and good to cover over and dismiss the thought of our own personal end, to keep in mind and heart always the good things that shall be done, rather than ourselves who shall or shall not have the doing of them, but also to our friends and loved ones we shall give the most worthy honour and tribute if we never say nor remember that they are dead, but contrariwise that they have lived; that hereby the brotherly force and flow of their action and work may be carried over the gulf of death and made immortal in the true and healthy life which they worthily had and used. It is only when the bloody hands of one who has fought against the light and the right are folded and powerless for further crime, that it is kind and most merciful to bury him and say, 'The dog is dead.'"'

'Brutal insolence!' Lestrange said. 'That is meant for Tories like you and me who have worn out health and nerves in fighting against the light of Positivism and the right of anarchy.'

Merton continued—' "But for you noble and great ones, who have loved and laboured yourselves not for yourselves but for the universal folk, in your time not for your time but for the coming generations, for you there shall be life as broad and far-reaching as your love, for you life-giving action to the utmost reach of the great wave whose crest you sometime were."'

Lestrange—' What utter twaddle! That last paragraph is but an insult to the instincts of the very men he means to flatter. "For you there shall be life as broad and far-reaching as your love"—life utterly unconscious, life that has ceased in every sense, life that is a prey to the worm, that is dissolved into the elements, life in the rotting carcase or the dried ashes! No—worse still, life in the memory of those who never knew us and whom we never knew; a metaphor, and a very stupid metaphor, dressed up to represent a fact. What man in his senses could care for such life as this? Is this posthumous immortality—this survival of the dead and rotten—merely what we call fame? If so, how few attain it, and they commonly those who least deserve it! Those who have done most for the future of mankind are mostly forgotten within a single generation. Philosophers, inventors, statesmen, those who have really bettered the condition of posterity, are unknown benefactors; those whose names are selected from the urn by chance are, nine out of ten, mere scourges of God; in the tenth case they are poets and artists who have contributed only to the amusement of their species. Of those who have really been benefactors of their kind, still more of those whom the Positivist would reckon as such, every one will have been forgotten before we have made three steps towards the Positivist Paradise. What man would not give all this fame of which he can know nothing for fifty years of renewed youth, of real life and activity upon this earth?

And if we are not to understand this metaphorical life as fame, but as the survival of our work, what is it to the point? It may be a good thing, it may be a pleasure while we live, to think that our works will live after us—though as matter of fact too often " the evil that men do lives after them, the good is oft interred with their bones." But to call this " *life* " is a lie, and a lie of the meanest and most cowardly kind; a lie intended to disguise the truth, to hide from the Agnostic himself and his disciples that plain hideous fact of annihilation which he has not the courage to contemplate. All this cant about an immortality of the dead, an immortality of something that is not we and indeed has little or nothing to do with ourselves, is the strongest possible proof of Agnostic cowardice. Not one of you dare tell yourselves what you know to be the truth, that death for the highest and the lowest, for the best and the worst, is one and the same thing—annihilation; that in place of the imaginary eternity of happiness proffered by Christianity on the one side or the eternity of horror and darkness threatened on the other, you have to offer something worse than either, something which would not be accepted by the spirits tormented in Hell! You are conscious that if you tell the truth you frighten away the world from the very consideration of your doctrines; that the truth is too ugly to be faced, that the flimsiest argument, the veriest rags of evidence will be accepted, will be caught at and fought for jealously, to hide this hideous prospect from the eyes of men. You know this, because as I say you have not courage yourselves to contemplate its naked horror. That this is so is proved by the passion with which you dilate on your metaphorical immortality; by all the artificial canonisations of Positivism, borrowed from Catholic ceremonial, as by the pile of verbiage stolen from Christian descriptions of Paradise wherewith mere Agnosticism endeavours to paint a tolerable picture upon the blackness of the final curtain.'

Sterne.—' Well, Lestrange, drop Clifford's last paragraph as mere verbiage; I may agree with you on that point; but the substantial argument lies in what precedes. Is not our dread of death, our horror of annihilation merely the animal instinct without which life would not exist, because none would struggle to preserve it? Is it a real desire for endless existence, or simply an instinctive shrinking from the termination of our present life, which is of course a necessary concomitant of life, since without it we should allow ourselves to die as individuals and probably to die out as a race?'

Lestrange.—' What does it matter? Be it what it may, the instinct is the deepest, most rooted, most invincible passion of our nature; and in proportion to the intellectual culture, to the energy of the mind, to the vitality of the whole being, is the intensity of its revolt from the horror of great darkness which, say what you will, hangs over the end. But it is not mere clinging to life, it is not fear of death as such—it is clinging to consciousness, the horror of annihilation, of ceasing to be. It is something more than the brute's fear of death, which the brute, if of a carnivorous race, generally overcomes so easily; it is a human feeling, and a feeling strongest in the highest races and I believe in the finest specimens of mankind.'

Cleveland.—' Do the aged desire death, or resurrection? Would not any man of eighty give any price to return to youthful manhood, and spend another sixty years on earth? If so, there is an end of Clifford's consolations and of his argument. If the aged cling to life as long as they have life in them, and would prefer renewed youth to unconscious rest, annihilation *is* the evil you hold it, and death the horror Clifford will not allow it to be.'

CHAPTER IX.

THE INVENTED DEITY.

'WILL you review it, Cleveland?' said Lestrange. 'As I observe you have read it twice through, I suppose you think it worth the trouble?'

Cleveland.—'I began it again because I doubted whether I quite understood it; and now I am sure I don't understand it at all.'

'I hope you do, then,' Lestrange observed, turning to myself.

A.—'I thought I did till this moment; but if Cleveland doesn't, and considering the author's previous reputation, I must suppose I don't. It is more likely that I am stupid, than that he has reiterated the most transparent fallacy of the age and contrived to obscure what was so simple.'

Lestrange.—'Either or both may be possible. *Ecce Homo* struck me as clever but paradoxical.'

Cleveland.—'Hardly that; but perhaps perverse. The author seemed pleased with the originality of his view on a subject so thoroughly discussed from all sides and all standpoints that originality must in all likelihood be sheer eccentricity. His conception of Christ's character and purpose was so unlike any other that he ought to have distrusted its soundness. He could never be stupid, but he is capable, I think, of going as far wrong as any man living.'

Lestrange.—'And after all, Gladstone's "Homer" is a signal example how very far wrong a very clever man may go on a favourite and familiar subject. If he had not himself told us so, we should hardly have believed that, busy as his life had been, the foremost scholar among English statesmen had never studied Max Müller or Cox. Scholars were still more surprised to find that not only had he read nothing of all the literature of comparative mythology, but had ventured to publish a book on Homer without knowing that comparative mythology had become a science since he was five-and-twenty.'

Ida.—'You don't mean to say that Mr. Gladstone—made a fool of himself?'

Lestrange.—'No; I will only say that the author of *Ecce Homo* has, in this new work, played the—Gladstone.'

Merton.—'Well, that Cleveland should pronounce the book unintelligible, and Lestrange call it original, equally surprise me. I have read it pretty carefully, and it seemed to me only to say a little more clearly and a good deal more cleverly, in new and telling terms, what the Comtists have been preaching for fifty years in vain.'

A.—'Then I fancy you render its meaning much as I do. Suppose he were to review it, Lestrange?'

Lestrange.—'No. Let Merton render it into English, and you shall review the translation.'

Merton.—'Surely I have rendered it, feebly and imperfectly, but *ad nauseam,* in many an argument in this room? Agnostics are not Atheists; Pantheism is, by the very force of the word, a form of Theism. A man's religion is in one sense his view of the Universe, in another his ideal of life. He who conceives of the Universe as an entity almost infinite, ruled by a law absolutely perfect, has a faith higher, a God far greater than any admitted by or compatible with supernaturalism. He who accepts Humanity as the ideal, its interest as the rule of life, is not irreligious but religious in the highest and directest sense. He who worships Nature is not without a God. He who serves Humanity is as true a devotee, and may be as real a martyr, as he who worships a God incarnate in human form.

Science and Humanity embody all that is true in the Old and New Testaments respectively. Science reiterates in a higher and stronger form the Jewish protest against anthropomorphism and its inherent idolatry; Agnosticism recognizes in Humanity the only rational Incarnation, the highest development of the Divine idea in Nature.'

Lestrange.—' *Vox, et præterea nil.*'

Ida.—' Please render that, Mr. Lestrange.'

Merton.—' If you can.'

Lestrange.—' I will try to render it for both, in your several senses. It is all words, words, words, and nothing more. The whole argument consists in the perversion of familiar words—the stealing of Christian phrases to express Atheistic and anti-Christian meaning—of which we have always accused the Positivists. Nature is not God, nor a God. Study of physical laws is not worship, whether of Nature or her supposed Maker. Humanity is not a thing but an idea —oftener a mere word; and used by Positivism in a double or treble sense, sometimes as a classification, and again sometimes as a quality. It seems too silly to say, " Worship mankind——" '

Merton.—' Why ?'

Lestrange.—' When you put that question to me, you answer it. We are, one and all, very much above the level of the thing you ask us to worship. Of course you fall back upon the other sense and say, "not mankind but the perfect Man." As well obey an imaginary monarch as worship a confessed ideal.'

Sterne.—' And yet what is God but man's ideal of superhuman perfection ?'

Cleveland.—' For once, Sterne, you have spoken first and thought afterwards. You can see the fallacy of that sophism without my help.'

Ida.—' But I cannot.'

Sterne.—' Cleveland means that to Theists, though God's character be ideal, His personality is real. They worship the real Person for His ideal character, as a lover the real woman for her imagined perfections. But to take up Lestrange's illustration, is not loyalty to an ideal monarch quite possible and even practicable ?—is not that very nearly the case of Thiers' constitutional royalty, " qui regne et ne gouverne pas " ?'

Cleveland.—' No doubt. And therein lies the absurdity of that very French saying. A king who in nowise governs in no sense reigns; and his people, as soon as they found him out, would feel for him not loyalty but contempt.'

Sterne.—' But a Republic is an idea; the State without a monarch is as pure an abstraction as Mankind or Nature.'

Cleveland.—' And that is the weakness of Republics. When once they outgrow the city, when they cease to be incarnate in a visible Athens or Sparta, patriotism tends to become as mere an idea as its object.'

Sterne.—' Mrs. Cleveland could teach you better. What truer loyalty was ever shown than that of those who fought and died for the Union on the one side, or for the South, for State rights and their several States, on the other ?'

Cleveland.—' Look at the strange contrast between North and South. Either cause was in some sense an abstraction. But while the Northerners fought partly for the Union—a grand political vision, but somewhat chilling in its magnificence—or against slavery, the South fought for very practical realities; for their personal freedom, for their homes, for the institutions interwoven with all their home-life, with their dearest associations as with their strongest interests. Therefore the South fought while she could stand: the North was more than once on the point of giving way, merely because the chances of success were so doubtful as to seem hardly worth the cost. On almost every point the two nations presented a striking contrast. The North had excellent Generals, and, after a while, gallant and stubborn soldiers; but her people were never in earnest, as was the entire

Southern nation. The North had no heroes; and no such *levée en masse* as that which maintained the Southern armies through three years of gradually increasing pressure, suffering, and disaster was, or ever seemed, possible in the North. In the field no Northern chief inspired anything approaching to the enthusiasm which well-nigh rose into a passion among the followers of Stonewall Jackson. Even after the victory, Northern adulation of Grant looks very artificial and very mean beside the Southern devotion to Lee. No one who has read the history can imagine a cry of " *Grant* to the rear !"—can fancy Northern battalions refusing to conquer till their leader was safe, insisting only that he should *not* share their peril. The conqueror had a court of personal adherents—a court as servile, dishonest, disreputable as that of Charles II. His antagonist, through privation, failure, ruin, was simply idolized by his soldiers and revered, as few hero-monarchs were revered in the days of Divine right, by the whole South. And yet the two peoples were of the same blood, the same religion, the same language, and moulded, save for a single distinction affecting after all but a small proportion of Southern families, by the same laws and nearly the same ideas.'

Lestrange.—' *Apropos ?*'

Cleveland.—' To this—that men fighting for home, land, and liberty will do their utmost, will die rather than yield; that such a cause develops heroes who win that personal loyalty which after all is the one motive that makes first-rate soldiers, and at need enthusiasts and martyrs, of all the military manhood of a people. But short of such feelings, short of the pride and passion of freemen in freedom, no enthusiasm for an abstract principle, a name, or a flag, will do more than make good Generals and gallant soldiers. Compare the last farewell between General Lee and the army he surrendered—the men who had fought, starved, shivered, perished of cold, wet, and hunger in the trenches of Richmond and in the terrible six days' retreat—with the grand review of the victorious army; compare the present feeling of either section towards the heroes of the war, and deny if you can that personal loyalty to General Lee was a far stronger, deeper, more telling passion than devotion to the Union; that even hatred of slavery inspired less enthusiasm than the feelings enlisted in its defence. And if the Union failed to create an enthusiasm equal or comparable to that of the South, what political ideal, what social passion can ever hope to approach the force of personal loyalty?'

Sterne.—'I thought the Puritans had settled that question.'

Cleveland.—'The Puritans! They prove my case, if ever instance could. The Rebels quailed before the Cavaliers. It was not till the enthusiasts in loyalty to the king were encountered by enthusiasts in loyalty to God that the troops of the Parliament won a victory or even made a decent figure in the field.'

Merton.—'What of the armies of the French Revolution?'

Cleveland.—'What would have become of them had the Vendeans equalled them in number? For my part, had Wellington commanded at Valmy with the army of the Peninsula, I doubt not that the White Flag would have been flying in Paris within a week, and that the Revolution would be remembered to-day not as the most awful tragedy in human history, but as the prime farce of democratic failure.'

Merton.—' *Vox* again. Illustration, not argument, and an allegory wanting even in analogy.'

Cleveland.—' Well, then, I leave the argument in Lestrange's hands for the present. To feel the full force of a negative, it should be pressed by one whose denial is not merely a step to positive conclusions.'

Lestrange.—'I don't know that. But I at

least have not denied Christianity to accept Comtism; have not given up a prayer-hearing and prayer-answering God to worship an abstract code of law that has not even the human interest of human legislation. I have not found faults in saints and martyrs, in Incarnate Deity and inspired prophets, to accept our Father Man and bow down to the lineal descendant of the typical Ape—a creature with all the vices and few of the virtues of his ancestor.'

Sterne.—' How much do you really deny, Lestrange ?'

Lestrange.—' Every jot and tittle, every point and principle of Merton's creed as he has just expounded it. I deny that Nature is God; I deny that man can or does worship it. I deny, scoff at, despise the religion of Humanity. As Christ taught it, the brotherhood of Man resting on the fatherhood of God was a noble idea if not a true one. Based upon common descent from the ancestral Ape, it is not only a lie but an absurdity. And finally, I deny that whether on Nature or on Humanity any moral obligation, any code of law can possibly be based; I deny that the future of mankind will or should be the supreme object of any one, man or woman, now or hereafter.'

Merton.—' The latter half of your negations

interest me the least for the moment. We have discussed them before, and I confess I find it hard to believe that any man can regard mankind as you profess to do. But why is Nature an insufficient object of reverence or worship; in what sense is she less, or rather in what sense is she not infinitely greater, than the God of Moses, or even of Jesus Christ? An Universe of which this world is but as an atom in that which Moses or Christ conceived—a scheme of law far higher, wiser, wider, more perfect than was dreamed of in the first century of our era—is surely a grander assertion, a nobler ideal, a fitter object of intense absorbing reverence than the Creator of one tiny globe among a thousand millions? Look at the question for a moment as one of arithmetic. Jesus Christ told us that no sparrow fell to the ground without the notice of the Creator; but His hearers probably regarded even that statement as a highly hyperbolical figure. Even the Teacher would probably have been startled at the assertion that each grain of sand on every sea-shore was an object of personal individual interest to its Maker. Yet the grains of sand in the Universe of His conception were not more numerous than worlds in ours; nor each grain more insignificant than Earth and all her inhabitants together in the

Universe of to-day. Earth and mankind are to the God of the astronomer what a single drop of water with its microscopic population would have been to the God of the Galilean Prophet.'

Ida.—' But, Mr. Merton, to repeat what I have heard often in this room and what you all seem to take for granted, the Creator is as infinite as His Universe, and nothing therein can be too small, no species too numerous for His individual observation. Is it a hyperbole or a metaphor that to the Infinite nothing is small and nothing great ?'

Lestrange.—' Perfectly true, Mrs. Cleveland. Logically, the infinitude of the Universe would not render us more insignificant in presence of an infinite Creator. But human imagination can hardly conceive of personal relations, personal interest, between the Ruler of millions of millions of worlds and individuals of the thousand millions of a single species existing for a short space upon one of those worlds. And I incline to think that, as astronomical knowledge is diffused among and realized by the people, Theism will, from this very defect of human imagination, be driven to fall back on Christianity ; on the Incarnate Deity who may conceivably interest Himself in every one of His fellow men. And yet the Incarnation itself becomes almost inconceivable when we realize the insignificance of mankind in the scheme of universal existence. Did the Creator of the Universe become flesh and die for one trillionth part thereof?'

Merton.—'Yet you maintain that the Nature which signifies, which includes this universal scheme and the laws that rule it, is a lower, meaner object of worship than the supposed Creator of a single small planet. As well maintain that the world and mankind are less divine than the maker of a toy globe peopled with animalcules!'

Lestrange.—'I said nothing of the kind. I said and I maintain that your Nature is not a God, and is not a possible object of worship. That which we worship must be wiser, nobler, loftier in an enormous degree than ourselves; and not one of these attributes does Nature possess.'

Merton.—'No?'

Ida.—'Even to me, Mr. Lestrange, that seems a startling paradox.'

Turning to her, Lestrange's tone changed at once. The scornful confidence with which he had thrown out the amazing negative that astounded his antagonist softened into respectful gentleness. 'Pardon me, Mrs. Cleveland, I meant the paradox for Merton, not for you; as a fair retort on the perverse paradox of his whole creed. I meant simply this: Wisdom, loftiness, nobility are personal, *I* should say human, qualities; not one of them is predicable of that *thing* which Merton calls Nature. A mindless, impersonal, soulless system—a machine, no matter how big, no matter how perfect—is not an object of worship or even of admiration.'

Ida.—' Not of admiration?'

Lestrange.—' I think not, Mrs. Cleveland. We admire not the machine itself but the genius that conceived and worked it out. But in a sense no doubt we do admire a marvellously-perfect machine: we feel a still higher admiration for the infinitely finer and more perfect because simpler mechanism of this stupendous Universe. But in that sense admiration is utterly different from, has no relation to, reverence or worship.'

Merton.—' " An undevout astronomer is mad." '

Lestrange.—' Mad with your own insanity, the insanity of Positivism; the insanity which in its negation at least I share with you. I cannot accept a Creator; above all, I see no reason to believe in a personal quasi-human Creator. At present human wisdom, science, investigation, stop far short of any point from which we could possibly 'look through Nature up to Nature's God.' But to apply the name of God to the Universe itself, or that of religion to the wonder and admiration which natural laws and the vastness of the Universe inspire, is simply to pervert and misapply language, to bewilder those who hear, and obscure the real thought of those who use the terms.'

Merton.—' How can you say that Nature is not wise? What more marvellous exhibition of wisdom could you ask than her every provision, from the law which keeps the stars in their courses to that which adapts the instincts of each habitant of earth, air, or water to its life and conditions?'

Lestrange.—' We say that a law is wise only in a secondary sense. Of law itself wisdom is not predicable, only of the mind which conceived the law.'

Merton.—' But you yourself admit as fully as I the marvellous completeness and grandeur of the Universal machine, if you chose to call it such. You admit that we have no right to infer a personal Creator and Governor, we have no reason to look beyond the Universe itself; and yet wisdom, intelligence of the highest kind—of a kind utterly beyond our conception—the Universe undoubtedly displays.'

Lestrange.—' Granted. By whom or by what that intelligence was exercised, to whom or to what it belongs, I do not know, and do not pretend to know. But you, who reproach the Theist with inventing a Being whom to invest with that intelligence, do the same yourselves. You personify Nature, and ascribe to it not an intelligence which it actually exerts, but one which you infer from it, or which is as you say "displayed" *in* it. If it be irrational, presumptuous to go beyond the Universe, the system we know, and infer a Creator so far like ourselves that we can reverence and worship Him, that we can ascribe to Him what we mean by wisdom and virtue—it is equally presumptuous, equally irrational, and incomparably more absurd to turn the Universe itself into a Being, an entity possessed of "an unconscious intelligence"—as if the two words did not neutralize each other, as if they did not express a contradiction in terms—and call upon us to worship the Nature of your imagination instead of the God of Theistic inference.'

Sterne.—'I fail, as I think Merton fails, to understand your allegation that wisdom is not predicable of Nature. And clearly that allegation is of paramount importance, for it is on that ground, if I understand you aright, that you deny the possibility of Nature-worship.'

Lestrange.—'Exactly: and the double use of your last word illustrates my meaning very aptly. Nature-worship, as applied to a worship that really once existed among men, meant anthropomorphism applied to Nature, the ascription of a human character, human or personal intelligence and emotion, to natural objects and natural forces; and this ascription is inevitable if Nature-worship is to mean anything. Reverence is applicable, is possible only for a personal conscious Intelligence, devotion possible only towards a moral Being; and if you could conceive Intelligence as non-conscious, morality certainly implies not only a person but conscience and consciousness.'

Sterne.—'*Is* unconscious intelligence a contradiction in terms? Is it not just what we mean by the word instinct, just what we see in the thing?'

Cleveland.—' I think not, though it is not easy to make that point as clear as I should wish. We distinguish instinct from intelligence: an act instinctively performed is non-intelligent. Observe how the question of animal cogitation is treated by the deepest thinkers aud closest observers. What is the question they ask with regard to any act put forward as a proof of proper thought in the brutes? They ask: " Is it conscious or unconscious, is it the fruit of an innate, determinate impulse, or an experimental adaptation of means to ends?" In one word, opposing the terms directly, they ask, "Is it instinctive or intelligent?" The bee is not intelligent when she stores honey for the winter, unless she knows with what purpose she stores it. Take, for example, the case of those creatures which provide by instinct for an offspring of whose wants they can have no memory and no foresight. The adaptation of means to ends is perfect. Nothing could be more admirably devised, no human invention could be cleverer than the act of the wasp which stings grasshoppers, not to death but to paralysis, that they may live and not rot, but live nevertheless as helpless prey for its grub. You cannot suppose the wasp to have any knowledge of what the grub will need, any perception of its inability to struggle with a grasshopper in full possession of its vital powers, or any knowledge of the period within which dead grasshoppers would become uneatable. I think, if I remember aright, that this same creature is so stupid that if you cut off the antennæ by which it is used to drag its prey, it abandons the grasshopper, not having the sense to seize it by the legs, which would serve its purpose just as well.'

Ida.—' But surely there is intelligence, conscious or unconscious, in the action by which the grasshopper is deprived of motion but left in life ?'

Cleveland.—' Very possibly. I cannot conceive such an exquisite adaptation of a special means to a special end without intelligent foresight; but that intelligent foresight does not reside in the wasp. Were it intelligent enough to perform such an action intelligently, it would be an absolutely different creature. It would have reason, mind enough for acts and habits which would have raised it almost indefinitely above its present level. The perfection of instinct is generally accompanied by a signal absence of intelligence, is limited absolutely to those actions which are essential to the preservation and multiplication of the species. The stupidity which such creatures manifest outside of their one special aptitude shows how utterly unintelligent that aptitude is. Sir John Lubbock has conclusively shown that ants, wasps, and bees are very stupid creatures; yet their instincts are about the most wonderful examples of cleverness that the brute creation exhibits.'

Merton.—' But is it not just as likely that their brains (or what serve them for brains) have been developed in one single direction, with intelligence enough for one single purpose, without the power to apply them further—in short, that one function absorbs the whole of the creature's mental capacity?'

Cleveland.—'No; there is no intelligence where there is no conscious purpose. The creature is an automaton worked by an impulse it doesn't understand to achieve a result of which it has neither experience nor foresight. At least, this is the fact in so many of the most striking examples of perfect instinctive adaptation that we have a right to assume it in all. The instincts are most perfect, generally, in the least intelligent creatures. The dog and the elephant have no instincts so marvellous as those of the bee and the wasp, but they commit no such stupid blunders. They can in a sense and to a certain extent reason and foresee, and therefore cannot be so governed by mere blind impulses as are the creatures that have no intelligence to ask why they do the one thing they have always done, or how they shall meet one little change in the conditions to which they are accustomed. The dog, used always to seize its prey in one particular fashion, has sense enough to resist the instinct when the instinct would lead to failure; as in the case of the retriever which, trained for generations never to kill or injure its booty, killed the wounded duck that would otherwise have escaped while the other was being carried over to the sportsman. Instinct and intelligence are contrasted rather than graduated the one into the other; intelligence supersedes instinct; instinct does not rise into intelligence.'

Sterne.—' Are you sure of that, Cleveland? It sounds to me a novelty if not a paradox.'

Cleveland.—' Observe that in the lower creatures which possess very little intelligence the instincts are imperious and absolute. Each generation of wasps makes its nest with equal perfection; they need no experience to guide them, and in the one act they never blunder. Those animals which have some feeble but real intelligence do learn by experience. Some naturalists tell us that the elder birds make better, more perfect nests than the younger. Every one who has kept rabbits must know how apt they are to lose their first brood, evidently for want of experience on the one hand and of an absolute mechanical instinct on the other.'

Merton.—' But these instincts, like our own intelligence, are parts of Nature. They constitute a portion of that whole which we admire and worship; and the highest intellect of the philosopher, as well as the most perfect instinct of the bee or bird, belong to, form part of Nature; are elements of her intelligence, whether conscious or not.'

Lestrange.—' Words again. Mankind may be a part of Nature, may be governed as a whole in a certain sense and to a certain degree by laws like those which rule the courses of the stars. But the intelligence of individual men is no part of that power, that system, that law, whatever it may be, which you personify under the name of Nature. In proportion to his intellect man stands apart therefrom and contemplates it from outside; and the idea that Man can worship that of which he is himself a part, and worship it because he is the highest, most intelligent part of it, if it could have a meaning at all, would be simply laughable.'

'*Ipse dixit*,' said Merton, mimicking the tone of Lestrange's Latin quotation awhile before.

'Well,' returned Lestrange, with perfect good temper, 'define this Nature you worship; what is it?'

Merton looked puzzled; but after a minute's thought answered firmly: 'The Universe as a whole, with the laws that rule it.'

Lestrange.—' Then keep the Universe as a whole distinct from its parts. Grant that its laws are part and parcel of the thing you call Nature. Human intelligence is a product, not a part, of the Universe in your sense; a result developed by that " unconscious intelligence " you ascribe to her. That the less should contain the greater, that unconscious intelligence should develop conscious thought—shall I call that absurd, or paradoxical?'

Merton.—'Why should conscious intelligence be higher than unconscious? Or, why do you rate human thought as higher in kind—it certainly does not even approach in power or grandeur—to that we discern and must discern in Nature?'

Lestrange.—'Discern *in* Nature! Once more the Positivist's perverse misuse of words. You discern in Nature the results of intelligence; but whether that intelligence reside in Nature or rule her, what it is, how far it resembles while it vastly surpasses our own, you have no notion, nor I. It is at least as likely that it stands outside of and rules Nature as that it forms a part of her. The one idea is conceivable and intelligible to us, the other is not. Man cannot conceive a mind diffused through all the stars, through all the individuals of all the races that inhabit the planets of each star, and yet capable of devising, regulating, developing the whole. Such diffusion is to us unintelligible, such a mind is to human thought unimaginable. The ascription of intelligence, conscious or unconscious, to Nature is as pure, as mere an invention as its ascription to a personal, extra-natural God; only the one idea is conceivable, does convey a thought, a meaning, to human minds, and the other does not.'

Sterne.—' Because the one conception is anthropomorphic and the other is not.'

Lestrange.—' Quite true; there is not a tittle of proof of either. But if Nature be not intelligent, the perfect system of law by which she is ruled excites no admiration for her. In that case she is a mere machine; and for a machine we can feel neither reverence nor worship. Our admiration is directed to the unknown maker, not to his work.'

Merton.—' But we know nothing of God; we have no reason to suppose that He exists. We know that Nature does.'

Lestrange.—' Pardon me; in your sense of the word you know just as little of Nature as of God. You know that there is an Universe; you know that that Universe as a whole is governed by certain laws, or rather that it is subject to one single law, the law of gravitation. You know that in one single planet there is a natural order of life, that there has been a development of life and organism from the lowest to the highest. But of Nature you know nothing, save that you have prefixed a capital letter to her name and attached to her the idea of personality.'

Merton.—' No, no.'

Lestrange.—' Yes. Speak of Nature as you know it, as a machine which may be as utterly inanimate, as dead, as incapable of self-action, of self-motion, as any Jacquard loom; and all your talk about worshipping, admiring, reverencing, even in your own eyes loses all meaning whatever. When you speak of Nature as an object of these feelings, as something you can substitute for God, you are speaking of a being as utterly imaginary as God Himself; a being moreover, as I said before, inconceivable. If the Universe has no mind, the Universe is less than I. And that it has a mind is a speculation utterly groundless.'

Merton.—' At least it has something which does infinitely better than any human mind, or any mind that humanity can comprehend.'

Lestrange.—' Once more, no! We cannot help fancying that such a mind has worked on, or through, or in Nature. But that may be merely because we are incapable of conceiving the kind of power that has really developed the Universe and its parts. Emphatically I say, we know nothing—nothing of Nature except as mechanism —nothing of God except as the supposed maker of that mechanism; and I have no great respect for either.'

Mrs. Cleveland's look of utter astonishment, moral as well as intellectual, showed how much the last cynical phrase had shocked and pained her; and Lestrange, who never spared an opponent in argument or respected a fallacy or prejudice, however dear to any other human creature, once more instantly softened his tone as he turned to explain for her a meaning which, if challenged by one of us, he would have enforced by fresh and yet more stinging cynicisms.

'I am speaking, remember, not of the God you conceive, Mrs. Cleveland, but of the Nature we know; that is, of the Power, be it what it may, that we have a right to infer from what we see of life in this one world out of thousands of millions. I have no respect for power as such, no more reverence for the force which now gives life and now destroys it than an intelligent insect might feel for the boy whom it sees at one moment feeding a robin, at the next crushing a worm with his foot. All I really see of the Power in or behind Nature is more or less ugly. It is utterly ruthless, intensely hard if not exactly cruel, and aristocratic to a degree that astounds and appals a Tory like myself. It deliberately, at every stage, in every generation, destroys, and destroys through torture, millions of sentient creatures for the benefit of one a very little better or more sensitive. To judge it by human life alone would be a monstrous immorality, a gigantic selfishness; and, judging it by human life alone, I see nothing for which to be grateful. On the whole, and taking history into account, the past as well as present, I believe that men suffer more than they enjoy; and with death, that is annihilation, hanging over each and over the whole, with the knowledge that mankind as well as man is mortal, I think the balance is heavily against—what Merton calls Nature.'

Merton.—' You forget the future.'

Lestrange.—' What is the future to me, or to those who have lived and suffered in the past? Mankind is not an unit, even now; but to treat it as an unit from first to last, to speak of the happiness of the few final generations—even were it probable, even were it sure to be all that you dream it—as if it would atone to the past for the past, is to push a fallacy of verbal logic to the utmost point of absurdity.'

Cleveland.—' Nature at any rate asserts the right to do evil that good may come.'

'And,' said Mrs. Cleveland, gravely, ' of course Mr. Lestrange leaves the future in another sense out of account.'

Sterne.—' But, Lestrange, you speak of Nature as a machine. How do you know that she is not an organism, a being with a mind of her own, or whether that mind be conscious or unconscious?'

Lestrange.—' I don't know, and I don't pretend to guess. But if she have such a mind, it must, I conceive, reside somewhere; must be a whole mind, not made up of infinitesimal infinitely dispersed fractions. The intelligence of man, the instinct of the bee may be, so to speak, nervous ganglia at the end of a finger, or rather something answering to the nervous centre of one tiny branch of some gigantic polype; but they form no part of Nature's mind, any more than the nerve of my little finger forms a part of mine.'

CHAPTER X.

'BY THEIR FRUITS.'

Lestrange.—' And, Merton, were your religion of Nature intelligible, it would not be practicable. In what sense can you worship an unconscious intelligence, except after the Buddhist fashion, by contemplation? You may stand on one leg like a *fakir*, or sit in your easy-chair after the preferable manner of the Positivist, contemplating the perfections of Nature. But you cannot pray to her; she cannot hear you; and if you praise her she neither knows nor cares. What is worship without prayer or praise? What is a religion of which worship, and worship without these, is the end and all? Nature cannot sympathize with you, cannot inspire or encourage you. She cannot give you a moral law, or a reason for obeying it.'

Merton.—' Why not? You must know that those who profess a natural religion believe also in a natural morality.'

Lestrange.—' Nature can neither give you a law nor enforce it.'

Merton.—' Assuredly she can. All true wisdom and virtue lies first in learning the law of Nature, and then in following it.'

Lestrange.—' That is to say, " Nature will crush you if you stand in her way; therefore stand out of it." I understand dimly the worship that throws itself in sacrifice before the car of Juggernaut: I see no sort of religion, reverence, or obedience in standing off the track lest Juggernaut should crush you.'

Cleveland.—' Nevertheless obedience to natural laws, if not virtue, is common sense, and sometimes a high and rare wisdom.'

Lestrange.—' But purely negative; it is neither moral nor religious. You cannot make either a virtue or an act of worship out of the morning tub or the temperate meal, out of careful drainage and sewage; still less out of that scientific skill which is applied to destroy a certain class of natural products because you have found that their function is to breed disease.'

Sterne.—' It is more useful, though, than all the morality of the Koran or all the ceremonial of Leviticus.'

Cleveland.—' Granted. Half, if not more than half, the ceremonial law of the East means what

Positivists call sanitation. But neither sanitary superstitions nor sanitary science have much relation to morality or any connection with religion.'

Sterne.—'Yet you have seen them made very essential parts of religion.'

Cleveland.—'Yes; and then their practical sense and part of their practical virtue is lost, and they become mere superstitions. I am not sure that the sanitary religion of the Positivists may not some day become a more intolerable bondage, a greater nuisance, than the ceremonial law of the Talmud itself.'

Lestrange.—'But natural religion or Nature-worship, can never be more moral than Nature; and Nature has no conscience, scruples at no crime.'

Merton.—'Another monstrous paradox.'

Lestrange.—'Is it? I hardly expected to hear that from one who, so far as he is a politician at all, I took for a democrat.'

Merton.—'Hardly. I believe that the despotism of the wisest is the one perfect government, the true aristocracy; and the only virtue of democracy is that it may lead up to that.'

Cleveland.—'Never! Envy is the root, the master-passion of democracy. It hates an aristocracy founded on any prowess, power, or pretension to which each and every man cannot lay claim. It hates an aristocracy of wealth rather more than one of birth, and an aristocracy of talent more than either. It can endure a superiority of chance better than one of merit, because the latter is to the democratic temper an insult as well as an injury. Happily a despotism of the wisest is impossible, for two excellent reasons. First, the wisest can never agree what is wise; and next, the really wise realize their unfitness to govern a world of fools.'

Sterne.—' But why should not a democrat worship Nature and obey her laws ?'

Lestrange.—' In one sense obey her laws we all must, or pay the penalty; and Nature's sentences are generally capital and always involve torture. But Nature is aristocratic to the core, aristocratic in principle and in detail, mercilessly, persistently, ruthlessly aristocratic. Her whole system both of production and of preservation rests on the sacrifice of the Many to the Few. She brings into existence ten times as many creatures of any species as can possibly exist, in order to preserve their *élite*. She creates millions where hundreds are wanted, in order that she may pick out the best hundred and let them live on the destruction of the million. Till she produced Man she had done the work directly. With her the millions exist for the few, are born to perish that the *élite* may survive ; each generation is sacrificed to an oligarchy of the strongest and healthiest, and each successive species is an aristocracy that has risen on extermination, to be one day exterminated in favour of a narrower but stronger one. And when Man was developed, Nature set him to work in the same ruthless way. Merton, do you mean anything by your obedience to natural laws, beyond getting out of Juggernaut's way? Do you mean that you will base a system of duty, of moral obligation, or even of practical life, upon the clearest indications of Nature's purposes?'

Merton.—' Of course.'

Lestrange.—' Then, look at the first consequence. Nature's first law is that the few shall eat the many, that the stronger shall slay or enslave the weaker; slavery being man's merciful modification of the harsher natural law of sheer extermination. War is man's knight-service to Nature, man's method of achieving progress through the perpetual destruction of the weaker by the stronger, of the more barbarous by the more civilized. Not only material but moral civilization has followed the same course. The weak, the cowardly, the undisciplined, the selfish, the anarchical tribes were beaten, destroyed by those which were a little braver, better disciplined, in one word more conscientious. The tribes which recognised no fatherhood, no marriage, were cleared out by those which had the *patria potestas*. The best, strongest, those which had the best law and morals, even more than those which had the best health, exterminated their inferiors, conquered and replenished the earth. We seem to be approaching a final, wholesale struggle between numbers and quality, between the hordes of Asia and the disciplined nations of Europe. Will you follow Nature, and say that we are first to kill out the eight hundred millions of non-Aryans in order to make room for an Aryan population; and then that the other Aryan races are to be killed out to make room for the Anglo-Saxon? If not, you are disobeying Nature, and your morality is what the *Spectator* calls supernatural, not natural.'

Merton.—' As if such atrocious cruelty were not utterly unnatural, an outrage to human nature; and as if human nature were not the clearest of natural indications to men, did not show most clearly what human conduct ought to be, was meant to be!'

Lestrange.—'Average human nature has no objection to wholesale killing, whatever it may think of murder by retail. Asia would have no scruple in exterminating Europe if she could; and when America and Africa are filled up, when we are short of room, and must either take or want, I fancy we shall find Aryans just as ruthless as Asiatics. At any rate, the course that man has taken thus far has been strictly in accordance with natural law, with Nature's own process; and if you refuse to carry it out to the end steadily and ruthlessly, the consistent logic of sterner and more orthodox worshippers of Nature will pronounce you not merely a heretic but an infidel.'

Sterne.—' Only an avowed Atheist can use that argument, for it tells as strongly against God as against Nature.'

Cleveland.—' No. Theism recognises a supernatural element in man, on which such reasoners as the *Spectator* justly and logically base a supernatural morality. But those who recognise nothing above Nature, who must find in Nature their highest law, can plead no logical answer to Lestrange's horrible dilemma.'

Lestrange.—'Worse still; can you say that Nature is not wise as well as logical? If it be a question between the existence of a thousand millions of Asiatics, or their gradual eradication to make room for as many Aryans; if we should ever come to a point at which the two things were clearly incompatible, at which two roads diverged, one leading the noblest races of the earth to seize the whole and people it to the full, the other limiting their numbers by the room they have already appropriated, I greatly doubt whether the total sum of human happiness would not be enlarged by the destruction of the inferior races to make room for their betters. The process of extermination, of course, would create a terrible debit of misery. But that process once complete, there would be far more, far higher, happiness in a world in which for ten or twenty generations its highest races were free to increase and multiply, were not pinched and dwarfed and demoralized by a palpably strictly-enforced Malthusianism.'

Ida.—' Would they not be far more fearfully demoralized by the monstrous crime on which their prosperity would be based ?'

Cleveland.—' I am not sure. It is just in these tremendous logical conclusions, these inferences which neither common-sense nor reason can well reject, but from which humanity revolts, that I see the logical weakness of Utilitarianism and Positivism—in a word, of all systems of purely natural or inferential, non-authoritative morality.'

Sterne.—' Utilitarianism ! The extirpation of eight-tenths of mankind seems a strange contribution to the greatest happiness of the greatest number.'

Cleveland.—'I reminded you once before how apt Benthamites are to leave out half that maxim in applying it to practice. To give Benthamism any logical meaning at all, we must treat the two elements as factors in one total, the amount of happiness multiplied into the number that enjoy it. Now the capacity of enjoying life is so vastly enlarged by all those qualities which constitute the superiority of the highest races that the total amount of happiness realized might be infinitely greater among a hundred millions of Aryans than among a thousand millions of Chinese, Hindoos, or Negroes. And that is not all. The extirpation of the inferior races would make room in the end for the same number of the higher race; and taking into account the thousand centuries during which the latter might enjoy the world they had conquered, I think the total of human happiness might probably be increased by Lestrange's process.'

Ida.—'Algernon! you are not in earnest?'

Cleveland.—'My dear child, I recognise the horror, the wickedness of the idea, as clearly as you do—but from your standpoint. It is un-Christian, Atheistic, if you will; but it is strictly natural, and, I think, sound Utilitarianism.'

Merton.—'But, Cleveland, the laws of Nature are from your standpoint the laws of God.'

Cleveland.—'In ethics, no. The instincts of human nature—the highest, deepest instincts of the highest human nature—are God's revelation to us of His purpose in us and for us.'

Merton.—'And why not Nature's?'

Cleveland.—'Obvicusly because you must take Nature as a whole; and so taking her, if you can ascribe to her any purpose at all—and if there can be unconscious intelligence, unconscious purpose is certainly a contradiction in terms—her purpose is, as Lestrange says, ruthlessly aristocratic. The extirpation of the Many for the benefit of the Few, of the inferior to make room for the superior, however small the superiority, is Nature's one visible, unmistakable, paramount law; and Nature-worshippers who disobey that, blaspheme their own deity, deny the fundamental tenet of their own religion.'

Sterne.—'I don't think you have much faith in your own argument. Paradox is never proof; and in morals at least a *reductio ad absurdum* is not so satisfactory or so conclusive as in mathematics.'

Cleveland.—'Perhaps not. At any rate, the case against natural morality, or even Utilitarianism, is too strong to need Lestrange's paradox, logical as it seems. Waive it then, and see what you can make of a natural morality even in practical working life. Does Nature teach tenderness to animals or to women, self-sacrifice, or even justice? With Nature might is right.'

Merton.—' Our instincts, like those of the lower creatures, are part of Nature, are Nature's guide for us as for them.'

Lestrange.—' Well, and what are real human instincts?'

Sterne.—' Sympathy, I suppose, is about the strongest.'

Lestrange.—' Certainly not. Cruelty is a deeper, a more tenacious, as an earlier instinct than sympathy.' Turning to me. ' I forgive you all the Theistic fallacies of your favourite book for that one saying. The child who has not to be slapped out of cruelty is a very exceptional child, and probably not very healthy either in mind or body.'

Ida.—' And why does the slapping cure it? Because it awakens the perception of sympathy. When the child learns what pain is, it learns not to inflict it wantonly. The one argument that goes home to infancy always is, " How would you like it yourself?" '

Lestrange.—' If you want to see what human instincts really are, you must infer them from human action when unfettered by artificial, social restraints. And wherever men are tolerably free —on the confines whether of civilization or of morality, in the collision of settlers with savages or in the mutual relations of nations—you find always the same rule; might makes right. The American acknowledges no honour, no public faith, no humanity as between the Anglo-Saxon and the Red Indian. From the Pilgrim Fathers down to President Garfield, the morality of American dealing with the aboriginal tribes has been the morality of the tiger; nay worse, as human falsehood and treachery have been coupled with the brute's indifference to suffering and lust of blood. The wars of Napoleon show how little the most civilized nations shrink from the worst crimes against one another; how little they really recognize any duty, any restraint of religion or morality, what fearful cruelties they will perpetrate and for what petty ends. And neither the present generation nor our own country is very much better. Judge Lord Beaconsfield's wars as Liberals judged them, or Mr. Gladstone's encouragement of Russian aggression and Bulgarian crime, his shameless injustice, his cruel inhumanity towards the Moslem as Tories judge them—and the Terrorists were hardly more lawless, Napoleon hardly more unscrupulous than our own chosen chiefs.'

Merton.—' I grant that our better instincts don't tell as they ought outside our own community. The community of nations is not yet recognized; the old traditions of patriotism—and its complement, hatred or selfishness towards foreign states—still defy the force of philosophy and of public law. But the social instinct is as strongly developed among men as among bees. We do recognize by instinct duties to our own community, duties of self-sacrifice as well as of mere justice, duties active as well as passive; and these afford the natural code of human morality.'

Lestrange.—'Not they. Agnostic science has disposed of the social instincts in tracing their origin. It suited each tribe to give honour and encouragement to the social, to suppress the selfish impulses of its members; and this tribal selfishness persisting for ages has imposed on mankind, has taught us what we call conscience. Conscience then means not our real native instincts of right and wrong, but the interest of the majority, the habits, the modes of thought which it has suited the majority to encourage. Sin means simply the habits it has suited the majority to punish and crush out for a thousand generations; and when we recognize this we recognize that conscience is a cheat and sin a phantom. We owe no allegiance to the majority, and only resent its pretensions the more because it has contrived to stamp them on our minds by hereditary education, and make us unrighteously uncomfortable when we defy them.'

Merton.—' You know that is the exact opposite of the doctrine which Nature-worshippers draw from Nature. In making us social creatures like bees or ants, Nature has made the social instincts supreme, has taught us instinctively to recognize the paramount claims of our kind, if not always to obey them.'

Lestrange.—' Nothing of the kind. Citizens living in a society which exists by virtue of what you call our social instincts, really our social habits, with everything to encourage those habits, with the strongest possible pressure put upon all contrary impulses, necessarily develop civil and social qualities. But take the tamest of those citizens. Set them free for a single generation from the social pressure, oppose them to Asiatics, Indians, Negroes, and you see what their natural instincts are. Once more might makes right; and the civilized conscience ceases to protest against a relapse into moral barbarism.'

Sterne.—' What does that prove ?'

Lestrange.—' Simply this : that conscience is not natural but artificial ; that our real instincts are not favourable to what even Agnostics feel obliged to call virtue, because it is essential or seems essential to the existence of civilized society. Humanity, civilization, sympathy are no part of Nature, hardly of human nature. They are the artificial developments of Society, and so artificial that they disappear as soon as men are released from social coercion.'

Merton.—' But you know that Positivism, Agnosticism, Atheism, call them what you will, have done nothing to relax morality.'

Lestrange.—' I admit nothing of the sort. Positivism dared not follow out its principles to their logical conclusion; still less dare the Agnostics of to-day. They shrink from the moral negation, the ethical Nihilism to which their principles clearly and logically lead, as two centuries ago their ancestors in innovation shrank from the Atheism which was the logical consequence of *their* negations. And as, Protestant or negative principles once accepted, two centuries have taught us to accept their religious consequences, so a shorter time will suffice to reconcile Agnostics to the moral results of Agnosticism. And in very truth Agnosticism has sapped the foundations of what we used to call morality, the morality even of the Ten Commandments. Measures distinguishable from open robbery only by the flimsiest sophisms are advocated by journalists and party leaders, and statesmen argue against instead of denouncing them; wholesale, wanton, cold-blooded murder is the method of modern revolutionists—avowed by desperadoes whom nevertheless international morality will not give up to the gallows; patronised, tacitly or directly, by the more outspoken Radicals, Clemenceaus and Rocheforts, Davitts and Rossas, and excused or tolerated by men of much higher standing and graver character. Between Bright's exultation in the flight of Irish landlords, and Most's apology for tyrannicide, there is barely a difference of degree; and the Gospel of Dynamite is the logical application of Agnostic morality by men whom Agnostic speculation has deprived of patience in depriving them of hope.'

Sterne.—' You gain nothing by calling names.'

Lestrange.—' Something however by calling a spade a spade. Communism is not robbery, of course, if it be made the rule of a new society where all start alike. But communism as applied to an old community where property exists—communism founded on confiscation—is theft pure and simple.'

Sterne.—' Communism is nothing new.'

Lestrange.—' But dynamite is. Till the Anarchists ceased to believe in God they did not destroy in mere promiscuous savagery. Regicide is Pagan or Christian, Catholic or Protestant; but massacre by bombs, slaughter by wholesale in order to kill one Prince without incurring certain death—attempts to blow up whole streets in order to terrorize a Government—utter indifference to innocent blood—these things are new, diabolical, and strictly traceable to the Atheism of the age. They are the crimes of Agnostics—the development of Agnosticism.'

Sterne.—'There have always been political maniacs.'

Lestrange.—'But in former days all decent men combined to hang them for their politics or lock them up for their madness. Now-a-days, one State shelters the fugitive assassins of another, and no statesman ventures to proclaim them *hostes humani generis.* Worse still, we are patient of the perpetration of such crimes within our own dominion. The agrarian assassin, the cowardly, bloodthirsty scoundrel who tries to butcher sleeping women and children by wholesale, no longer fears being torn to pieces by an outraged nation. We do try, though very feebly and irresolutely, to punish the actual assassins; we make no effort whatever to reach the far more guilty instigators. To me there seems something horribly immoral in the offer to accept as Queen's evidence any but the actual perpetrators. Surely, instead of offering to pardon the instigator if he will betray his hireling, we should offer pardon to the hireling if he will betray his employer, especially as the hanging of one instigator or accomplice, one leader in the system of crime, would do more to stop it than the punishment of a dozen mere instruments. Is this no proof that Agnosticism has shaken the foundations of morality?'

Sterne.—' All which amounts only to this: that people are becoming more tolerant of political differences however deep and wide, of new views of social right however startling.'

Lestrange.—' Rather that morality has disappeared from politics. Agnosticism has so sapped our ethical faith that we cannot cordially abhor, and therefore cannot hang, men who are murderers and robbers on principle.'

Cleveland.—' The mischief is not confined to politics. We are tolerant of almost any vices, of those that our fathers most reprobated. Fifty or thirty years ago, men and women of notoriously evil character and life were as a rule excluded from society, were almost invariably hooted from the hustings and the stage. Now-a-days some of the most popular personages in social and still more in professional life are what the Church calls notorious evil-livers. Report says that two of the favourite singers of the day, two who are cheered and covered with flowers wherever they appear, are living in a double adultery, an adultery public as it is flagrant. It may not be true, but it is notorious; and the public which fully believes it applauds and pays them none the less. Any one of us could mention a dozen similar cases. In short, we have reached that point of liberalism, latitudinarianism in practice if not in theory, that people may live as they please in private—and even in public if they can give the public something it desires—without interference or practical reprobation.'

Merton.—' Agnostics would probably pelt your examples, certainly excommunicate them.'

Lestrange.—' They have no right. Agnosticism has destroyed the foundation of social intolerance; an Agnostic can give no reason why men and women should not choose their own partners at pleasure and change them at will; and in this respect as in others the public is becoming practically Agnostic. It knows no certain morality, none sure enough to be enforced by persecution.'

Cleveland.—' I am afraid we always persecute when we are thoroughly in earnest. Moral, like religious, tolerance means moral indifferentism—the recognition of opposite views as equally entitled to respect; and once recognise that, sin or license ceases to be punishable, is no longer infamous, and we have made a vast step towards adopting and accepting it. The liberties we allow others to take we shall not long refuse for ourselves. First tolerance, then indifference, then actual license, are the inevitable fruits of Agnosticism—of any system that renders morality matter of inference, whether from Nature or from the interests of society.'

Merton.—' And why ?'

Cleveland.—' Obviously because, when morals become matter of inference, they become matter of speculation, and all ethical speculations are placed on an equal or quasi-equal footing. Positivism indeed did propose a kind of despotic Court of Review, an Agnostic Inquisition, to decide *ex cathedrâ* what moral speculations were or were not admissible, what ethical principles were *de fide*. But that part of Comte's system scarcely any Positivist of this day attempts to uphold.'

Sterne.—' All revolutions involve a period of anarchy.'

Lestrange.—' A very strong argument against any revolution whatever, so long as the existing system is not worse than anarchy; and " anarchy is the worst tyranny." '

Sterne.—' Still you cannot say that no revolution in morals can ever be justifiable; and therefore you cannot condemn a new religion because it involves a moral revolution and a consequent period of flux and anarchy in ethical convictions.'

Cleveland.—' Not if it promised to afford a firm future basis for a new and better moral code. But only Frenchmen and madmen have ever conceived of revolution as a permanent condition; and it is with the *revolution en permanence*, with a perpetual moral flux, a persistent ethical anarchy, that you menace us.'

Merton.—' Surely not!'

Cleveland.—' Surely yes; unless you intend and can find means to put down speculation, to impose finality on moral science. Whether your future code is to be drawn from Nature or from humanity, from the apparent order of the Universe, or from the apparent interests of mankind, it can never be established, never be authoritative, because it is matter of inference. Men will draw the most opposite conclusions from the same set of facts, and will never agree what the facts are, or what respective weight should be allowed to each. If you base a new morality upon the laws of Nature, not only will there be several permanent schools inferring the most opposite doctrines from different sides of Nature, but some new and vital discovery in Natural law may upset the very basis of all. It matters not whether Nature or Humanity be your idol or your

God, whether science or philanthropy be your law-giver. In either case you build upon a quicksand the one edifice whose stability is essential to mankind. Accept the fundamental principle of Utilitarianism, and what sort of morals can it give us? We see already that theft is the fundamental principle of one school of Utilitarians, as strict economic law resting on self-interest is the basis of another; and though we know which the founder of Utilitarianism would have adopted, we have no means of deciding between the two. We cannot deny to the Communist and the confiscator the license we have given to speculation in general. The thief ceases to be a criminal, he becomes at worst a moral heretic; and the time is gone by when you could punish heresy, in speculation or in action.'

Sterne.—' I don't see that.'

Cleveland.—' You may have *law* without a common basis, a common conviction, but not morality. You may punish, but you cannot abhor; and punishment without abhorrence ceases to be effective, and will soon cease to be possible.'

Sterne.—' But, Cleveland, after the period of anarchy we grant you, will there be, need there be, any serious permanent difference on any practical question of morals?'

Cleveland.—' That means, from your standpoint,

can there be any doubt what conduct really conduces to the greatest happiness of the greatest number?'

Sterne.—'I suppose so.'

Cleveland.—'Does not that question answer itself? You reduce morals to a branch of political speculation—do you expect men ever to agree about politics? There are two severally coherent, mutually irreconcileable ideas of that which will really conduce to the welfare of mankind, the democratic and the aristocratic, the socialist and the economic. The one looks to equality, the other to inequality as the permanent state of human society; and looking to exactly opposite ends, either must perforce recommend an exactly opposite method. The morality of Communism and the morality of Individualism are not merely diverse but divergent, become more and more clearly contradictory the more frankly and logically they are carried out. Their very ideals of duty are opposite. The one holds as the very guide of practical life that he who provideth not for his own is worse than an infidel; the other recognizes no ownership even in the family, no closer tie between father and children than between citizen and citizen. The one merges all duties in the sole duty owed to the community at large; the other, starting from the family, only subordinates the family to the State in a few extreme cases, which hardly affect in practice the life of one man in a thousand, and affect that one life but once or twice in fifty years.'

Sterne.—' But, except a few stubborn Tories like yourself, a few cynics like Lestrange, does any one seriously believe that social inequality is good in itself, ought to or can permanently endure ?'

Cleveland.—' We discussed that point the other day, and no one answered my argument that equality means stagnation.'

Sterne.—' I should imagine that that question will be settled to the satisfaction of mankind during the revolution; and after that, why should not Utilitarianism or Naturalism furnish as sure a basis of morals as theology ?'

Cleveland.—' The judicial maxim, " Give your decisions, they will be right; don't give your reasons, they are sure to be wrong," goes to the root of that question. Law, moral or municipal, cannot and must not argue. " Thou shalt not steal,"—that is plain, intelligible, practical enough to direct us all, if we earnestly want to know what is right. But " Don't steal, because stealing will injure the interests of humanity " is open to two fatal replies. Lestrange says, " I care nothing for humanity. I won't go without my dinner to bring your paradise nearer by half an hour." The Communist says, "Property is robbery; the interest of mankind is involved not in its maintenance but in its abolition." You cannot answer either objection—that is, you cannot so answer them as to put the objector obviously, unquestionably in the wrong. He simply holds a different opinion from yourself on a question of pure speculation. Now Law, social and moral, holds society together; must be strong and absolute if civilized society is to exist. You cannot build it on a shifting foundation; you cannot rest the world on the elephant of morals and the elephant on the quicksands of speculative inference.'

Sterne.—'You can tell both the Cynic and the Communist, "You may think what you please; but if you steal you shall be hanged."'

Cleveland.—'Pardon me, that is just what you can't do. You could do it while the vast majority of mankind held to the Eighth Commandment. But when the righteousness of property becomes an open question, when, as I said, the thief is simply a moral heretic, that power is cut from under you. You cannot hang a man whom Society does not abhor; and the time has gone by when society abhorred a heretic.'

MALA PROHIBITA.

Lestrange.—'But after all, on what does the Commandment rest?'

Cleveland.—'On two strong grounds: a supreme authority and a supreme sanction. First, "God spake these words and said," and next, "If you do steal, you incur a punishment you cannot escape from a Judge you cannot deceive."'

Sterne.—'You cannot found morality on punishment. To use a favourite retort of your own—If you do that, what if the Devil got the upper hand?'

Cleveland.—'General rebellion. But till the law is so bad as to provoke general rebellion, we know that severe punishment does establish a sort of moral right. So long as Society respects the law on the whole, it associates infamy with severe legal punishment.'

Sterne.—'Don't confuse logic and prejudice, philosophy and practice. A thing is not wrong, and no thoughtful man can believe it wrong, merely because the State will hang him or the Church damn him for it.'

Cleveland.—'On the contrary, I hold many things wrong simply because the State forbids them. But after all that kind of morality might survive religion; not for ever, but for some time.'

Sterne.—'And how much stronger after all is your other foundation? Can God make right and wrong?'

Cleveland.—' He is so infinitely wiser, so incomparably more likely to know what is right and wrong than we, that no believer in God will ever raise that question. That is the inalienable, irreplaceable advantage of a morality that rests on religion. Our duty is settled for us by an authority we neither can nor wish to dispute.'

Sterne.—' Well; *if* you can believe that " God spake these words and said." But if He did, He spoke a good many other words you refuse to accept. You might quite as well found morality on Utilitarian or Naturalistic theory as on private judgment, dividing the canon of Scripture into inspired oracles and Prophetic or Apostolic errors.'

Cleveland.—If I thought so—and in some measure I do think so—I should doubt whether it were not the duty of every man, sceptic or believer, to hold by and uphold the strongest form of authoritative religion, the Church Catholic. After all, even Papal despotism is better than moral anarchy.'

Lestrange.—' " If God did not exist men would have to invent Him." But an invented God won't serve your purpose. France has shown you what happens when a Church rests on the support of popular ignorance and sceptical acquiescence.'

Cleveland.—' The French sceptics did not hold their tongues—and our sceptics won't. But after all, Theism does involve a certain revelation on the main lines of morality ; it is difficult to doubt what the will of God really is, what He meant and exacts from us.'

Merton.—' Through Nature ?'

Cleveland.—' No ; through those human instincts and impulses which are not natural but supernatural.'

Merton.—' If your God be only the God of Nature, you must seek the revelation of His will in Nature and in history ; and then you incur all the objections you allege against a Natural morality.'

Cleveland.—' No : I have what you have not, the right to distinguish—to seek His highest revelation, His command, in the highest human conceptions, in the best human instincts.'

Lestrange.—' But after all you see Him throughout history doing evil that good may come, just as ruthlessly as Nature herself.'

Cleveland.—' Blindly the wicked work the righteous will of Heaven.'

Merton.—' But if God's purposes are only to be worked out through wickedness, it doesn't say much for His own moral character.'

Cleveland.—' If we were to sift that argument to the bottom, we should come to the old inscrutable problem—the existence of Evil. Now, I have solved that difficulty to my own satisfaction, and I don't think it ever seriously embarrassed a believer who had once realised the possibility that even Omnipotence may be conditioned; that perhaps God, like ourselves, cannot think a contradiction. It seems to me not only possible but probable that that inability is a condition not of human but of all intelligence; and if so, free-will may be incompatible in the nature of things with perfection. It may be that the very best God could think or desire for His creatures may be an upward gradual approach to excellence rather than excellence conferred upon them at the outset.'

Lestrange.—' After all, there are fatal objections to your view, as to all others I ever heard. 1 cannot believe either in God or in conscience, because I know how both have been developed. Evolution accounts for both; traces your God back to the Negro's Fetish, and your morality to tribal selfishness.'

Cleveland.—'I don't undertake to prove, to the satisfaction of men who have thought out the problem for themselves and come to an opposite conclusion, the truth either of religion or of morality. I admit your absolute denial of both as at least a possible, a thinkable conclusion. What I affirm, and think I can prove and have proved, is that the two are mutually indispensable, must stand and fall together. There can be no law without a law-giver, therefore no morality without a God.'

Sterne.—' I don't see the "therefore."'

Cleveland.—' What is your law-giver ?'

Sterne.—' Conscience, I fancy.'

Lestrange.—' And how did you come by conscience ?'

Cleveland.—' After all, I fancy that you and Merton, if you work out your ideas, will come to the same conclusion: "Nature is God, and Humanity is His Prophet."'

Merton.—' That sounds like truth.'

Cleveland.—' Well, then, the God is a machine, or, for aught we know, may be a machine—is not a God that we can understand or that can understand us; and the prophet has no mission and no credentials. If Humanity be your law-giver, where is his right, whence did he receive authority to bind me ?'

Sterne.—' The prophet of course takes his authority from the God.'

Cleveland.—' And the God—what deference, what obedience do we owe to Nature ? The Ruler of the Universe has a right divine to my allegiance; my Creator, till I know that He has wronged me, has at least a *prima facie* claim to my obedience. Nature has neither. If I follow her example, I become a demon. If I recognize her law in the whole body of human instincts—observe, deriving them from Nature I cannot pick and choose among them, I can recognize none as higher than others—what sort of morality will they furnish? And even if mine—the instincts of a cultivated, thoughtful, happy man—were a safe guide, what would be the common morality of common men? Their instincts are too often low and base, and the stronger the baser they are. But above all they are divergent, contradictory in different ages and among different races; and the natural morality of one age or country, of one race or class would be diametrically opposed to that of another.'

Sterne.—' But you affirm with Lestrange that Nature is ruthlessly aristocratic. Well, then, the instincts which Nature meant for your guide must be those of the highest forms of humanity, the best and wisest of mankind.'

Cleveland.—' When we have settled who the best and wisest are.'

Sterne.—' Take the great body of those whose right to either title you would yourself admit. Whatever their tenets, whatever their theology, whatever their moral theories—are not their instincts the same?'

Lestrange.—' Certainly not. Take three or

four of the best and wisest among our fathers living and dead—Cardinal Newman, John Mill, Darwin, and any gentlemen you may select to represent the medical profession on the one hand and the Antivivisection crusade on the other—you will admit that among the latter there are one or two men wise as well as good. Their instincts are opposite, their ideas of right and wrong on vital points as directly contradictory as their theology.'

Sterne.—' Are they really so? Or do you not confound their instincts and their theories?'

Cleveland.—' No, I think not. If there be a point on which instinct is likely to have governed conviction, it is a question like that of vivisection. Yet the best and gentlest as the wisest and noblest of men evidently may and do come to exactly opposite conclusions; and not only their thoughts but their feelings are in strong mutual contradiction. H—— utterly abhors what seems to him the atrocious cruelty of vivisection, can hardly believe a man to be good or gentle, just or generous, who approves it. I know many and many a man quite as gentle, quite as tenderhearted as H——, who can hardly speak with patience of the brutal insensibility to human suffering, to human welfare which H——'s opposition to vivisection involves. Newman is perhaps the purest and most honest man of the age; but Newman's ideas about truth drove a man like Kingsley, an enthusiast on the subject, utterly frantic, drove him beyond the bounds alike of decency and common-sense. And if you say that Kingsley, though a lofty professor, was not a strict practitioner—that few men violated the command not to bear false witness more recklessly, however unconsciously—you must own that most high-minded Englishmen dislike Newman's doctrine almost as much as he did. If these things are not matters of instinct, what are?'

Lestrange.—' Cleveland, for once I think you have put your foot in it. You said just now that the best human instincts were the revelation of God's will.'

Cleveland.—' It looks like contradiction, I admit; yet I am sure that in fact and in truth it is none. Take these instincts as given by Nature, take them as a whole, and you find the mass of confusion and mutual conflict I have alleged and tried to illustrate. Take those alone that are not natural but human—those especially that we can conceive of most easily as given from above rather than developed from below—and I believe that we shall all find in them a guidance for our own life, and a guidance not so divergent as might seem at first.'

Lestrange.—' Obedience to instinct—with nine men in ten that would mean yielding to impulse; and if you escape that pitfall, if you construct a coherent scheme of morals upon the higher instincts alone—will they not lead us very far apart and very far astray? Nay, do we not know that they have often done so ?'

Cleveland.—' I doubt it. They may have led former generations very far apart from the course in which they would lead us. But holding as I do to all the leading principles of Evolution, to all except the theory of accidental variation, I see nothing strange, nothing contrary to the Creator's system or to my idea of Providential government, in a gradual development of human morality. After all, I but apply to natural, what has been long since recognized as the truth by those who believe in supernatural, revelation; the truth of revelation by degrees as men could bear it.'

Lestrange.—' Are you convinced, Merton ?'

Merton.—' Certainly not.'

Lestrange.—' Exactly. You might talk for ever and never convince one another; never come nearer together, never arrive at a principle, a truth, hardly even a method, you hold in common. What is the fitting inference? First, of course, that there is much to be said on both sides; but secondly, I fear, either that there is no truth on these subjects or that it lies utterly beyond our reach. If you, and men wiser, abler, more fully informed than you, come to the most opposite conclusions on all the primary questions of morals and religion, I, trying to be impartial, must infer that there exist either no moral certainties or no means of attaining them. You are each so successful in damaging your opponent's case, so feeble when you come to set up a doctrine of your own—your denials are so forcible and so plausible, your affirmations so weak and incoherent—that I can only be confirmed in universal doubt, if not universal negation. The only safe conclusion seems to be my own—perhaps because it has been so long my own—that we know and can know nothing; that "there is nothing new and nothing true, and it don't much matter." The longer I listen to you, the more I disbelieve you all.'

CHAPTER XI.

THIN ICE AND SNOW-BRIDGES.

WE had had three days of continuous and very sharp frost, and Mrs. Cleveland felt sure that a neighbouring lake would be so frozen as to bear securely. Cleveland, whose experience was longer, whose observation was perhaps a little more careful and accurate than hers, was doubtful, but agreed at her request that we should all go down thither next morning. We had tried the ice in several places before the little phaeton in which she drove Lestrange appeared on a narrow drive, between the foot of the hill overlooking the water and the lake itself; a drive accessible only through private roads, or to pedestrians by a somewhat longer and more difficult route, and therefore the most quiet and secluded access to the ice.

'Will it bear?' she asked, as I, who happened to be nearest and had first caught sight of the phaeton, came within hail.

'I don't know, Mrs. Cleveland. It will bear us singly: whether it would bear your chair and your escort at once I doubt. You see there are but few men on, and we have not yet tried the dangerous parts, by the island and where the current begins to be felt above and below.'

'It won't bear below the reeds,' observed Lestrange, who had been scanning it narrowly, shading his eyes with his hand. 'It is like Agnostic morality, safe for one light weight here and there, but sure to give way with the crowd or under any unusual stress.'

'You forget, Lestrange,' I said, 'Mahomet's declaration that we must each appear before the Judgment Seat alone. So with conscience. Each, even in a crowd, must judge for himself, and the moral rule that will bear each will bear all.'

'You may say that only one man can stand on each square foot of ice, but the ice does break with a crowd that will bear a few scattered skaters. So in ethics: the weight of a common temptation, a common error, is multiplied, not merely added.'

Just then a skater came from behind the island, apparently from the point of greatest danger save one, that where the river entered the lake. The current there, however, was gentler than at foot, the stream along the upper valley being stiller and deeper than below, where it ran for some distance over a steep incline. By his black dress and black felt hat we knew, even before we could recognise his face, our clerical friend and frequent interlocutor, Vere. As Lestrange assisted Mrs. Cleveland from her phaeton, Vere quickened his pace, raising his hat as soon as he came within hearing.

'No, Mrs. Cleveland,' he called, 'it will not do for you.'

'You think not?' Cleveland asked, coming up. 'Merton is trying near the reeds, but I thought it was pretty firm across the open here.'

'Yes,' Vere answered, 'ten to one you might run Mrs. Cleveland over in her chair; but is it worth the one chance in ten of a dangerous accident?'

'Certainly not, if there be one in twenty; and you think there is?'

'I am afraid so.'

Evidently much disappointed, Mrs. Cleveland yielded at once, without even a remonstrance or a sullen look, only asking,

'Will you not take me across on foot to the island, Algernon?'

'You think it safe?' he asked, turning to Vere.

'I suppose so, or——'

He was interrupted by a scream from below,

near the point which Lestrange had indicated as certainly unsafe, but beyond our sight. Vere, an excellent skater, accomplished in all exercises which the popular prejudice he was careful never needlessly to offend permitted to his cloth, started at once for the spot; and some five minutes later returned with Merton, who had, as we knew, been in the immediate neighbourhood of the danger, and for whom therefore we had been a little uneasy.

'As usual,' the latter said. 'A foolish boy venturing not only his own life, which may be of no great consequence, but the horror and misery of such an accident, a terrible shock, a lifelong grief to his mother; and merely for bravado's sake. The ice was too rough for skating, there was nothing to see—no attraction except the danger.'

'You should have more sympathy with those who love to skate on thin ice,' Lestrange rejoined. 'Your whole philosophy consists in leading your disciples over ice that has just borne you without breaking.'

'They will always have benefit of clergy,' Merton retorted. 'There will be plenty of sound theologians, like Vere, at hand to do what he did for that young ass.'

'Aye, but,' said Vere, 'they may have caught

a mortal chill before we can bring them out on safe ground. You ought to know how the ice breaks round and round as they try to regain their footing.'

'Are you wet, Mr. Vere?' Mrs. Cleveland asked. 'As I must not venture after this warning, I was going to ask you to return with us to lunch; but I am afraid you ought to go home and change at once.'

'Oh, no! I should have dried myself skating, and a long walk over the hills will do as well.'

'Thank you,' she said, resuming her seat in the phaeton. 'Mr. Lestrange, you will drive back with me?'

'And then Merton would say I had thrown my glove and shirked my own challenge. No, as I miss the skating, I shall not be sorry for the walk.'

The groom who had brought the chair entrusted it to one of the multitude of boyish loungers who are always to be found in the neighbourhood of ice, especially when unsafe; and mounted the back seat of the phaeton as Mrs. Cleveland drove off, intending to make the circuit of the valley and to return home by a route considerably longer than our own. Two or three threatening cracks warned the skaters off the lake, and in five minutes more our whole party, Vere included, had turned homeward.

'You must own, Lestrange,' Merton said, 'that no Agnostic of the day has broken the ice yet. Our creed has proved firm enough to bear us through all the trials and temptations of life as creditably as our neighbours of the straitest sects.'

Lestrange.—'Granted, as regards your practice. But what has borne you is not your creed but the survivals of superstition that linger with you in spite thereof; and may long remain imbedded like fossils in your philosophy, if not so long as the many survivals of barbaric ideas and customs—omens and lucky usages—have persisted in the midst of a civilization that has forgotten their meaning.'

Merton.—'For instance?'

Lestrange.—'Well, as I said before, conscience is for you a survival not only of superstition but of barbarism.'

Cleveland.—'Nay, Lestrange, a development is not a survival.'

Lestrange.—'It matters nothing which you call it: conscience has no place in the creed of a consistent Agnostic. But we won't go over that ground again. Only, I will say, and Merton must admit, that for an Agnostic cruelty is about the only sin.'

Vere.—'Or rather, Agnosticism knows no sin, but only crime.'

Merton.—' How so ?'

Cleveland.—' Judging you out of your own mouth, Humanity is your God—I will not say your idol—the sole object of duty; the interests of society or mankind your sole standard of right and wrong.'

Merton.—Well ?'

Cleveland.—' Then Vere is right, and you recognise nothing but crimes. A sin against society, a sin which society can punish of right, whether or not it be found prudent or possible to punish, is a crime. The sins which are not crimes are those which do not injure others.'

Merton.—' I think your definition is defective. Ingratitude, for example, injures others, but it is not a crime.'

Cleveland.—' I beg your pardon; a crime, but a crime too indefinite for legal punishment. It is amenable to social judgment, to social censure, and is therefore a crime in morals if not in law.'

Merton.—' So, then, must be all sins that fall under social censure.'

Cleveland.—' No; only those that so fall of right; that is, those which injure society collectively, or your neighbour, whom society is bound to protect; only those which infringe some social right.'

Merton.—' For example ?'

Cleveland.—' *Volenti non fit injuria.* That is a rule of social ethics as well as of law. Therefore all those wrongs to others to which the others are willing parties are to a consistent Agnostic no sins at all.'

'Say rather no wrong-doing,' interposed Vere. 'Sin is a term properly religious and has no place in the Agnostic vocabulary.'

Merton.—' Still I don't see your drift.'

Cleveland.—' This—that a large class, or rather several large classes of sins, and some of the worst sins, are not injurious to society and do not infringe any right, moral or legal, of your neighbour; therefore from your standpoint, by your own definition, they are not wrong. From your standpoint no self-regarding actions can be wrong, and no acts which, though they regard others, are done with the full consent of those they regard.'

Merton.—No one willingly submits to an injury; therefore an action injurious to your neighbour must either be done without his consent or by deception; and to deceive is to wrong him.'

Cleveland.—' Many and serious injuries are done to others with their full and knowing consent. Duelling, for example, is murder from the Christian standpoint, may be murder from yours, in so far as it is an injury to society; but, so far as each duellist is concerned, it is a wrong done with his own consent, a consent at once willing and sensible.'

Merton.—' How can consent be insensible?'

Cleveland.—'Not insensible, but induced by deception. Now the duellist is neither forced nor deceived. Again, the same rule includes all sexual sins, where the woman is old enough to know her own mind and appreciate the consequences.'

Merton.—' They are injuries to society.'

Cleveland.—'Very remotely if at all, as the manner in which the world regards them proves. Why does society deal so severely with the one sex, so lightly with the other? Obviously because it regards the matter not from a social but from a personal standpoint; not as an injury to the community—in which aspect society finds it too remote, too dubious for practical censure—but as a violation of purity, which is a strictly personal virtue. Social opinion, human instincts regard purity as the primary virtue of woman, as a very secondary virtue in man. Therefore, and on no other conceivable or intelligible ground, opinion punishes feminine unchastity and leaves the male accomplice almost unscathed. Now the Agnostic has no right, no reason to censure impurity at all.'

Merton.—' Why not?'

Cleveland.—'Clearly because it is not an injury to society.'

Merton.—'Certainly it is.'

Cleveland.—'No—not if it be concealed, if no scandal, no bad example be created, if no child be born to bear the punishment of its parents' violation of social usages. Therefore, it is not the sin but the scandal alone that you have a right to censure.'

Lestrange.—'As I said, if a man like pig-wash, he has a right to be a swine.'

Merton.—'No; Nature made him a man.'

Lestrange.—'Nature? Once more, you borrow a Theistic term and twist it out of its Theistic and only meaning. When Vere or Cleveland say, "Nature made me man," they mean something: they use the phrase from a sort of reverence, to avoid saying God. But for you Nature is a mechanism or a metaphor, not a person.'

Merton.—'What difference does personality make?'

Lestrange.—'Just this: that Nature not being a person, but either a personification of physical law or an elliptic expression for the collective frame of existing things, has no rights, can impose no obligations. From your standpoint, moreover, the phrase is a falsehood. Nature did *not* make me man: I growed, as Topsy says—

grew like a tree, and am no more amenable to moral laws than a tree; except, you would say, in so far as I am a member of a community or of the human race, and have no right to wrong my fellow-men. I don't admit even that; but, accepting that, I repeat you must admit my right to be a swine if I please. It concerns none but myself. For when you say Nature made me man, you mean merely I happen to be man.'

Merton.—' Well, perhaps—if it concern none but yourself.'

Lestrange.—' Look a little further. Drunkenness is no sin, it affects no one but the drunkard, unless he have a wife to beat; and then it is the beating not the drunkenness that makes him a sinner. Meanness, selfishness, greed, idleness, all self-regarding vices, all evil feelings and dispositions, are utterly indifferent by your rule.'

Merton.—' Till they take shape in action, and then they injure others.'

Lestrange.—' But what matter though they injure others, so the injury infringe no right ?'

Merton.—' A man is bound to do his best for mankind.'

Lestrange.—' How bound? By what law, by what sanction ? Conscience, as you have shown, is simply the transmitted will of the majority; social and legal penalties simply give effect to the present will of the majority. Can that will make right and wrong? But pass that over as a point already sufficiently argued—only bear in mind your fundamental admission, that nothing is wrong which does not injure others; consequently no self-regarding sin, and no sin to which all concerned are consenting parties, can be a sin at all. Do you not see that, even as regards social action, your rule inverts many fundamental principles of existing morality, outrages some of our strongest moral instincts?'

Merton.—' I don't see it at this moment, but it is likely enough. A true code of ethics must invert many rules derived from a false one; and our existing moral instincts, as you call them, are but the impressions of personal and hereditary training, the mental habits formed by ages of superstition.'

Lestrange.—' Then look here. Avarice is no sin, for in its effects it is, if not exclusively, mainly beneficial to society. Political economy leaves no doubt of that. Charity, on the contrary, is one of the worst of vices; for, on the whole again, nothing is more noxious. Avarice injures only the miser, it enriches the community. It saves, and applies to the wages-fund of the present, to the capital of the future, all that the miser might, had he been a spendthrift, have consumed or wasted. Charity, for one innocent sufferer that it saves, demoralises and ruins a dozen families.'

Merton.—' By misapplication.'

Lestrange.—' Oh, I do not mean to say that all charity is necessarily wicked, but only that from your standpoint charity at large is one of the worst sins, and avarice a very considerable virtue.'

Merton.—' Intention must of course determine merit. That which is done with a selfish, unjust end must be wrong, culpable in itself; that which is meant to benefit others is meritorious in the individual even if it be noxious in result.'

Lestrange.—' Sound Christian morality, but very unsound Agnostic logic. What have you to do with intent, with a man's thought or the inward state of his mind? For you, that is wrong which is injurious, that is right which is beneficial to mankind. Charity does not less demoralize and pauperize a population because the money is given by tender-conscienced men and soft-hearted women; because the desire of the givers is to relieve suffering and not to encourage idleness. Avarice does not accumulate less capital, does not less increase the wages-fund of the country, because the miser's motive is pure unadulterated selfishness. Can you not see that a code which is based upon consequences must ignore motives? that a philosophy which makes consequence the standard, nay, the constituent principle, of right and wrong, can take cognizance of nothing else, cannot go behind the consequence and enquire into the intention?'

Merton.—' You are confounding two different things; right, in the sense of expedient, and right, in the sense of just and holy.'

Lestrange.—' What have you who deny a Deity, whose conscience is the opinion, whose morality is the interest of mankind, to do with holiness? The word has no meaning on your lips. But it is not I who confound right and expediency; that confusion is the very essence of your creed. That is right in your eyes which is expedient: nay, by your own axiom, it is the expediency, conduciveness to the general welfare, that makes right.'

Merton.—' Still, society might justly make a law to forbid charity, to encourage avarice; but in the man's own conscience, and in others' estimation of the man not of his act, the intent is everything. If he intend the welfare of mankind, he is doing right according to his own conscience, be the consequences what they may.'

Lestrange.—' That is, it may be the duty of

society to make a law which it is the duty of individuals to break?'

Merton.—' Certainly. Would you not admit that Marcus Antoninus did well from his standpoint in persecuting the Christians, that they did well in refusing to yield?'

Lestrange.—' No. I should say that Antoninus was culpably, almost criminally, ignorant. But that is not a parallel case. There, the law-giver and the law-breakers were governed by different or opposite principles. It was Cæsar's political duty to punish revolt against the religion of Rome: it was the Christians' duty to refuse to Cæsar what belonged to God. The contradiction was possible only because the morality of the two parties was drawn from distinct irreconcileable principles. Your argument is that an Agnostic society may be bound to pass laws which an Agnostic conscience would be bound to violate.'

Merton.—' For want of enlightenment. An enlightened conscience would know that charity, unless very carefully and vigilantly discriminated, was not a virtue.'

Lestrange.—' Nor avarice a vice? Come now, Merton! Agnostic society should encourage avarice; the avaricious man should obey the law because it is wise; and his miserliness, though founded on pure selfishness, is therefore a high virtue.'

Cleveland.—'I think you are pushing a mere verbal advantage too far, Lestrange. Grant that Agnosticism can show no basis, no code of personal, self-regarding morality—that seems to me a clear irrefragable deduction from the doctrine that the interest of mankind is the sole standard of right and wrong, of vice and virtue. Still the judgment of society and the judgment of the individual may honestly conflict, and then the individual must follow his own judgment. On actions that affect society the majority must make the law to suit their estimate of social interests; the individual is doing right when he does that which he believes beneficial to mankind at large.'

Lestrange.—'There is another inference that occurs to me as following logically from the Utilitarian dogma; if that be right which is beneficial to mankind, conduct is virtuous or vicious, right or wrong, in *proportion* to the benefit or injury it confers upon mankind. And again, since error often does more harm than wickedness, ignorance—perhaps we should make an exception as the Roman Church does for inevitable or invincible ignorance—would seem to be the unpardonable sin.'

Merton.—' How can that be sin which is involuntary?'

Lestrange.—' But ignorance or misjudgment is by no means involuntary. Take the case of charity, for example. Women might know, if they would but listen, how mischievous it is. They will not be guided by masculine counsel, they will not study political economy; and they sin—that is, they injure society—from *wilful* ignorance, from petulant self-will and self-conceit, or from something worse, a preference of feeling to judgment. Surely from your standpoint, Merton, the first duty, the paramount virtue, is knowledge. Before we presume to act, we ought to have mastered the philosophy of life, to have studied thoroughly the principles of political economy and social science. We have no right to be careless, thoughtless, or idle; to do anything less than our best to master the philosophy on which depends the consequence, and therefore the morality, of our conduct.'

Vere.—' I think the truth lies far deeper than Lestrange's cynicism cares to follow it. For an Agnostic there may be right and wrong as forms of wisdom or folly—a wisdom or folly which we may call moral. But sin in the Christian sense, holiness as believers in God use the word, there can never be.'

Merton.—' I cannot see it. Surely you will admit that the leading Agnostics of this age are men of lives at least as stainless, of thought at least as pure as the leaders of any other school can boast?'

Cleveland.—' But that is nothing to the point. You know that the Agnostics of to-day, with scarcely an exception, have been educated as Christians.'

Merton.—' But in discarding Christianity they have shown no disposition to discard holiness.'

Lestrange.—' No, they want to steal it as they steal every other Christian phrase, to give it a sense or nonsense of their own.'

Merton.—' By their fruits ye shall know them.'

Lestrange.—' Aye, but the fruits are not ripe yet, and will not be for a century to come. Agnostic morality is as yet wholly undeveloped, is in bud, not even in flower. You practise purity because, in the first place, you are for the most part men of cold temperament, powerful intellects, and hard constant brain-work; and such men, whatever their opinions, are rarely profligates. And secondly, you preach and practise it for the sake of your creed, because any admission that Agnosticism involves a great relaxation of morality would be fatal to your cause. But, after all, you know that we could quote one or two signal examples of scandal among your foremost leaders. The ablest woman of your sect was what the Church calls a notorious evil-liver.'

Merton.—' For shame !'

Cleveland.—' It is literally true as Lestrange puts it. She set at naught both Christian and English law. But waive that point. We admit that you practise, we admit that you preach, a morality as strict as our own. We say that you have no right to it, that it is as unreal as your Paradise, your "immortality," and will, in the logic of your successors, in the lives of your pupils, disappear as a survival of superstition.'

Merton.—' Vice is pernicious to mankind, and therefore immoral from an Agnostic or Utilitarian as from a Christian point of view.'

Vere.—' Wrong, perhaps, but not sinful : inexpedient, hardly even wicked—certainly not unholy, abominable, as it is in Christian eyes. For you wickedness, however great, is finite ; for us it is infinite in its evils.'

Merton.—' How so ?'

Vere.—' Because the loss of one immortal soul is an infinite evil. For you, right and wrong are mere matters of expediency. An evil action, however atrocious, is evil only to the extent of the practical injury it does; and that injury is limited by the lifetime of the sufferers, or at most of the evil-doer also.'

Merton.—' No, it is eternal as the Universe. Every act produces effects which are felt, or at least which extend, through infinite space and infinite time.'

Lestrange.—' Just in the same sense in which a pebble thrown by a child into the sea produces an infinite disturbance.'

Merton.—' Metaphor is not argument.'

Cleveland.—' In this case it is. For your theory of infinite consequences is a physical, not a moral one; and the analogy is strict and complete, is something more than an analogy. Your consequences, like the circles made by the stone's splash, widen and widen, but become fainter and fainter as they extend, till a yard or a year off they vanish altogether.'

Merton.—' Vanish from sight; they do not cease to be.'

Cleveland.—' Practically they do. Your infinite propagation of consequences is an infinite series of perpetually diminishing fractions; is it not?'

Merton.—' Well, I suppose so.'

Cleveland.—' Then I need not remind you, surely, that an infinite series of infinitesimals *may*—an infinite series of rapidly diminishing fractions *must*—have a finite limit. Your universal Cosmic extension of consequences is exactly like the typical series of mathematical tyros— $1+\frac{1}{2}+\frac{1}{4}+\frac{1}{8}+$ etc., of which the limit is 2.'

Vere.—' For you, then, Merton, the wickedness of the worst action is finite, and very small indeed. Your standard of evil is injury done to mankind; you measure actions moral and other by their consequences—is it not so?'

Merton.—' Hardly, I think.'

Vere.—' Can you name any other standard? An action is evil because its consequences are harmful, for no other reason. You admit that? Well then, it is evil *in proportion* as it is harmful. But its wickedness from *our* standpoint has no relation to its consequences. A Napoleon loses his temper for five minutes, and the consequences are, it may be, half a million deaths and the misery of nations prolonged for years. A private man bears bitter animosity, we will say, to his father, who has been patient, forgiving, generous to him for a lifetime, and avenges imaginary wrongs by parricide. He is an ingrate, a murderer, a criminal of the deepest dye; but from your standpoint, by your measurement, his guilt is infinitely less than that of the Emperor who lost his temper at a critical moment.'

Merton.—' " Unto whom much is given, of him shall much be required." Loss of temper on the part of an Emperor, who knows that the lives of millions depend on his judgment, is, if not a great crime, a very grave fault.'

Vere.—' Granted, as compared with similar ill-temper in a private man, not with parricide. Yet the consequences of parricide may be very trivial, may cost only a few years of one not very useful life.'

Cleveland.—' It seems to me, Vere, that you are not proving your point. You reduce the Utilitarian standard of morals to an absurdity, no doubt; you do not prove that Agnosticism cannot recognise sin.'

Vere.—' No; I was led a little astray, though my argument bears strongly, if indirectly, on that point. Sin is something wholly apart from consequence. It is not mere evil-doing, it is not, as an immoral action must be to the Agnostic, something comparable with an error of judgment in kind if not in degree; it is not a moral blunder, a misconception or disregard of practical expediency. It is for us a thing utterly distinct, infinitely deeper and different in nature, in essence. Cardinal Newman scarcely exaggerated when he said that the destruction of the world was a less evil than a single mortal sin. After all, Merton, what can be for you the very worst guilt of the very worst action, under the most aggravating circumstances of position and power? Grant that it might conceivably influence for evil the fortunes of mankind as long as mankind exists, that it will hurt a little some fraction of mankind till the world cools and becomes uninhabitable—what then? It is still an evil of the same kind with the introduction of a new disease, with the error of a statesman which embroils two great Powers in a needless war. So much for the greatest, gravest sins of men the most highly placed and powerful. What of the worst crimes of ordinary offenders? Practically their consequences are limited to a very few years and a very few individuals.'

Merton.—' It may be; but that does not take from them the character of sinfulness. I have no more right to inflict unprovoked, unjustified injury upon a single fellow-creature than a Sovereign to engage in an unprovoked unjustified war.'

Vere.—' Granted; but for you the evil of the action is limited to its consequences. It cannot by possibility be worse than those. For you, then, an evil action that has no ill consequences, if there can be such, is hardly in any true sense evil at all.'

Merton.—' Yes; it is a violation of Law, and of a law necessary to the welfare of mankind. Therefore its guilt is proportionate not to its own immediate consequences but to the importance of the law violated, to the consequences which the habitual neglect of that law would bring about. The responsibility of the offender is measurable not by the consequences of his own act, which may be matter of accident, but by the necessity, the value to mankind of the law he has broken.'

Lestrange.—' But that responsibility covers one-billionth part of the whole mischief possible from systematic universal violation of the law. He is responsible only in proportion to his power of mischief. Suppose that the total abrogation of the law would produce an amount of evil we will call x. The violation of that law by A., one individual out of a thousand millions of one generation in a thousand, can only cause one-billionth part of x. That is the measure of his fault.'

Merton.—' Be as cynical as you like, Lestrange; but don't argue as if morals could be measured by mathematics.'

Vere.—' The fact remains, Merton, that morally as well as mathematically, from your standpoint, the evil of an action must be measured by its consequences; if not by its individual consequences, then by the evil tendency of such actions. But that evil tendency is limited to the lifetime of mankind, which, on the showing of modern scientists, is certainly finite and probably brief; and again, it is evil of a kind strictly analogous to all other physical and social evils. *You* can draw no broad, deep, impassable distinction between sin and folly, between error and wickedness.'

Merton.—' Can you ?'

Vere.—' Yes. Folly may be virtuous : though a truly virtuous man or woman is seldom or never a thorough fool. Do you not see how forcibly, intensely, the instincts of mankind revolt from your theory, how you yourself refuse to measure the wickedness of an act by its consequences, or even by its tendencies ? Nothing, probably, can be more evil in consequence than misplaced heroism, or mistaken martyrdom. A man, again, whose life is of great value to a whole nation, risks and loses it to save that of an idiot child who will never be anything but a burden to the world. He is doing a positive injury to mankind, both in saving the idiot and in casting away his own life. The more valuable his own life, the worse from your point of view the action; yet the more mankind perforce admire it.'

Merton.—'Because the tendency is good; the law he has obeyed is the highest of all, self-sacrifice; the temptation he has overcome is the strongest of all, selfishness fortified by just self-appreciation.'

Vere.—' Even if we allow you to judge acts by their tendencies, to look only at the consequences of law or lawlessness in the abstract and not in each particular case, Utilitarianism will still bring you into frequent and violent conflict with the strongest human instincts.'

Merton.—' It must be, then, because the motives of evil actions are pure; because, in short, the error has been a mistake and not a crime.'

Cleveland.—' Not at all. Is there any law more general, more absolute, more necessary to the welfare of mankind than "Thou shalt not kill"? Avarice, again, is, from any standpoint, a light, a comparatively venial vice; from yours it is no vice at all. Revenge is always an evil motive; yet, which act is more venial in the estimation of the universal conscience of mankind,—that of the man who murders his daughter's seducer, or that of the wealthy miser who refuses food to a child dying of want under his eyes ?'

Merton.—' The one is guilty of wild justice, the other of intense consummate selfishness; and selfishness is, in the creed of most Agnostics, the sum, the essence, of all sin. The preference of self to the welfare of mankind—of egotism to altruism—is our definition of sin.'

Vere.—' Still, what I say remains true, and I think unanswerable. Evil-doing from your standpoint is little more than aggravated blundering. You can nowhere draw a clear, definite, moral line distinguishing wickedness from recklessness, or recklessness from sheer ignorance. The difference is for you one of degree; for us of kind, of essence. Sin is for Theists disobedience, rebellion, treason against God ; for Christians faithlessness, ingratitude to Christ. For you, it is at worst the violation of a right which, if there be no God, is at best doubtful—the right of mankind at large to the fealty of individual men. Sin as sin, apart from the special heinousness of this or that guilt in particular, is not to you abhorrent and abominable, is not an infinite, imperishable evil.'

Cleveland.—' Imperishable, Vere ?'

Vere.—' From your ground of Natural Theism, yes ; from mine naturally imperishable, reparable only by a miracle, and the one supreme Miracle of miracles.'

Merton.—' Well, grant that we do not attach to sin the special religious importance, the superstitious significance, as we consider it, that it bears in your eyes—need that be an evil ? May we not be right and you wrong ?'

Vere.—' Possibly, as matter of argument. I only care to insist on that vital distinction between our ethics and yours. With you, morals are a branch of policy ; with us, something superhuman and infinite in importance. For you, sin is a temporary, practical, limited evil; for us, evil in an exclusive, absolute, infinite sense.'

Cleveland.—' And the consequence of that difference is also almost infinite. You lose the sanction, the penalty, you lose almost the sense of guilt. Your future disciples will very soon shake off your subtle distinction between abstract tendencies and concrete consequences; will measure, at least under temptation, every act by its own individual immediate effects, and will never think those effects serious enough to induce remorse or even repentance, seldom serious enough to exercise a present restraint upon passion or desire.'

Merton.—' Do you think then that practically, in every-day life, in ordinary cases, ordinary men are restrained from sin by the fear of God, the dread of Hell, or the hope of Heaven?'

Cleveland.—' Directly and immediately, no; ultimately, yes. From faith in God the Law-giver they have learned to regard a breach of His laws as something far graver, far worse than a breach of mere human ordinances. From your standpoint, human ordinances are the highest we can have. You can draw no distinction between that Natural Law which has been insensibly impressed upon conscience by the will of the majority in past ages, and those present ordinances which we call artificial local municipal law—between *malum in se* and *malum prohibitum*. You lower all law to the level of national legislation. And the dread of Hell as an indirect influence you must not overlook. Can you doubt that the horror with which nine men in ten regard murder—the modern English horror of it, so much stronger than is felt in Asia or Russia—arises in great part from the capital penalty? Few men think, "I must not commit murder lest I should be hung," most men think of murder as something impossible, atrocious beyond other crimes; and if they sought out their reason, it would be that the State hangs for murder and for that alone. So the thought that sin is an offence against God, punishable by everlasting perdition, has impressed upon Christians age after age an unconscious, unreasoning dread, shame, repentance of mortal sin; utterly distinct from that mild repugnance with which they regard breaches of human law—which alone will be left when you have reduced all morals, all conscience to the level of human legislation, direct or indirect, present or hereditary.'

Merton—' I cannot see that much practical harm would follow the disappearance of that superstitious fear of particular evil actions, even were it as general as you assume.'

Lestrange.—' You think then, when men come to regard morals as matter of expediency, to measure wrong-doing by its consequences,—that the rein will not be given to passion, the restraint not taken from vice?'

Merton.—' Why so ?'

Lestrange.—' Because all human actions matter so very little. The worst of all, murder, what is it? To shorten a useless, worthless, perhaps mischievous, life by a few months or years. The clerk has in his hands £5,000, a fortune to him, a provision for his family, which his millionaire master will never miss. How great to him the value, how little to others the harm, of theft! He makes his wife and children comfortable for life, and who is hurt? And in many sins there may be no palpable harm at all. Looked at coarsely, plainly, brutally, what harm does seduction do a woman? It injures her seriously in the estimation of society—but what if it be not known? She is leading a miserable life of hardship, insult, humiliation, as a governess or shop-girl under harsh employers. How is she injured if a rich man persuade her (or half a dozen girls) to remain with him till he is tired of her, securing to her a provision better than the situation she loses? Sweep away the mystical significance, the superstitious sanctity that Christianity, or rather universal Religion, has attached to feminine chastity; regard it practically, physically :—and who—what man at least—will feel scruple in tempting or remorse when the mischief, such as it is, is done? Can you not see that the actual practical evil consequences of human actions are, in one large class of cases, imaginary or artificial; in all so small, so limited, so petty, that they will never restrain a man from vice, even if they still put some check on the worst class of crimes? Humanity itself is so small and vile a thing; our individual power to injure it so slight, the result of our acts so uncertain, the direct positive, inevitable harm of most sins so dubious and so trifling—that to rest morality on consequences, to measure sin by injury, is to abolish morality *in toto.*'

Vere.—' At least to strike Sin, the thought and the word, out of the vocabulary and the conscience of mankind.'

CHAPTER XII.

CÆTERUM CENSEO.

In politics, in theology, even in science, most men are partisans, and nothing irritates partisans like impartial criticism. A man who sees the weak points of both sides—who will point out one day how much there is to be said for those orthodox doctrines which the extreme votaries of negative criticism or destructive science consider themselves to have demolished, on the next how completely orthodoxy fails to maintain its case, how many of its favourite dogmas are clearly untenable—is pretty sure to be credited with inconsistency, insincerity, or indifference, or with one and all. And yet such a man is very likely to be right in each and either view; and his impartiality, even his indecision, if not a happy or satisfactory mood, may surely indicate a clearer insight and a more judicial temper than the consistent convictions of either extreme. It irritates, however, even cool and candid men who have arrived at definite conclusions, or cherish strong but unexamined convictions. The conversation here recorded was the last of many in which our host of Ferndale Holm had maintained on the whole this mainly negative attitude; and more than one of his friends were determined, partly from genuine curiosity, partly perhaps in retaliation for many argumentative defeats, to extract from him some positive avowal; if not a declaration of agreement with either side, yet a definition of his own position between them, an outline of his own convictions, or a confession that he had none. For some time Cleveland defended himself vigorously, and, as I thought, not unjustly.

'In politics,' he said, ' a man must take a side, or he must stand aloof; but even in politics thorough-going partisanship should be confined to action, and that public utterance which is a part of action. A man who in private and confidential conversation affirms his entire agreement with either side, accepts every article either of the Tory or the Liberal creed, must be but half sincere; or must have derived his opinions from prejudice and passion, not from thought.'

Merton.—' Perhaps; but in science, and in those philosophic speculations which are so largely based on science, a man should take one side or the other.'

Cleveland.—' Why ?'

Merton.—' Because the creed of either side is a consistent whole; rests upon one or two general principles, and is in the main a fair logical deduction from the premisses. I understand the orthodoxy which is based on Faith, which refuses to submit itself to Reason; I understand of course thoroughly the negative, or, as you call it, destructive logic which will accept nothing that Reason cannot prove, which denies everything that cannot stand the test of Reason. But I cannot understand, I can hardly believe in any middle course.'

Cleveland.—' Can you not understand that I may find destructive logic often illogical, and the conclusions even of unreasoning orthodoxy on some points reasonable ?'

Sterne.—' Then I wish you would tell us clearly what those points are. When you argue against orthodoxy you seem to accept the conclusions of science, to believe to the full in Darwin and Wallace, if not in Huxley and Tyndall. When you assail Positivism, you speak now and then as if you half believed in the Christian evidences and even in the Christian miracles.'

Cleveland.—' I don't believe—I say you have not disproved them. Your negations may be true: I only say you have not shown them to be so.'

'Aye; but,' said Sterne, 'here are half-a-dozen of your oldest and most intimate friends, men who have known you for more than twenty years, and talked over with you all the most exciting questions of the hour, all the deepest problems of life and thought. Is it a credit to you that not one of us can say what you do believe?'

Cleveland.—' Is it fair to ask any man for his creed? Could any of you give yours?'

Sterne.—' I think so.'

Merton.—' And I am sure.'

Cleveland.—' Positive, as usual. And you, Lestrange?'

Lestrange.—' " I believe nothing—no, not even that I believe nothing." '

Cleveland.—' In politics, in economic science, I know what I believe; so I think do you. But when it comes to those deepest, most fundamental problems on which turn the highest interests not of nations but of mankind, our views not of a temporary expediency but of universal truth, I am not fool enough to be a partisan, nor passionate enough to be positive. If on these subjects a man is clearly, firmly, surely convinced, it is almost always—I will not say that he has decided without study but—that his mind was practically made up before he had mastered more than half the elements of the question.'

Lestrange.—'Then you accuse all clergymen at least of judging without hearing; for they, I suppose, are bound to be sure.'

Cleveland.—'They have to make up their minds at four-and-twenty; and who at that age can have studied half the case? If they have mastered the evidences in favour of Christianity, they are content; if they have really investigated the great issues of Biblical criticism, they have been exceptionally careful and conscientious. But they have not taken in one half, hardly perhaps a tithe, of the vast ground their propositions really cover. A Christian believes in the Resurrection; and believing in that he looks no further, he is dispensed from studying anything that conflicts with the doctrines on which that puts the seal of miraculous attestation.'

Lestrange.—'You don't believe that?'

Cleveland.—'Nor disbelieve. I cannot think that it happened; I cannot explain, can hardly conceive, how if it did not happen the Apostles came to believe it as they assuredly did—to live and die for that belief.'

Vere.—'And can you be content to remain in doubt on that fundamental question of all?'

Cleveland.—'Fundamental for you, who are satisfied of it. But your phrase "content to doubt" conveys the fundamental fallacy of all orthodox reasoning; the idea that belief is matter of will. On that as on most other questions of paramount importance I am *forced* to doubt, because the evidence is always conflicting and often incommensurable.'

Lestrange.—'Then, like me, you believe nothing?'

Cleveland.—'By no means. I believe—but I hardly know why I believe; I can very seldom say how much I believe it. I believe—but I can quite believe that I may be mistaken. I believe— yet I can see strong reasons for disbelieving. I believe—and yet I doubt. Can that be called belief at all?'

Vere.—'I suppose that few—save those who have resigned their intellect to some despotic authority outside themselves—fail to see, I will not say strong grounds for disbelief, but strong arguments against their firmest beliefs.'

Cleveland.—'Aye; but your doubts are temporary, or do not amount to doubt. Where you believe with full conviction, on the fundamental points of your creed, you never think it possible that you should be wrong.'

Vere.—'I don't know. What right have I to hold that the Church of eighteen centuries is wrong and I right when we differ?'

Cleveland.—'I don't know what right you have to differ from the Church Universal; but you *do.*

You may have no adequate ground for your belief, but—you believe. Now, on nearly every point of vital moment, I see both sides so clearly that, if I can feel which is the weightier, I cannot feel certain of either.'

Lestrange.—' Well, if you cannot say what you believe, say what you think.'

Cleveland.—' Well, I will try; but it will not be exactly what I thought last year; nor can I say that I shall think the same to-morrow. I believe then in a Creator; because I cannot conceive creation without intelligence, or law without a Law-giver; but I fully admit the force of the one strong Agnostic argument, that in this case we are reasoning from ourselves to something infinitely different from and greater than ourselves, reasoning from the finite to the infinite, from our own conceptions to absolute existence. I believe in God; because I can no more help it than I can disbelieve in your existence or your presence; but I admit that I have no such tangible evidence to support my conviction.'

Lestrange.—' You believe in creation ?'

Cleveland.—' Yes. Not in creation by miracle, but in creation by law. I believe that God made Man, as I believe that He made me—through a more recondite, less ordinary everyday law, but equally through law. I believe, because the logic, the evidence in favour of that belief seems to me irresistible, that Evolution has been the Creator's method. I cannot read the evidence otherwise, nor can I imagine that the evidence has been arranged to mislead us. Moreover, it seems to me a far more consistent and a far more reverent conception than the old orthodox idea. "Let there be light, and light was," sounds a very grand phrase. There is something to our first impressions sublime, because awful, in a Power that has called the Universe and the order of life in this world into being by one absolute *fiat*. But I think this is but our human weakness of reverence for power. A God who has given law to the Universe—and such a law that without miraculous interference it has developed, age after age and step by step, the wonderful simplicity of order, the wonderful complexity of existence that we behold—seems to me a far loftier and incomparably wiser Being than He who should have called it into instantaneous existence by a single or a repeated miracle. After all, it equally emanates from Him, is equally dependent upon Him. And, moreover, Development explains—if not absolutely yet as no other theory has ever explained—the arch puzzle of Theism, the existence of Evil. Again, creation by fiat, by miracle, is inconceivable to human imagination, and inconsistent with everything we know. If there be two axioms we may lay down with confidence they are the two: *Ex nihilo nil;* and *Natura non facit saltum.* To believe that matter within the Universe is indestructible, and yet that the material Universe was called out of nothing and may be resolved into nothing is not indeed a contradiction but a very startling inconsistency. To believe that He who is patient because eternal, whose method of working is always gradual, who seems to have forbidden that violent and sudden change shall ever be successful or lasting, chose rather to bring a complete Cosmos into instant perfection than to evolve it by law and by degrees, would be improbable, implausible, even if we did not know that there has been gradual evolution from the point to which we can trace back the records of life upon Earth. But I cannot carry the doctrine out to Darwin's full length. First, so far as I understand the reasonings of astronomers and physicists, we have no right to assume the existence of life on Earth for more than twenty-five millions of years: we know that it can hardly have existed for four times that period. The shorter term is palpably incompatible with Darwin's idea of minute accidental variations and infinitely slow accumulation thereof by Natural

Selection; even the longer is in his belief and that of all the best authorities far too short. There has been time, I conceive, for the evolution of species, but not for their evolution by infinitely slow accumulation of infinitesimal variations occurring by chance.'

Merton.—' I hardly understand.'

Cleveland.—' The law of chances renders accidental variations rare, accidental variations in the right direction still rarer, and development by their accumulation inexpressibly, almost inconceivably slow. But variation by law directed constantly upward—variation so to speak in a straight line—may well have produced even the present infinite variety of existence within the time allowed, without a single startling or violent change. Again, I cannot think that the great puzzle of hybridity is to be explained without the interposition of a law providentially directed to prevent the intermingling of species—to protect the process of development. I fail to understand how Darwin's explanations can have fully satisfied himself. That specific difference should prevent interbreeding is conceivable enough; what is utterly inconceivable to me is that— without the interposition of a special law for which confessedly Evolution cannot account— species should interbreed, yet (with a few doubtful exceptions) always produce offspring incapable of breeding. It almost looks as if there had been not merely a Providential prevention of confusion and intermingling, but Providential proof thereof; as if the Creator had intended to show us His intention. What we should have expected would have been a refusal of species to intermix; what we find is interbreeding of parent species, and as a rule perfect and perfectly inexplicable sterility in the offspring. Again, for reasons I have given before, I cannot believe, upon the evidence at present before us, in the development of Man by slow and gradual degrees from the ape. And here, if I venture to dissent from Darwin, I am supported by an authority only second to his, that of Wallace. The same great authority demurs to the accepted estimate of geological time as calculated from the thickness of deposits. I could not have ventured to set my own reasoning from evidence against Darwin's authority. Even when he does not make out his conclusions clearly, it is *prima facie* very improbable that so judicious and cautious an enquirer is mistaken where he seems confident. But it is not grossly improbable that Wallace, who has studied the subject from a somewhat different point of view, and accumulated evidence from wider and more varied if not equally profound investigation, should be right where he differs from Darwin.'

Sterne.—' What does he say about the thickness of the strata—a thing on which Geology has always seemed to me to prove too much ?'

Cleveland.—' This, in substance. Geologists estimate the age of the world and the duration of organic life by taking the thickness of each stratum at its utmost, and assuming them to have been deposited in strict succession. Wallace shows that strata treated as successive may often have been contemporaneous. Again, geologists calculate the duration of each stratum from the known average rate of denudation, and assume the rates of denudation and deposition to be identical or nearly so. Wallace shows that the waste brought down by rivers and otherwise from vast continental areas was deposited in narrow belts in shallow waters near the shore; so that the rate of deposition may have been ten, twenty, fifty times as rapid as that of denudation. Thus, though he hardly draws the inference, the geological estimate of time may be enormously exaggerated, may be ten or twenty times too great. Here observe that from two utterly distinct sources, from two unconnected classes of witnesses, we obtain the same general correction. Physicists infer from the rate of cooling that the Earth cannot have been inhabited for a tithe of the time assumed by geologists: Wallace shows from geological considerations that the geological estimate is probably vastly exaggerated. The concurrence of two such pieces of independent testimony has incomparably greater weight than attaches to each witness, is not double but perhaps a hundredfold the worth of either separately. So, as against the theory of infinitely slow development by accidental variations, we find on the one hand grave objections to it in the details of physiology, and again we find it incompatible, on its author's showing, with the age of the world as determined by wholly independent considerations. Two such concurrent objections drawn from distinct uncorrelated sources have enormously greater force than any evidence that could be drawn from any single field of enquiry. Again, not Evolution, but Evolution by accidental variation, involves the absolute limitation of development, of adaptation, to changes directly beneficial to the species in which they take place. Darwin says that a single proven case of instinct beneficial not to its possessor but to some alien creature would overturn his whole theory. I estimate the strength of his theory too highly to accept this statement; but at any rate one such case clearly proven would present a difficulty if not fatal to the theory yet incompatible with it, a problem which it could not solve. Now, one such instinct Darwin himself has mentioned, the excretion of the aphis only under pressure of the ant's antennæ and for the benefit of the ant. The excretion may benefit the aphis; but what benefit can it be to the aphis to wait till the ant finds and milks it? Naturalists indicate a far stronger case, though without noting its bearing on Evolution. It would seem that the bee, and I think other insects, go not from flower to flower promiscuously, but from snapdragon to snapdragon, and as a rule from a red snapdragon to a red, not from a red to a yellow or white one. Here, as in the case of hybridity, is a palpable provision to prevent the confusion of species. All diœcious and most hermaphrodite flowers depend on insects for their fertilization. If the insect flew from flower to flower promiscuously, the pollen it carries would be wasted, in ninety-nine instances out of a hundred, long before it reached the first flower it could fertilize. Darwin's several works on fertilization show what marvellous and various provisions have been made to fix on the insect a mass of pollen from the male organs of certain flowers. These provisions would fail, could never have been developed, but for the instinct that takes the insect straight to another flower of the same species. If it went to a totally different flower the pollen would be wasted. In many instances among orchids the attachment is of such a kind as to be available only for a very short period—assumes, so to speak, that within a minute or two the insect will visit a flower of the same kind possessing female organs. If it flew from flower to flower promiscuously, pollen would be wasted in a manner which it is the express object of these provisions to prevent. If it flew to a flower of a different but kindred species or variety, confusion of species would be inevitable. We have, then, an instinct of no importance, apparently of no value whatever, to the insect, but absolutely essential to the flowers; essential to the development and permanent distinction of species as well as to the fertilization of flowers in sufficient number and with due economy of pollen; a provision, observe, analogous in one of its purposes to the law of hybridity.'

Sterne.—' How do you know that the instinct is not important to the insect itself ?'

Cleveland.—' How can it be? There is no reason to suppose any essential difference between the nectar of one flower and another; still less can we suppose that that of a red pea or rose differs from that of a white one; and if there were such difference, the nectar of the different flowers is worked up all together into the honey stored in the cells by different bees of the same hive. If there were any such benefit to the insect —and it is almost inconceivable—it must be very trivial. In the absence of any reason to suppose such a benefit, you have the very case Darwin regarded as fatal to his scheme—an instinct bestowed on the insect for the benefit of the flowers. If the insect derive some trivial advantage from it, you have an almost equally extraordinary provision of Nature. An instinct that can at most be slightly beneficial to it is bestowed on the bee or moth, and upon this instinct, thus doubly accidental in its origin and character, thus unimportant to its possessor, depends the very existence of the whole kingdom of flowers. There could have been no development as there could have been no distinction of species, hardly any provision for the cross-fertilization of flowers, but for this curious instinct belonging to an infinitely remote department of Nature. The whole scheme, the fundamental law of the life of flowers, is founded on this trivial peculiarity of a few distinct races of insects. The instinct is either useless or of very little use to its possessors; it is absolutely essential to one of the largest, most highly developed, and most exquisite realms of terrestrial life. The whole sexual system of the flowers—a system full of the most marvellous and most perfect as well as most varied mechanism, full of contrivances of every degree of complexity and beauty—is built upon, adapted to this single instinct; would fall into ruin and confusion at once if the visits of insects were promiscuous, if the bee flew indifferently from a red snapdragon to a white, or from a pansy to a primrose.'

Ida.—' Has each flower its own insect ?'

Cleveland.—' No. A few flowers and insects are specially adapted to one another, but that case the Evolutionist can easily explain. The instinct of which I speak does not direct one kind of bee to one kind of flower, but directs each bee of a hive to confine itself for the day or the hour, or it may be only for the single journey, to one species and variety of flower; while every flower in the garden adapted to their visits is visited by one bee or another of a single hive.'

Merton.—' Is not that merely a consequence of the insect's colour-sense ? First attracted by red, is it not natural that it should go on from red to red ?'

Cleveland.—' That might be, but it is not so. If the colour-sense alone guided it, it would go from a red snap-dragon to a red rose, from a blue lobelia to a blue campanula. But it does nothing of the kind; it goes to the same species as well as to the same colour. There is another point, by the way, on which I should greatly have liked to question Darwin or one of his scientific disciples. I think I state his doctrine fairly, viz., that Natural Selection can only act by giving to a species or a breed a larger number of surviving offspring, favouring it by enlarging its numbers.'

Merton.—' Or giving it strength, speed, or other advantages which prolong individual existence.'

Cleveland.—' Aye, but how does that tell? Surely by enabling it to leave a larger number of offspring. Is it not so? In one word, Natural Selection preserves a variety, creates a new and superior species, by increasing not necessarily the number born, but the number that survive.'

Merton.—' Well?'

Cleveland.—' Natural Selection, then, must increase, not diminish, the prolific power of a new species. If it diminishes the number of births, it must increase the strength; so that on the whole the number of offspring surviving in each generation shall be increased.'

Merton.—' I suppose so.'

Cleveland.—' Then how is it that in raising the grade Nature generally diminishes, and diminishes rapidly, the rate of breeding?'

Merton.—' The higher creatures have not need of the lavish reproductive force of the lower. Of the eggs of insects or fish probably not one in a thousand reaches maturity, of even the lower mammals perhaps one in ten.'

Cleveland.—' Aye; that would be perfectly intelligible if the lower grades descended from the higher. The power of multiplication would be given, of course, as the liability to destruction was increased, or else the species would be exterminated. But the progress has taken place by elevation, not degeneration; the higher creatures on the Darwinian theory have been evolved from the lower. How has Natural Selection steadily diminished their reproductive power?'

Merton.—' Because they cease to require it, and it would have been waste of vital force.'

Cleveland.—' Granted. One understands clearly why a Creator, an intelligent Director of the evolutionary process, should have diminished the number of births and increased the period of gestation with each upward step. But how can Natural Selection, acting as you assume it to act, blindly, have done so? Examine the process practically and in detail. Out of genus A starts variety B with certain advantages, competing with A. There will be at first, say for a century, a thousand A's for one B; there is room, then, for as many B's as can be born till A is exterminated. It tends, then, to the advantage of B in the struggle for existence to retain the full prolific power of A; and at no stage can it become advantageous to B so long as it has competitors to diminish in numbers.'

Merton.—' I am not sure of that.'

Cleveland.—' The first principle of the theory is that that species or variety prevails or survives which leaves in each generation the greatest number of offspring that attain maturity. Of two closely allied varieties, that *ceteris paribus* will survive which breeds fastest; the diminution of prolific power is, then, a disadvantage to a nascent species, a disadvantage so long as the species has competitors for the same kind of food. It may be for its ultimate advantage to breed slowly, but only when competition has ceased. Till then, of the competing species that will survive which is the most prolific.'

Merton.—' No, for other advantages may make up for the diminution of births.'

Cleveland.—' But the diminution of births is in itself a loss, a disadvantage, and therefore could not have been conferred by Natural Selection; and yet it is precisely the quality which Nature most certainly and invariably bestows on a new and higher grade. It is perhaps the most universal accompaniment and characteristic of upward development; and if, as I contend, Natural Selection cannot have bestowed that characteristic, it seems unreasonable to ascribe to Natural Selection the development of which this characteristic is always and, we must suppose, necessarily the attendant.'

Merton.—' It is natural and reasonable to suppose that elevation of grade should in itself involve diminished fertility; the greater the expenditure of vital power in other directions the less is left for reproduction.'

Cleveland.—' True, but Natural Selection can confer and does confer increase of total vital power. Therefore those genera should survive to which Nature has given increased vital power *without* diminished reproduction. There ought to be many such cases; there are I fancy very few. Either then upward development cannot take place without diminished reproduction—which would mean that Nature cannot supply increased vital power or cannot turn it in this direction—or some other power than Natural Selection has been at work in controlling the upward course of Evolution; which is precisely the point for which I contend, and which the Evolutionists refuse to admit.'

Lestrange.—' I don't know that I quite understand you, or see to what your argument tends.'

Cleveland.—' In the absence of destructive agencies, if there be no enemies to eat the young, and abundant food for them, a pair of fish will in six years leave perhaps a million descendants or more; a pair of birds or of rabbits several hundreds. Oxen or horses might double their numbers every three or four years; man every twenty-five; whales and elephants have, I believe, one or two children in the course of three years. In one word, the highest creatures breed the slowest.'

Lestrange.—' *I* agree with you. But most people put man at the head, and man breeds, as you say, much faster than the elephant.'

Merton.—' The elephant must breed slowly or would over-people a country very rapidly.'

Cleveland.—' Of course. Intelligence can foresee and provide for that: Natural Selection cannot. Natural Selection cannot take from the earlier generations the power of rapid multiplication because it will not increase the happiness or welfare of their descendants. It can deal only with the immediate advantage of each successive generation, and in each generation rapid multiplication is an advantage.'

Merton.—' I don't see that. If food is falling short it is certainly the reverse. The elephant would be stunted if it produced as many offspring as man or the rabbit, for all would be half-starved.'

Cleveland.—' Some would starve. The principle of Natural Selection is that the majority *shall* be killed or starved for the benefit of the select few. Observe, the question is, which of two nearly allied varieties shall survive, shall exterminate the other? *Ceteris paribus* clearly that will survive which breeds most rapidly.'

Merton.—' But *ceteris non paribus?*'

Cleveland.—' *Ceteris paribus* always at the moment, unless you can show a clear, necessary, natural connection between slow breeding and compensating advantages. That you cannot do, even in the strongest case of all, that of the elephant. Nature was giving it small advantages over its congeners. If she left it at the same time their rate of breeding, it would conquer them the more rapidly; in slackening its breeding rate Natural Selection inflicted a present disadvantage for the sake of an ultimate gain: exercised foresight, which is the one thing Natural Selection cannot do. Evidence of foresight, of preparation for remote generations at the expense of the present, is fatal to the Evolutionist theory. Now, my contention throughout has been that we have evidences of this kind recurring in different instances, in different fields, in unconnected, widely distinct modes of action. And this combination of proofs from separate independent quarters is just that kind of indication which science recognizes as establishing a theory beyond reasonable doubt. 1˙contend that in scores of cases, in the most remote quarters, we do find evidence of Creative foresight; and foresight once established, the sufficiency of Natural Selection is disposed of.'

Merton.—' What is foresight but adaptation? and adaptation is the proper function of Natural Selection.'

Cleveland.—' No; there are two vital, impassable distinctions. Natural Selection can only act in and for the present, cannot give an advantage to the future at the cost of the present. Natural Selection, as Darwin himself with his usual frankness declares, cannot adapt one species to its environments except for its own benefit. Natural Selection could not teach the bee to take honey in the way most advantageous to the flowers, making no difference to the bee. Natural Selection could not provide for the limitation of the number of elephants in Asia at a time when there was as yet room for as many elephants as could possibly be born for many centuries. These and a score of similar cases are instances of foresight.'

Lestrange.—' But, Cleveland, you believe in the Origin of Species? You believe that Natural Selection has brought about the present variety of vegetable and animal life from at most a very few aboriginal types?'

Cleveland.—' No doubt. But I say that Natural Selection has been the method, not the Director; the blind instrument of an intelligent, probably infallible foresight. ' Natural Selection gave the wind; the sail was furnished, the helm has been held throughout by a higher Power.'

A.—' If you believe in Natural Selection, how can you say that the Evolutionist Theory is overthrown?'

Cleveland.—' It would be much more correct as well as more becoming to say, the critical inference of the Darwinian school is invalidated. Few men of sense, however strong their religious convictions or prejudices, could be seriously disturbed by learning that in creation as in all else Providence has acted through law; that there has been no creative miracle, at least within that part of this world's existence which Science can trace back. What the scientific Agnostic affirms, what is in popular parlance the Darwinian doctrine, is that Natural Selection has been the *sole* creative agency, that it has worked *blindly* upon materials supplied by accident.'

Merton.—'I deny the accident.'

Cleveland.—'Well, upon variations infinitesimal and occurring equally in every direction. In one word, the Darwinian doctrine, as understood both by its advocates and its opponents, denies creative intelligence, creative foresight; affirms the all-sufficiency of Natural Selection to accomplish all that has been done since the beginning of life upon this earth. *That* I dispute; that—I do not pretend to say I have disproved—but I think I have given reasons why it should not be accepted, and reasons which the Agnostic physiologist, the believer in mere Natural Selection is bound to answer.'

Lestrange.—'If I grant that you could prove a Creator—and of course I deny it altogether—what, after all, have you done? The Creator works by law, thinks not of the individual but of the species, not even of the species but of the entirety, developing species only to supersede and exterminate them. What part has He in your life or mine? What have we to do with Him or He with us? A God who has made the machine and now sits seeing it go is no more a God to your mind, to your feeling, no more the possible object of a religion, than Nature herself.'

Cleveland.—'I believe in Providence as well as in Creation; in a Providence visible alike in the course of history and in our own individual lives. The Providence of history has worked no doubt as in Creation, chiefly through Natural Selection but not through Natural Selection alone. The decisive struggles of the world have not always terminated in favour of the party strongest, best, fittest to survive at the time; but always in favour of ultimate civilization, always in favour of the race whose victory tended to raise in the long run the level of mankind. So also I hold that each human life is a long education, a course of discipline in which we can trace a Power that is not Chance, because it has a definite course and purpose; that is not general Law, because its course is adapted to individual character.'

Vere.—'But if this life be education, it must be education for a better and a higher.'

Cleveland.—'It should seem so.'

Merton.—'Can you believe in a soul apart from the body, in a life after death, in face of all the proof furnished by Science that physical, intellectual, and moral life are more than intertwined and interdependent, that they are but parts of one whole? How can you believe in an independent soul that can be extinguished for hours or weeks by a blow on the head, that can be disordered, demoralized by a lesion of the brain; whose moods, nay, whose character can be affected

—altered—by such coarse material agents as opium and alcohol? Do you seriously believe in immortality?'

Cleveland.—' I cannot answer the question. I feel as forcibly as you do the weight of the physical evidence in the negative; feel it so strongly that when I look at it alone I can hardly doubt the negation. When I regard the moral evidence, I can hardly hold it possible or conceivable that Nature is guilty of such wholesale habitual waste; that Providence takes such pains to teach lessons never to be applied. All physical proof lies in the one scale, all moral probability, I might almost say possibility, in the other.'

Merton.—' Can you doubt which should prevail? Physical impossibility is surely conclusive?'

Cleveland.—' Aye; but physical improbability, however gross, is not. I find it equally hard to imagine that Nature tells a lie, and that God has made Man in vain.'

Sterne.—' Why in vain, even if we admit the Maker? Is not life worth having, was not mankind worth making, if only as the culmination of physical conscious being, the highest form, the supreme development of organic existence upon Earth? To put it popularly or humanly—would it not have been a pity, a mistake for God or

Nature to leave Man unmade, terrestrial life uncrowned, Evolution incomplete?'

Lestrange.—' Man is Nature's supreme blunder —the one creature God would not have made. All other life is in a sense at least perfect in itself, honest, true, innocent, rational. Every other creature does what it should do, fulfils its purpose, enjoys and makes the most of its life. Man alone flounders from folly into folly, from vice into vice; is the one discord in the harmony of existence, the one life that is broken, disordered, false; incomparably the most powerful of animals, and the only one that turns its powers to no account, or worse than none.'

Vere.—' The only one that sins, because the only one that can understand duty or conceive of law.'

Lestrange.—' Is it better to do wrong by reason than to do right by instinct?'.

Ida.—' Algernon once said that paradox is the salt of argument; but yours, Mr. Lestrange, is all salt.'

Cleveland.—' To preserve ours, perhaps, or make it worth preserving.'

Vere.—' Cynicism, as I think Lestrange feels at heart, is worse than a paradox, it is a fallacy. The brutes no more do right than wrong; it is only Man that is capable of sin or virtue.'

Sterne.—' What do you say, Cleveland ? Is life worth having if it be confined to this world ?'

Cleveland.—' God knows—not I. If there be no other, He thought it was, since He gave it.'

Lestrange.—' Is it immortality, or the belief in it, that you need to make life worth living ?'

There was a long pause, much to my surprise, before Cleveland answered :

' To give what seems to me the true, at least the honest, reply—to answer as I feel—would be to say that a lie may give savour to life: that a delusion may not merely be more precious than reality, but give reality its whole value. And yet it is, I think, the terror of annihilation that makes us doubt if life on earth be worth having for itself alone. After all, if mine were to end now, it has been full of interest and enjoyment, and to doubt its worth were to seem very ungrateful for its many blessings. On the other hand, if I knew that I must part with them for ever, the best, the choicest, would seem almost intolerable. Who believes that he must so soon cease to be, can hardly dare to love.'

Vere.—' Then, if this life be all, either God tortures or He cheats us. The worth of His choicest gifts depends on, nay is, a lie. Can you believe that ?'

Cleveland.—' No. The whole problem is to me

an inscrutable and intolerably painful mystery.'

Sterne.—' Are we to look at what is or what should be? At the practical effect of divergent influences, or their theoretical tendencies? I cannot see why Atheism should make a man more selfish or Theism less so, nor why a man should think less of his own life because he believes that it will last for ever. On the contrary, if we have but fifty years, it is hardly worth while to be selfish. If we have to enjoy or suffer eternally, if our choice lie between inconceivable bliss and inconceivable torture for countless millions of years, I think we should hardly dare to consider anything but our own salvation.'

Vere.—' Happily, we know the best way to that is to forget it.'

Sterne.—' I think you are the first Christian I ever met who thought so. Surely the common tenet, the universal practice of the Saints was to neglect all duties, to renounce all human charities, in order to provide in solitary selfishness for their own souls?'

Cleveland.—' Yes; in that as in so many other things, as Mrs. Browning says—" Now, may the good God pardon all good men."'

Sterne.—' But for yourself, Cleveland. Put aside the ideas, the lives of men like Vere, who believes, as few men do believe, in his Faith, and men like myself, enthusiasts for ours. Would *your* life have been different, would it be different now, if you were ever so sure that there is or that there is not another?'

Cleveland.—' I think so;—very different. Had I disbelieved in my youth, I should have regarded love, domestic happiness, as a thing to be shunned, feared; a joy which would be poisoned, would be changed into torture by the thought of its certain and speedy ending. I think that one's choice of life, of a career, should be utterly different as one believes or disbelieves in God and in futurity, in responsibility and in retribution. If this life be all, and if we do not owe it to a Giver who claims our service, then the one aim of existence must be personal enjoyment. Then the one thing I should expect to repent at the end of life would be self-denial or self-restraint, the loss of any pleasure I might have enjoyed without consequent pain. Above all, if life end at the grave, self-concentration, if not selfishness, seems true wisdom. It is not worth while to contract strong ties that must be torn asunder, not worth while to work except for the means of enjoyment, folly even to sacrifice the present to a precarious future. Self-improvement becomes a matter of taste; culture and even science almost a waste of time. " If the dead rise not, let us eat and drink, for to-morrow we die." '

Sterne.—' You agree with him, Lestrange ?'

Lestrange.—' Of course.'

Sterne.—' Then why don't you ?'

Lestrange.—' Partly because I did not agree with him in time. Before I was convinced of the folly of love, the security of selfishness, the time was past when I had the choice, the right to be selfish. And again, my habits were formed; I had learnt to work, or rather to fight, and to take more pleasure in fighting than in drinking. And finally, eating and drinking—and in the wider sense as much as the narrower—give me disgust as well as dyspepsia; and I know no earthly pleasure worth the pain that follows excess.'

Sterne.—' I see cynicism is not only a paradox, not only, as Vere said, a fallacy, but a fiction. The only consistent cynic I ever met is just as inconsistent as any Christian. *Why* is it too late to repent of morality, to turn even for a few years to the better way of pure unmitigated selfishness ?'

Lestrange.—' Too late to repent when it is too late to change, too late to enjoy.'

Sterne.—' Aye; but, Lestrange, you spoke of having no right to be selfish.'

Lestrange.—' If there be one obligation, one duty a cynic cannot deny, it is a parent's duty to those he brought into the world without choice of their own.'

Cleveland.—' There lies the solution of the only difficult problem, the only knotty point in the evidence, as regards Agnostic morality. Agnostics say that unbelief, scepticism, does not practically make people worse; I say it does and must; and yet by reference to instances they seem to prove their case. It seems to be true that man's opinions do not greatly affect their lives, because we look chiefly at the lives of men who have fixed their place in the world; men whose opinions are now made up, but too late to act upon them. A man of five and forty with a family, with duties, with fixed habits, with ties from which he can only loose himself by a violent and painful effort, with responsibilities he cannot wholly shake off, will probably go on to the end as he has begun, whatever his opinions may now be. But the man who has the world before him, who has to choose a life of steady decorous social service, a life in and with others, or one of independent unburdened unrestrained selfishness, will be governed very largely by his conception of existence. If he believe that conscience is an illusion, God a fiction, and Heaven a dream, that a life of self-indulgence prudently regulated involves no penalty, that a life of service to others has no reward, he would seem to himself a fool to choose the hard beaten highway instead of rambling at will in whatever direction the grass may be greenest, the flowers fairest, the fruits most plentiful. You cannot measure the influence of Atheism till you have a generation educated, if not in Atheism, at any rate without Christianity. Its full power for evil you can never see till men so educated have been the fathers and grandfathers of children brought up by precept and example in pure selfishness, or at least in the full conviction that selfishness entails no penalty and service has no payment worth the name. Whether we have or have not a Master and a Judge, whether we are or are not bound by a law, whether or not virtue and vice be mere names, mere matter of individual taste—these are questions that cannot be without influence on conduct, if once they are allowed to exercise that influence at an age when choice of conduct is still really open. You say that you will educate children to believe in Nature and serve Humanity. But, in the first place, you can teach the idea of God and Heaven to a child of six; you can scarcely make a boy of sixteen or a girl of any age understand Nature and Humanity. To the rude and practical they will be empty names; to the thoughtful and sceptical invented *eidola*, artificial substitutes for the Deity and the Judgment you have discarded. Your abler, more clear-sighted, more independent pupils will be much more than indifferent to your teaching; they will resent and revolt from it. They will feel and see that you are imposing on them, that you have devised an unreal, illusive, insecure scheme, a religion without meaning, a morality without sanction, to coerce them. They will rebel as the unbelieving child of a Calvinist revolts from his father's Hell, a bugbear invented to frighten him. By no possibility can you bridge the stupendous gulf between convinced Theism and convinced Atheism, between Chance and Providence, between mortality and immortality. The difference is the widest that human mind can conceive; the questions have a close, intimate, unmistakable bearing on every practical issue of life and conduct; and it is equally illogical and irrational, unphilosophic and unpractical, to dream that opposite ideals will not lead to exactly opposite courses. Men who believe that they have fifty years to enjoy or not to enjoy, that they have no other master than the society in which they live, no other law than the opinion of their fellows, no punishment or reward but such as the chance of human opinion can bestow, will not live as men who firmly believe that they have fifty years wherein to prepare for eternity, that they are responsible to an Almighty and

All-seeing Master, that they will reap as they sow, and that for every illicit enjoyment here they will pay in tenfold suffering here or hereafter. Above all, no man of spirit will care for the strongest, deepest, most universal convictions of mankind as he cares for the lightest word of a Supreme Being. Only Satan dared in his own heart rebel against and defy the Almighty. Every man of spirit tends both by temper and experience to despise and defy Society. Humanity at large is too false, too mean, too irresolute to command obedience from the better sort of men; and say what you may, Agnostics rest their moral code on the assent of humanity, their very conscience on the past consent of generations duller and more ignorant than our own. If you really think that a change of opinion so vast, the removal of motives so powerful, the substitution of motives so utterly different in quality and tendency, will not change the conduct of men, what do you think of your pupils' intelligence? The man to whom such questions are matter of indifference must be dull and insensible; the man who will act without a God, a Divine law, a Judgment, a Future as he would act in face thereof must be all fool or half a brute. Your religion a fantasy, your Deity a personification, your Law-giver a mob, your creed a theory, your

Heaven an acknowledged dream, your salvation the approval of the average herd of men—your highest reward, your most precious hope, the phantom of posthumous fame—what have you to win men to virtue or strengthen them against temptation, to rouse their enthusiasm or govern their passions? The very passion with which you insist on your denials shows that you feel the vastness, the momentousness of that which you deny. Your negations alter, destroy the guiding principles, the leading motives of human life, and offer no substitute more substantial than a dream. You ask us to give up, you bid the world at large give up, all that has guided and governed it heretofore; and you can offer us nothing in return which any one of us cares to have at a gift, much less to earn by the devotion of a life.'

Vere.—' Suppose for a moment that you can succeed; that you can destroy all on which the faith, the hope, the sympathy, the conduct of men are now based, the whole structure of personal and social morality—sweep clean to the foundation. Grant that for a moment you can construct your own scheme of thought, your own code of morals, and make them the sole guide of life, the sole governing, coercing, inspiring law of the home and the community. Can you not see yourselves that your materials are rotten, unsubstantial, unreal; your edifice a crazy shell in place of the solid fortress that has endured the storms of two thousand years? How long will it shelter the weak or restrain the strong? You are re-building not only human society but human life, not only law but conscience, the whole structure of human nature; and you are building on the sand. When the storms of passion and temptation, of enquiry and denial beat upon your edifice, will it not fall at once and with a crash that will be heard to the uttermost ends of the earth? And when it has fallen, what will be left to Man?'

Extract from Cleveland's last Letter.

'Professor Cayley's Address does not affect our views at all. The metaphysical issue—what is and is not conceivable—any thoughtful man can understand; and I reaffirm that linear or superficial experience could conceive surface or solid, but that space of four dimensions, or space limited by curvature, is not only unimaginable but impossible—a contradiction in terms. The great mathematician alone can tell what would happen *if* Space had four dimensions; whether, on the curved surface of the Infinite Void, two and two make five. I affirm only that three-dimensioned Space includes the Universe; and that in the Universe two and two are always and necessarily four—God could not make, because He could not think, a plane triangle including more than two right angles . . . Agnostic virtues are those of the few earnest Agnostics true or zealous enough to live and fight for their creed. What are the lives of the many who hold and practise that creed in silence?'

THE END.

By the same Author.

THE DEVIL'S ADVOCATE. 2 vols. Trübner & Co. 1878.

"The series of assaults against modern ideas and institutions . . . are conducted with great spirit and persistency . . . but so managed that the brilliant pessimist has generally rather the best of it."—*Saturday Review.*

"Remarkable shrewdness and power, and a style at once lucid and precise."—*Standard.*

"Every page is pregnant with the gravest and most anxious suggestions."—*Daily News.*

"Full of thought, and of the particular kind of thought which rarely gets itself uttered."—*Manchester Guardian.*

"Full of thought, and of thought which goes to the very kernel of most of the questions discussed."—*Spectator.*

ACROSS THE ZODIAC: The Story of a wrecked Record. Deciphered, Translated, and Edited by PERCY GREG. 2 vols. Trübner & Co. 1880.

"Shows great powers of description, no small constructive imagination, and the general merits of practised and forcible writing."—*Saturday Review.*

"There is reason to suppose that Mr. Greg and his Innominate believe themselves to have been dipping far into the future, and to have seen 'a vision of the world and all the wonders that shall be.' This question their readers—and they should have many—must settle for themselves."—*Pall Mall Gazette.*

"Can hardly be read without pleasure, and will certainly add to the literary reputation of its author. . . . The voyage was a long one; but the reader will allow that the people and the climate of the planet Mars were worth the effort."—*Standard.*

"The verisimilitude is well maintained, and it is clear that the author must have been at considerable pains in working out the minute details of Martial life and character. The proverbial philosophy of the interesting community strikes us as particularly well done."—*Globe.*

"Even as a story the latter part of the book is very entertaining."—*Academy.*

"Mr. Greg is a thinker of earnestness and no little depth; and his power of realising in his own mind, and as it were objectively seeing, every particular of a wholly imaginary scene or order of things has been surpassed by few contemporary writers. Not the least among the merits of the story is the quiet and matter-of-fact manner in which it is told. Circumstances the most astounding are related with a simplicity and naïveté which greatly enhance their effect.—*Spectator*, Jan. 31, 1880.

"That strange and powerful book of his, 'Across the Zodiac.'"—*Spectator*, May 1, 1880.

"Full of a wide and varied fancy and deep philosophy."—*Melbourne Argus.*

IVY: COUSIN AND BRIDE. 3 vols. Hurst & Blackett. 1881.

"The work of a man of genius, and capable of affording more pleasure at a fourth or fifth perusal than an ordinary novel at the first."—*John Bull.*

"There is something very touching in the conception of Ivy's character. Her unfaltering loyalty to her husband, her abnegation of self, her sweetness and gentleness make a very pathetic picture."—*Spectator.*

"A book that may be likened to a piece of ancient tapestry. The figures are few; they loom unduly large against the background, and are slightly unnatural and distorted—yet with an originality and vigour which render them worth more than a hundred specimens of conventional modern correctness."—*Morning Post.*

"Can be strongly recommended to persons who are able to recognize accurate drawing of character, whatever it is, and still more strongly to those who appreciate pathos."—*Saturday Review.*

"Deserves warm praise and welcome, both for its literary qualities and its interest as a subtle study of what we trust is not altogether an ideal aspect of the possibilities of human nature."—*Graphic.*

"A sweeter picture of maiden innocence and wifely devotion has perhaps never been drawn."—*Morning Advertiser.*

SANGUELAC.   3 vols.   Hurst & Blackett.   1883.

"A powerful and original novel . . . throws upon a subject little understood all that fresh light which can only be thrown by a powerful imagination sustained by accurate and far-reaching knowledge."—*John Bull.*

"Really deserves warm praise."—*Figaro.*

"The various episodes of the war are well described."—*Graphic.*

"Scrupulous fairness . . . an interesting and in parts exceedingly interesting novel uniting the powers of sketching feminine character, of a certain kind which Mr. Greg showed in 'Ivy,' with the faculty of depicting battle scenes which he showed in 'Errant.'"—*Saturday Review.*

"Spirited and moving story."—*Spectator.*

"Absolutely impartial."—*Globe.*

"Everyone who begins to read will desire to finish it."—*Advertiser.*

"The character of Rose, the devoted white slave, is one of real beauty and power. The growth of her affection for Clarence, her jealousy towards his chosen wife . . . . and finally the scene of her death and funeral, are touched with a pathos and delicacy which make one forget the controversial bearings of the story in its sheer human interest."—*Pall Mall Gazette.*

ERRANT : A Life-story of Latter-Day Chivalry. 3 vols. Sampson Low & Co.   1880.

"More incident and adventure than is usually spread over twenty ordinary novels."—*Academy.*

"A story of great power, originality, and variety of incident."—*Court Circular.*

"The battle scenes . . . are among the most vigorous and stirring things of the kind which have found a place in prose fiction for some years."—*Saturday Review.*

"A really interesting and even exciting story . . . exceptionally well written . . . and contains some incidental poetry which in point of both form and spirit is excellent in its way."—*Graphic.*

"In one respect it is a genuine study of life, worked out with a skill and truth which deserve recognition. . . . The episode of Zela . . . is painful enough and more than enough, but it is managed with delicacy and tact, and made to point a moral of no ordinary significance and value."—*Pall Mall Gazette.*

"The American part of 'Errant' is a singularly beautiful story, ... an idyl of the sweetest as well as of the saddest character."—*Morning Advertiser.*

INTERLEAVES IN THE WORK-DAY PROSE OF TWENTY YEARS. Trübner & Co.   1875.

"A little volume of thoughtful and manly verse, always spirited and graceful, and which at times rises to the higher strains of meditative poetry."—*Saturday Review.*

"Every poem in this little book which breathes either indignation or defiance or scorn is full of vigour and eloquence, and generally also of a sort of intensity of emotion, which together make the verse rememberable."—*Spectator.*

MESSRS. HURST & BLACKETT'S

LIST OF NEW WORKS.

LONDON:
13, GREAT MARLBOROUGH STREET, W.

WORKS by the AUTHOR of 'JOHN HALIFAX.'

Each in a Single Volume, with Frontispiece, price 5s.

JOHN HALIFAX, GENTLEMAN.
A WOMAN'S THOUGHTS ABOUT WOMEN.
A LIFE FOR A LIFE.
NOTHING NEW.
MISTRESS AND MAID.
THE WOMAN'S KINGDOM.

CHRISTIAN'S MISTAKE.
A NOBLE LIFE.
HANNAH.
THE UNKIND WORD.
A BRAVE LADY.
STUDIES FROM LIFE.
YOUNG MRS. JARDINE.

WORKS by GEORGE MAC DONALD, LL.D.

Each in a Single Volume, with Frontispiece, price 5s.

DAVID ELGINBROD.
ROBERT FALCONER.

ALEC FORBES.
SIR GIBBIE.

WORKS by MRS. OLIPHANT.

Each in a Single Volume, with Frontispiece, price 5s.

THE LAIRD OF NORLAW.
ADAM GRAEME OF MOSSGRAY.

A ROSE IN JUNE.
PHŒBE, JUNIOR.
AGNES.

THE LIFE OF THE REV. EDWARD IRVING.

WORKS by the AUTHOR of 'SAM SLICK.'

Each in a Single Volume, with Frontispiece, price 5s.

NATURE AND HUMAN NATURE.
WISE SAWS AND MODERN INSTANCES.

THE OLD JUDGE; OR, LIFE IN A COLONY.
TRAITS OF AMERICAN HUMOUR.

THE AMERICANS AT HOME.

HURST & BLACKETT, PUBLISHERS.

MESSRS. HURST AND BLACKETT'S
LIST OF NEW WORKS.

THE REAL LORD BYRON: NEW VIEWS OF THE
POET'S LIFE. By JOHN CORDY JEAFFRESON, Author of "A Book about Doctors," &c. 2 vols. demy 8vo. 30s.

CONTENTS:—Misconceptions about Byron—The Byrons of Rochdale and Newstead—Byron's near Ancestors—More of "Mad Jack Byron"—Aberdeen—Nottingham and London—Harrow—Harrow Holidays—Lord Byron of Trinity—Cambridge Vacations—Peer and Pilgrim—"Childe Harold"—The Rival Cousins-in-Law—The Turning of the Tide—Byron's Married Life—The Separation—The Storm—Switzerland—Venice: Byron's Depravation—Teresa Gamba Guiccioli—Ravenna—Pisa—Genoa—Cephalonia—Missolonghi—The Destruction of "The Memoirs"—Byronic Womankind—A Parting Note.

"Mr. Jeaffreson comes forward with a narrative which must take a very important place in Byronic literature. Almost every chapter contains material which may be fairly called new, and the book differs from many biographies of Byron in one very important point—it is scrupulously just to every person concerned, the facts dealt with being placed before the reader in a judicial spirit. Mr. Jeaffreson had a specific work to do, and he has done it fully, conclusively, and well; and it may reasonably be anticipated that these volumes will be regarded with deep interest by all who are concerned in the works and the fame of this great English poet."—*The Times.*

"No other book relating to the history of English literature in the nineteenth century has appeared of recent years that can claim to contain so much novel information as Mr. Jeaffreson's. He has had access to new sources of information, and he may be congratulated on the use he has made of his good fortune. He has produced a work that throws a flood of new light on the most critical periods of Byron's life, and that every future critic of modern English poetry will have to read and re-read."—*Athenæum.*

"Everybody will read these volumes, many for the sake of the great poet, whose biography forms the subject, and others simply on account of the extraordinary amount of interesting gossip which it contains about the famous personages who flourished in the days of our grandfathers. It is a very able book admirably written, thoughtful, and evidently entirely unprejudiced."—*Morning Post.*

"This is a masterly performance, and one of the most important contributions to literary biography published for many years. Mr. Jeaffreson writes not only like a student, but a man of the world, and his entire analysis of the relation between Byron and his wife is admirable."—*The World.*

"Byronic literature receives an important accession in Mr. Jeaffreson's new work, an ably-written review of the great poet's character and life. It abounds with facts and new matter worthy of careful reflection. The author has had access to valuable sources of information, and he has used his material with great skill and judgment."—*Daily Telegraph.*

"Mr. Jeaffreson may claim to have produced a work which establishes itself at once as standard, and which, for grace of style and intrinsic value will retain a permanent place in literature. It is not easy to imagine a narrative more dramatic, more stirring, and at the same time more trustworthy, than this."—*Notes and Queries.*

"The admirers of Byron will read these volumes with interest, and may flatter themselves that they have got a version of his history which no future revelations are likely to add much to or impugn."—*Graphic.*

MESSRS. HURST AND BLACKETT'S NEW WORKS—*Continued.*

WITHOUT GOD: NEGATIVE SCIENCE AND NATURAL
ETHICS. By PERCY GREG, Author of "The Devil's Advocate," "Across the Zodiac," &c. 1 vol. demy 8vo. 12s.

> "What can ye give us for a Faith so lost,
> For love of Duty and delight in Prayer?
> How are we wiser that our minds are tost
> By winds of knowledge on a sea of care?"
> LORD HOUGHTON's *Palm Leaves.*

SIBERIAN PICTURES. By LUDWIK NIEMOJOWSKI.
Edited, from the Polish, by MAJOR SZULCZEWSKI. 2 vols. 21s.

"This book contains a good deal of interesting matter. M. Niemojowski's description of Siberian game and the hunting of it is clearly valuable, and shows that he really has lived among the people. His work is not without interest to ethnographers, for it deals with almost every race that inhabits Siberia—Tunguzes and Tartars, Samoyedes and Ostiaks, the Buriats of Lake Baikal, and the Gilliacks of the Pacific coasts."—*Saturday Review.*

"Major Szulczewski has done a service by translating from the Polish the interesting account which Mr. Niemojowski has given of the dreary land in which he spent so many years of exile. The book contains a number of very interesting stories."—*Athenæum.*

"This book contains by far the most exhaustive and reliable account which has yet been given in English of Siberia."—*British Quarterly Review.*

"There is an unwonted freshness and novelty of standpoint in M. Niemojowski's varied reminiscences of his long and dismal Siberian sojourn."—*Pall Mall Gazette.*

REMINISCENCES OF MILITARY SERVICE
WITH THE 93rd SUTHERLAND HIGHLANDERS. By SURGEON-GENERAL MUNRO, M.D., C.B., Formerly Surgeon of the Regiment. 1 vol. demy 8vo. 15s.

"This is a book of interesting recollections of active military campaigning life. It is told in a frank, simple, and unpretentious manner."—*Illustrated London News.*

"This book is not only bright and lively, but thoroughly good-natured. What makes these reminiscences exceptionally readable is the amount of illustrative anecdote with which they are interspersed. The author has a keen appreciation of humour, with the knack of recalling appropriate stories."—*Saturday Review.*

"There is much in these interesting reminiscences that will gratify while it pains the reader. A book like this, which portrays the horrors and not merely the showy side of war, has distinct usefulness. Dr. Munro recounts many incidents with pardonable pride."—*Pall Mall Gazette.*

"Dr. Munro served thirteen years with the 93rd, during which time he took part in the Crimean war, the Indian Mutiny, and the Sitana campaign. He saw much, recorded much, and noted much, and the result is the book before us. It is an interesting collection of reminiscences."—*United Service Gazette.*

THE FRIENDSHIPS OF MARY RUSSELL
MITFORD: AS RECORDED IN LETTERS FROM HER LITERARY CORRESPONDENTS. Edited by the REV. A. G. L'ESTRANGE, Editor of "The Life of Mary Russell Mitford," &c. 2 vols. 21s.

"These letters are all written as to one whom the writers love and revere. Miss Barrett is one of Miss Mitford's correspondents, all of whom seem to be inspired with a sense of excellence in the mind they are invoking. Their letters are extremely interesting, and they strike out recollections, opinions, criticisms, which will hold the reader's delighted and serious attention."—*Daily Telegraph.*

"In this singular and probably unique book Miss Mitford is painted, not in letters of her own nor in letters written of her, but in letters addressed to her; and a true idea is thus conveyed of her talent, her disposition, and of the impression she made upon her friends. It seldom happens that anyone, however distinguished, receives such a number of letters well worth reading as were addressed to Miss Mitford; and the letters from her correspondents are not only from interesting persons, but are in themselves interesting."—*St. James's Gazette.*

MESSRS. HURST AND BLACKETT'S
NEW WORKS—*Continued.*

COURT LIFE BELOW STAIRS; or, LONDON UNDER THE FIRST GEORGES, 1714—1760. By J. FITZGERALD MOLLOY. *Second Edition.* Vols. 1 and 2. Crown 8vo. 21s.

"Mr. Molloy's pages contain abundance of amusing anecdote. He writes in a brisk and fluent style."—*Athenæum.*

"Well written, full of anecdotes, and with its facts admirably grouped, this excellent work will prove of the greatest value to all who desire to know what manner of men the first Electors of Hanover who came here really were. Pictures of Court life so drawn cannot fail to be very instructive. Some of the word pictures are wonderfully well drawn"—*Daily Telegraph.*

"Mr. Molloy produces some curious anecdotes which have not before appeared in print, and he is always lively."—*Pall Mall Gazette.*

VOLS. III. and IV. of COURT LIFE BELOW STAIRS; or, LONDON UNDER THE LAST GEORGES, 1760—1830. By J. FITZGERALD MOLLOY. 21s. Completing the Work.

WITH THE CONNAUGHT RANGERS IN QUARTERS, CAMP, AND ON LEAVE. By GENERAL E. H. MAXWELL, C.B., Author of "Griffin, Ahoy!" 1 vol. 8vo. With Illustrations. 15s.

"General Maxwell has, in the course of his military career, seen much of the world, taken part in a considerable amount of fighting, and experienced many adventures. He writes in a genial fashion."—*Athenæum.*

"A warm welcome may be presaged for General Maxwell's new work. It is an eminently readable book, quite apart from the special attraction it must possess for all who are, or who have been, connected with the gallant 88th."—*Daily Telegraph.*

"When General Maxwell made his *début* in that capital book, 'Griffin, Ahoy!' we expressed a hope that we should soon meet him again. This expectation is now fulfilled, and again we have to congratulate the author on a distinct success. Scarcely a page in his volume but has its little anecdote, and these stories have a real touch of humour in them."—*Globe.*

GRIFFIN, AHOY! A Yacht Cruise to the LEVANT, and Wanderings in EGYPT, SYRIA, THE HOLY LAND, GREECE, and ITALY in 1881. By GENERAL E. H. MAXWELL, C.B. One vol. demy 8vo. With Illustrations. 15s.

"The cruise of the *Griffin* affords bright and amusing reading from its beginning to its end. General Maxwell writes in a frank and easy style.—*Morning Post.*

PRINCE CHARLES AND THE SPANISH MARRIAGE: A Chapter of English History, 1617 to 1623; from Unpublished Documents in the Archives of Simancas, Venice, and Brussels. By SAMUEL RAWSON GARDINER. 2 vols. 8vo. 30s.

"For the first time in our literature the real history of the Spanish match, and what took place when Charles and Buckingham were at Madrid, is here revealed. Mr. Gardiner has brought to bear upon his subject an amount of historical reading and consultation of authorities which we believe to be almost without a parallel."—*Notes and Queries.*

PLAIN SPEAKING. By Author of "John Halifax, Gentleman." 1 vol. crown 8vo. 10s. 6d.

"We recommend 'Plain Speaking' to all who like amusing, wholesome, and instructive reading. The contents of Mrs. Craik's volume are of the most multifarious kind, but all the papers are good and readable, and one at least of them of real importance."—*St. James's Gazette.*

MESSRS. HURST AND BLACKETT'S
NEW WORKS—*Continued*.

LIFE OF MOSCHELES; WITH SELECTIONS FROM HIS DIARIES AND CORRESPONDENCE. By HIS WIFE. 2 vols. large post 8vo. With Portrait. 24s.

"This life of Moscheles will be a valuable book of reference for the musical historian, for the contents extend over a period of threescore years, commencing with 1794, and ending at 1870. We need scarcely state that all the portions of Moscheles' diary which refer to his intercourse with Beethoven, Hummel, Weber, Czerny, Spontini, Rossini, Auber, Halévy, Schumann, Cherubini, Spohr, Mendelssohn, F. David, Chopin, J. B. Cramer, Clementi, John Field, Habeneck, Hauptmann, Kalkbrenner, Kiesewetter, C. Klingemann, Lablache, Dragonetti, Sontag, Persiana, Malibran, Paganini, Rachel, Rouzi de Begnis, De Beriot, Ernst, Donzelli, Cinti-Damoreau, Chelard, Bochsa, Laporte, Charles Kemble, Schröder-Devrient, Mrs. Siddons, Sir H. Bishop, Sir G. Smart, Staudigl, Thalberg, Berlioz, Velluti, C. Young, Balfe, Braham, and many other artists of note in their time, will recall a flood of recollections. Moscheles writes fairly of what is called the 'Music of the Future,' and his judgments on Herr Wagner, Dr. Liszt, Rubenstein, Dr. von Bülow, Litolff, &c., whether as composers or executants, are in a liberal spirit. He recognizes cheerfully the talents of our native artists: Sir S. Bennett, Mr. Macfarren, Madame Goddard, Mr. J. Barnett, Mr. Hullah, Mr. A. Sullivan, &c. The volumes are full of amusing anecdotes."—*Athenæum.*

MONSIEUR GUIZOT IN PRIVATE LIFE (1787-1874). By His Daughter, Madame DE WITT. Translated by Mrs. SIMPSON. 1 vol. demy 8vo. 15s.

"Madame de Witt has done justice to her father's memory in an admirable record of his life. Mrs. Simpson's translation of this singularly interesting book is in accuracy and grace worthy of the original and of the subject."—*Saturday Review.*

MY OLD PLAYGROUND REVISITED; A TOUR IN ITALY IN THE SPRING OF 1881. By BENJAMIN E. KENNEDY. Second Edition, with Appendix. 1 vol. crown 8vo. With Illustrations, by the Author. 6s.

"It is no small merit of Mr. Kennedy that he has rendered an account of a journey over such familiar ground as that lying between London and Naples remarkably readable. These pages are full of really useful information, and travellers 'going South' cannot do better than take Mr. Kennedy's experiences as their rule of conduct."—*Morning Post.*

"'My Old Playground Revisited' will repay perusal. It is written with the ease that comes of long experience."—*Graphic.*

WORDS OF HOPE AND COMFORT TO THOSE IN SORROW. Dedicated by Permission to THE QUEEN. Fourth Edition. 1 vol. small 4to. 5s.

"The writer of the tenderly-conceived letters in this volume was Mrs. Julius Hare, a sister of Mr. Maurice. They are instinct with the devout submissiveness and fine sympathy which we associate with the name of Maurice; but in her there is added a winningness of tact, and sometimes, too, a directness of language, which we hardly find even in the brother. The letters were privately printed and circulated, and were found to be the source of much comfort, which they cannot fail to afford now to a wide circle. A sweetly-conceived memorial poem, bearing the well-known initials, 'E. H. P.', gives a very faithful outline of the life."—*British Quarterly Review.*

MEMOIRS OF QUEEN HORTENSE, MOTHER OF NAPOLEON III. Cheaper Edition, in 1 vol. 6s.

"A biography of the beautiful and unhappy Queen, more satisfactory than any we have yet met with."—*Daily News.*

HURST AND BLACKETT'S
SIX-SHILLING NOVELS

THE BRANDRETHS.
By the Right Hon. A. J. B. BERESFORD HOPE, M.P.,
Author of " Strictly Tied Up."

"In 'The Brandreths' we have a sequel to Mr. Beresford Hope's clever novel of Strictly Tied Up,' and we may add that it is a decided improvement on his maiden effort. Mr. Hope writes of political life and the vicissitudes of parties with the knowledge and experience of a veteran politician. The novel is one which will repay careful reading."—*Times.*

"'The Brandreths' has all the charm of its predecessor. The great attraction of the novel is the easy, conversational, knowledgeable tone of it; the sketching from the life, and yet not so close to the life as to be malicious, men, women, periods, and events, to all of which intelligent readers can fit a name. The political and social sketches will naturally excite the chief interest among readers who will be attracted by the author's name and experience."—*Spectator.*

SOPHY:
OR THE ADVENTURES OF A SAVAGE.
By VIOLET FANE,
Author of "Denzil Place," &c.

"'Sophy' is the clever and original work of a clever woman. Its merits are of a strikingly unusual kind. It is charged throughout with the strongest human interest. It is, in a word, a novel that will make its mark."—*World.*

"A clever, amusing, and interesting story, well worth reading."—*Post.*

"This novel is as amusing, piquant, droll, and suggestive as it can be. It overflows with humour, nor are there wanting touches of genuine feeling. To considerable imaginative power, the writer joins keen observation."—*Daily News.*

"'Sophy' throughout displays accurate knowledge of widely differing forms of character, and remarkable breadth of view. It is one of the few current novels that may not impossibly stand the test of time."—*Graphic.*

MY LORD AND MY LADY.
By Mrs. FORRESTER,
Author of "Viva," "Mignon," &c.

"This novel will take a high place among the successes of the season. It is as fresh a novel as it is interesting, as attractive as it is realistically true, as full of novelty of presentment as it is of close study and observation of life."—*World.*

"A love story of considerable interest. The novel is full of surprises, and will serve to while away a leisure hour most agreeably."—*Daily Telegraph.*

"A very capital novel. The great charm about it is that Mrs. Forrester is quite at home in the society which she describes. It is a book to read."—*Standard.*

"Mrs. Forrester's style is so fresh and graphic that the reader is kept under its spell from first to last."—*Post.*

HIS LITTLE MOTHER: and Other Tales.
By the Author of "John Halifax, Gentleman."

"This is an interesting book, written in a pleasant manner, and full of shrewd observation and kindly feeling. It is a book that will be read with interest, and that cannot be lightly forgotten."—*St. James's Gazette.*

"The Author of 'John Halifax' always writes with grace and feeling, and never more so than in the present volume."—*Morning Post.*

"'His Little Mother' is one of those pathetic stories which the author tells better than anybody else."—*John Bull.*

"This book is written with all Mrs. Craik's grace of style, the chief charm of which, after all, is its simplicity."—*Glasgow Herald.*

Under the Especial Patronage of Her Majesty.

Published annually, in One Vol., royal 8vo, with the Arms beautifully engraved, handsomely bound, with gilt edges, price 31s. 6d.

LODGE'S PEERAGE
AND BARONETAGE,
CORRECTED BY THE NOBILITY.

THE FIFTY-SECOND EDITION FOR 1883 IS NOW READY.

LODGE'S PEERAGE AND BARONETAGE is acknowledged to be the most complete, as well as the most elegant, work of the kind. As an established and authentic authority on all questions respecting the family histories, honours, and connections of the titled aristocracy, no work has ever stood so high. It is published under the especial patronage of Her Majesty, and is annually corrected throughout, from the personal communications of the Nobility. It is the only work of its class in which, *the type being kept constantly standing*, every correction is made in its proper place to the date of publication, an advantage which gives it supremacy over all its competitors. Independently of its full and authentic information respecting the existing Peers and Baronets of the realm, the most sedulous attention is given in its pages to the collateral branches of the various noble families, and the names of many thousand individuals are introduced, which do not appear in other records of the titled classes. For its authority, correctness, and facility of arrangement, and the beauty of its typography and binding, the work is justly entitled to the place it occupies on the tables of Her Majesty and the Nobility.

LIST OF THE PRINCIPAL CONTENTS.

Historical View of the Peerage.
Parliamentary Roll of the House of Lords.
English, Scotch, and Irish Peers, in their orders of Precedence.
Alphabetical List of Peers of Great Britain and the United Kingdom, holding superior rank in the Scotch or Irish Peerage.
Alphabetical list of Scotch and Irish Peers, holding superior titles in the Peerage of Great Britain and the United Kingdom.
A Collective list of Peers, in their order of Precedence.
Table of Precedency among Men.
Table of Precedency among Women.
The Queen and the Royal Family.
Peers of the Blood Royal.
The Peerage, alphabetically arranged.
Families of such Extinct Peers as have left Widows or Issue.
Alphabetical List of the Surnames of all the Peers.
The Archbishops and Bishops of England and Ireland.
The Baronetage alphabetically arranged.
Alphabetical List of Surnames assumed by members of Noble Families.
Alphabetical List of the Second Titles of Peers, usually borne by their Eldest Sons.
Alphabetical Index to the Daughters of Dukes, Marquises, and Earls, who, having married Commoners, retain the title of Lady before their own Christian and their Husband's Surnames.
Alphabetical Index to the Daughters of Viscounts and Barons, who, having married Commoners, are styled Honourable Mrs.; and, in case of the husband being a Baronet or Knight, Hon. Lady.
A List of the Orders of Knighthood.
Mottoes alphabetically arranged and translated.

"This work is the most perfect and elaborate record of the living and recently deceased members of the Peerage of the Three Kingdoms as it stands at this day. It is a most useful publication. We are happy to bear testimony to the fact that scrupulous accuracy is a distinguishing feature of this book."—*Times.*

"Lodge's Peerage must supersede all other works of the kind, for two reasons: first, it is on a better plan; and secondly, it is better executed. We can safely pronounce it to be the readiest, the most useful, and exactest of modern works on the subject."—*Spectator.*

"A work of great value. It is the most faithful record we possess of the aristocracy of the day."—*Post.*

"The best existing, and, we believe, the best possible Peerage. It is the standard authority on the subject."—*Standard.*

HURST & BLACKETT'S STANDARD LIBRARY

OF CHEAP EDITIONS OF

POPULAR MODERN WORKS.

ILLUSTRATED BY SIR JOHN GILBERT, MILLAIS, HOLMAN HUNT, BIRKET FOSTER, LEECH, SANDYS, TENNIEL, ETC.

Each in a Single Volume, with Frontispiece, price 5s.

I.—SAM SLICK'S NATURE AND HUMAN NATURE.

"The first volume of Messrs. Hurst and Blackett's Standard Library of Cheap Editions forms a very good beginning to what will doubtless be a very successful undertaking. 'Nature and Human Nature' is one of the best of Sam Slick's witty and humorous productions, and well entitled to the large circulation which it cannot fail to obtain in its present convenient and cheap shape. The volume combines with the great recommendations of a clear, bold type and good paper, the lesser, but attractive merits of being well illustrated and elegantly bound."—*Morning Post.*

II.—JOHN HALIFAX, GENTLEMAN.

"The new and cheaper edition of this interesting work will doubtless meet with great success. John Halifax, the hero of this most beautiful story, is no ordinary hero, and this his history is no ordinary book. It is a full-length portrait of a true gentleman, one of nature's own nobility. It is also the history of a home, and a thoroughly English one. The work abounds in incident, and many of the scenes are full of graphic power and true pathos. It is a book that few will read without becoming wiser and better."—*Scotsman.*

"This story is very interesting. The attachment between John Halifax and his wife is beautifully painted, as are the pictures of their domestic life, and the growing up of their children; and the conclusion of the book is beautiful and touching."—*Athenæum.*

III.—THE CRESCENT AND THE CROSS.
BY ELIOT WARBURTON.

"Independent of its value as an original narrative, and its useful and interesting information, this work is remarkable for the colouring power and play of fancy with which its descriptions are enlivened. Among its greatest and most lasting charms is its reverent and serious spirit."—*Quarterly Review.*

"Mr. Warburton has fulfilled the promise of his title-page. The 'Realities of Eastern Travel' are described with a vividness which invests them with deep and abiding interest; while the 'Romantic' adventures which the enterprising tourist met with in his course are narrated with a spirit which shows how much he enjoyed these reliefs from the ennui of every-day life."—*Globe.*

IV.—NATHALIE.
BY JULIA KAVANAGH.

"'Nathalie' is Miss Kavanagh's best imaginative effort. Its manner is gracious and attractive. Its matter is good. A sentiment, a tenderness, are commanded by her which are as individual as they are elegant. We should not soon come to an end were we to specify all the delicate touches and attractive pictures which place 'Nathalie' high among books of its class."—*Athenæum.*

V.—A WOMAN'S THOUGHTS ABOUT WOMEN.
BY THE AUTHOR OF "JOHN HALIFAX, GENTLEMAN."

"These thoughts are good and humane. They are thoughts we would wish women to think: they are much more to the purpose than the treatises upon the women and daughters of England, which were fashionable some years ago, and these thoughts mark the progress of opinion, and indicate a higher tone of character, and a juster estimate of woman's position."—*Athenæum.*

"This excellent book is characterised by good sense, good taste, and feeling, and is written in an earnest, philanthropic, as well as practical spirit."—*Morning Post.*

HURST & BLACKETT'S STANDARD LIBRARY

VI.—ADAM GRAEME OF MOSSGRAY.
BY MRS. OLIPHANT.

"'Adam Graeme' is a story awakening genuine emotions of interest and delight by its admirable pictures of Scottish life and scenery. The plot is cleverly complicated, and there is great vitality in the dialogue, and remarkable brilliancy in the descriptive passages, as who that has read 'Margaret Maitland' would not be prepared to expect? But the story has a 'mightier magnet still,' in the healthy tone which pervades it, in its feminine delicacy of thought and diction, and in the truly womanly tenderness of its sentiments. The eloquent author sets before us the essential attributes of Christian virtue, their deep and silent workings in the heart, and their beautiful manifestations in the life, with a delicacy, a power, and a truth which can hardly be surpassed."—*Morning Post.*

VII.—SAM SLICK'S WISE SAWS AND MODERN INSTANCES.

"We have not the slightest intention to criticise this book. Its reputation is made, and will stand as long as that of Scott's or Bulwer's novels. The remarkable originality of its purpose, and the happy description it affords of American life and manners, still continue the subject of universal admiration. To say thus much is to say enough, though we must just mention that the new edition forms a part of the Publishers' Cheap Standard Library, which has included some of the very best specimens of light literature that ever have been written."—*Messenger.*

VIII.—CARDINAL WISEMAN'S RECOLLECTIONS OF THE LAST FOUR POPES.

"A picturesque book on Rome and its ecclesiastical sovereigns, by an eloquent Roman Catholic. Cardinal Wiseman has here treated a special subject with so much generality and geniality that his recollections will excite no ill-feeling in those who are most conscientiously opposed to every idea of human infallibility represented in Papal domination."—*Athenæum.*

IX.—A LIFE FOR A LIFE.
BY THE AUTHOR OF "JOHN HALIFAX, GENTLEMAN."

"We are always glad to welcome Mrs. Craik. She writes from her own convictions, and she has the power not only to conceive clearly what it is that she wishes to say, but to express it in language effective and vigorous. In 'A Life for a Life' she is fortunate in a good subject, and she has produced a work of strong effect. The reader, having read the book through for the story, will be apt (if he be of our persuasion) to return and read again many pages and passages with greater pleasure than on a first perusal. The whole book is replete with a graceful, tender delicacy; and, in addition to its other merits, it is written in good careful English."—*Athenæum.*

"'A Life for a Life' is a book of a high class. The characters are depicted with a masterly hand; the events are dramatically set forth; the descriptions of scenery and sketches of society are admirably penned; moreover, the work has an object—a clearly defined moral—most poetically, most beautifully drawn, and through all there is that strong, reflective mind visible which lays bare the human heart and human mind to the very core."—*Morning Post.*

X.—THE OLD COURT SUBURB.
BY LEIGH HUNT.

"A book which has afforded us no slight gratification."—*Athenæum.*
"From the mixture of description, anecdote, biography, and criticism, this book is very pleasant reading."—*Spectator.*
"A more agreeable and entertaining book has not been published since Boswell produced his reminiscences of Johnson."—*Observer.*

HURST & BLACKETT'S STANDARD LIBRARY

XI.—MARGARET AND HER BRIDESMAIDS.
BY THE AUTHOR OF "THE VALLEY OF A HUNDRED FIRES."

"We recommend all who are in search of a fascinating novel to read this work for themselves. They will find it well worth their while. There are a freshness and originality about it quite charming, and there is a certain nobleness in the treatment both of sentiment and incident which is not often found."—*Athenæum.*

XII.—THE OLD JUDGE; OR, LIFE IN A COLONY.
BY SAM SLICK.

"A peculiar interest attaches to sketches of colonial life, and readers could not have a safer guide than the talented author of this work, who, by a residence of half a century, has practically grasped the habits, manners, and social conditions of the colonists he describes. All who wish to form a fair idea of the difficulties and pleasures of life in a new country, unlike England in some respects, yet like it in many, should read this book."—*John Bull.*

XIII.—DARIEN; OR, THE MERCHANT PRINCE.
BY ELIOT WARBURTON.

"This last production of the author of 'The Crescent and the Cross' has the same elements of a very wide popularity. It will please its thousands."—*Globe.*

"Eliot Warburton's active and productive genius is amply exemplified in the present book. We have seldom met with any work in which the realities of history and the poetry of fiction were more happily interwoven."—*Illustrated News.*

XIV.—FAMILY ROMANCE; OR, DOMESTIC ANNALS OF THE ARISTOCRACY.
BY SIR BERNARD BURKE, ULSTER KING OF ARMS.

"It were impossible to praise too highly this most interesting book, whether we should have regard to its excellent plan or its not less excellent execution. It ought to be found on every drawing-room table. Here we have nearly fifty captivating romances with the pith of all their interest preserved in undiminished poignancy, and any one may be read in half an hour. It is not the least of their merits that the romances are founded on fact —or what, at least, has been handed down for truth by long tradition—and the romance of reality far exceeds the romance of fiction."—*Standard.*

XV.—THE LAIRD OF NORLAW.
BY MRS. OLIPHANT.

"We have had frequent opportunities of commending Messrs. Hurst and Blackett's Standard Library. For neatness, elegance, and distinctness the volumes in this series surpass anything with which we are familiar. 'The Laird of Norlaw' will fully sustain the author's high reputation. The reader is carried on from first to last with an energy of sympathy that never flags."—*Sunday Times.*

"'The Laird of Norlaw' is worthy of the author's reputation. It is one of the most exquisite of modern novels."—*Observer.*

XVI.—THE ENGLISHWOMAN IN ITALY.
BY MRS. G. GRETTON.

"Mrs. Gretton had opportunities which rarely fall to the lot of strangers of becoming acquainted with the inner life and habits of a part of the Italian peninsula which is the very centre of the national crisis. We can praise her performance as interesting, unexaggerated, and full of opportune instruction."—*The Times.*

"Mrs. Gretton's book is timely, life-like, and for every reason to be recommended. It is impossible to close the book without liking the writer as well as the subject. The work is engaging, because real."—*Athenæum.*

HURST & BLACKETT'S STANDARD LIBRARY

XVII.—NOTHING NEW.
BY THE AUTHOR OF "JOHN HALIFAX, GENTLEMAN."

"'Nothing New' displays all those superior merits which have made 'John Halifax' one of the most popular works of the day. There is a force and truthfulness about these tales which mark them as the production of no ordinary mind, and we cordially recommend them to the perusal of all lovers of fiction."—*Morning Post.*

XVIII.—LIFE OF JEANNE D'ALBRET, QUEEN OF NAVARRE.
BY MISS FREER.

"We have read this book with great pleasure, and have no hesitation in recommending it to general perusal. It reflects the highest credit on the industry and ability of Miss Freer. Nothing can be more interesting than her story of the life of Jeanne D'Albret, and the narrative is as trustworthy as it is attractive."—*Morning Post.*

XIX.—THE VALLEY OF A HUNDRED FIRES.
BY THE AUTHOR OF "MARGARET AND HER BRIDESMAIDS."

"If asked to classify this work, we should give it a place between 'John Halifax' and 'The Caxtons.'"—*Standard.*
"The spirit in which the whole book is written is refined and good."—*Athenæum.*
"This is in every sense a charming novel."—*Messenger.*

XX.—THE ROMANCE OF THE FORUM; OR, NARRATIVES, SCENES, AND ANECDOTES FROM COURTS OF JUSTICE.
BY PETER BURKE, SERJEANT AT LAW.

"This attractive book will be perused with much interest. It contains a great variety of singular and highly romantic stories."—*John Bull.*
"A work of singular interest, which can never fail to charm and absorb the reader's attention. The present cheap and elegant edition includes the true story of the Colleen Bawn."—*Illustrated News.*

XXI.—ADÈLE.
BY JULIA KAVANAGH.

"'Adèle' is the best work we have read by Miss Kavanagh; it is a charming story, full of delicate character-painting. The interest kindled in the first chapter burns brightly to the close."—*Athenæum.*
"'Adèle' will fully sustain the reputation of Miss Kavanagh, high as it already ranks."—*John Bull.*
"'Adèle' is a love-story of very considerable pathos and power. It is a very clever novel."—*Daily News.*

XXII.—STUDIES FROM LIFE.
BY THE AUTHOR OF "JOHN HALIFAX, GENTLEMAN."

"These 'Studies' are truthful and vivid pictures of life, often earnest, always full of right feeling, and occasionally lightened by touches of quiet, genial humour. The volume is remarkable for thought, sound sense, shrewd observation, and kind and sympathetic feeling for all things good and beautiful."—*Morning Post.*
"These 'Studies from Life' are remarkable for graphic power and observation. The book will not diminish the reputation of the accomplished author."—*Saturday Review.*

HURST & BLACKETT'S STANDARD LIBRARY

XXIII.—GRANDMOTHER'S MONEY.
BY F. W. ROBINSON.

"We commend 'Grandmother's Money' to readers in search of a good novel. The characters are true to human nature, and the story is interesting."—*Athenæum.*

XXIV.—A BOOK ABOUT DOCTORS.
BY JOHN CORDY JEAFFRESON.

"A book to be read and re-read; fit for the study as well as the drawing-room table and the circulating library."—*Lancet.*

"This is a pleasant book for the fireside season, and for the seaside season. Mr. Jeaffreson has, out of hundreds of volumes, collected thousands of good things, adding thereto much that appears in print for the first time, and which, of course, gives increased value to this very readable book."—*Athenæum.*

XXV.—NO CHURCH.
BY F. W. ROBINSON.

"We advise all who have the opportunity to read this book. It is well worth the study."—*Athenæum.*

"A work of great originality, merit, and power."—*Standard.*

XXVI.—MISTRESS AND MAID.
BY THE AUTHOR OF "JOHN HALIFAX, GENTLEMAN."

"A good wholesome book, gracefully written, and as pleasant to read as it is instructive."—*Athenæum.*

"A charming tale, charmingly told."—*Standard.*

"All lovers of a good novel will hail with delight another of Mrs. Craik's charming stories."—*John Bull.*

XXVII.—LOST AND SAVED.
BY THE HON. MRS. NORTON.

"'Lost and Saved' will be read with eager interest by those who love a touching story. It is a vigorous novel."—*Times.*

"This story is animated, full of exciting situations and stirring incidents. The characters are delineated with great power. Above and beyond these elements of a good novel, there is that indefinable charm with which true genius invests all it touches."—*Daily News.*

XXVIII.—LES MISERABLES.
BY VICTOR HUGO.
Authorised Copyright English Translation.

"The merits of 'Les Miserables' do not merely consist in the conception of it as a whole; it abounds with details of unequalled beauty. M. Victor Hugo has stamped upon every page the hall-mark of genius."—*Quarterly Review.*

XXIX.—BARBARA'S HISTORY
BY AMELIA B. EDWARDS.

"It is not often that we light upon a novel of so much merit and interest as 'Barbara's History.' It is a work conspicuous for taste and literary culture. It is a very graceful and charming book, with a well-managed story, clearly-cut characters, and sentiments expressed with an exquisite elocution. The dialogues especially sparkle with repartee. It is a book which the world will like. This is high praise of a work of art, and so we intend it."—*The Times.*

HURST & BLACKETT'S STANDARD LIBRARY

XXX.—LIFE OF THE REV. EDWARD IRVING.
BY MRS. OLIPHANT.

"A good book on a most interesting theme."—*Times.*
"A truly interesting and most affecting memoir. 'Irving's Life' ought to have a niche in every gallery of religious biography. There are few lives that will be fuller of instruction, interest, and consolation."—*Saturday Review.*

XXXI.—ST. OLAVE'S.
BY THE AUTHOR OF "JANITA'S CROSS."

"This novel is the work of one who possesses a great talent for writing, as well as experience and knowledge of the world. The whole book is worth reading."—*Athenæum.*
"'St. Olave's' belongs to a lofty order of fiction. It is a good novel, but it is something more. It is written with unflagging ability, and it is as even as it is clever. The author has determined to do nothing short of the best, and has succeeded."—*Morning Post.*

XXXII.—SAM SLICK'S TRAITS OF AMERICAN HUMOUR.

"Dip where you will into this lottery of fun, you are sure to draw out a prize. These 'Traits' exhibit most successfully the broad national features of American humour."—*Post.*

XXXIII.—CHRISTIAN'S MISTAKE.
BY THE AUTHOR OF "JOHN HALIFAX, GENTLEMAN."

"A more charming story has rarely been written. It is a choice gift to be able thus to render human nature so truly, to penetrate its depths with such a searching sagacity, and to illuminate them with a radiance so eminently the writer's own."—*Times.*

XXXIV.—ALEC FORBES OF HOWGLEN.
BY GEORGE MAC DONALD, LL.D.

"No account of this story would give any idea of the profound interest that pervades the work from the first page to the last."—*Athenæum.*
"A novel of uncommon merit. Sir Walter Scott said he would advise no man to try to read 'Clarissa Harlowe' out loud in company if he wished to keep his character for manly superiority to tears. We fancy a good many hardened old novel-readers will feel a rising in the throat as they follow the fortunes of Alec and Annie."—*Pall Mall Gazette.*

XXXV.—AGNES.
BY MRS. OLIPHANT.

"'Agnes' is a novel superior to any of Mrs. Oliphant's former works."—*Athenæum.*
"Mrs. Oliphant is one of the most admirable of our novelists. In her works there are always to be found high principle, good taste, sense, and refinement. 'Agnes' is a story whose pathetic beauty will appeal irresistibly to all readers."—*Morning Post.*

XXXVI.—A NOBLE LIFE.
BY THE AUTHOR OF "JOHN HALIFAX, GENTLEMAN."

"Few men and no women will read 'A Noble Life' without feeling themselves the better for the effort."—*Spectator.*
"A beautifully written and touching tale. It is a noble book."—*Morning Post.*
"'A Noble Life' is remarkable for the high types of character it presents, and the skill with which they are made to work out a story of powerful and pathetic interest."—*Daily News.*

XXXVII—NEW AMERICA.
BY W. HEPWORTH DIXON.

"A very interesting book. Mr. Dixon has written thoughtfully and well."—*Times.*
"We recommend everyone who feels any interest in human nature to read Mr Dixon's very interesting book."—*Saturday Review.*

HURST & BLACKETT'S STANDARD LIBRARY

XXXVIII.—ROBERT FALCONER.
BY GEORGE MAC DONALD, LL.D.

"'Robert Falconer' is a work brimful of life and humour and of the deepest human interest. It is a book to be returned to again and again for the deep and searching knowledge it evinces of human thoughts and feelings."—*Athenæum.*

XXXIX.—THE WOMAN'S KINGDOM.
BY THE AUTHOR OF "JOHN HALIFAX, GENTLEMAN."

"'The Woman's Kingdom' sustains the author's reputation as a writer of the purest and noblest kind of domestic stories."—*Athenæum.*

"'The Woman's Kingdom' is remarkable for its romantic interest. The characters are masterpieces. Edna is worthy of the hand that drew John Halifax."—*Morning Post.*

XL.—ANNALS OF AN EVENTFUL LIFE.
BY GEORGE WEBBE DASENT, D.C.L.

"A racy, well-written, and original novel. The interest never flags. The whole work sparkles with wit and humour."—*Quarterly Review.*

XLI.—DAVID ELGINBROD.
BY GEORGE MAC DONALD, LL.D.

"A novel which is the work of a man of genius. It will attract the highest class of readers."—*Times.*

XLII.—A BRAVE LADY.
BY THE AUTHOR OF "JOHN HALIFAX, GENTLEMAN."

"We earnestly recommend this novel. It is a special and worthy specimen of the author's remarkable powers. The reader's attention never for a moment flags."—*Post.*

"'A Brave Lady' thoroughly rivets the unmingled sympathy of the reader, and her history deserves to stand foremost among the author's works."—*Daily Telegraph.*

XLIII.—HANNAH.
BY THE AUTHOR OF "JOHN HALIFAX, GENTLEMAN."

"A very pleasant, healthy story, well and artistically told. The book is sure of a wide circle of readers. The character of Hannah is one of rare beauty."—*Standard.*

"A powerful novel of social and domestic life. One of the most successful efforts of a successful novelist."—*Daily News.*

XLIV.—SAM SLICK'S AMERICANS AT HOME.

"This is one of the most amusing books that we ever read."—*Standard.*

"'The Americans at Home' will not be less popular than any of Judge Halliburton's previous works."—*Morning Post.*

XLV.—THE UNKIND WORD.
BY THE AUTHOR OF "JOHN HALIFAX, GENTLEMAN."

"These stories are gems of narrative. Indeed, some of them, in their touching grace and simplicity, seem to us to possess a charm even beyond the authoress's most popular novels. Of none of them can this be said more emphatically than of that which opens the series, 'The Unkind Word.' It is wonderful to see the imaginative power displayed in the few delicate touches by which this successful love-story is sketched out."—*The Echo.*

HURST & BLACKETT'S STANDARD LIBRARY

XLVI.—A ROSE IN JUNE.
BY MRS. OLIPHANT.

"'A Rose in June' is as pretty as its title. The story is one of the best and most touching which we owe to the industry and talent of Mrs. Oliphant, and may hold its own with even 'The Chronicles of Carlingford.'"—*Times.*

"In 'A Rose in June' Mrs. Oliphant is at her very best again. The book is full of character, drawn with the most delicate of touches."—*Athenæum.*

XLVII.—MY LITTLE LADY.
BY E. FRANCES POYNTER.

"There is a great deal of fascination about this book. The author writes in a clear, unaffected style; she has a decided gift for depicting character, while the descriptions of scenery convey a distinct pictorial impression to the reader."—*Times.*

"This story presents a number of vivid and very charming pictures. Indeed, the whole book is charming. It is interesting in both character and story, and thoroughly good of its kind."—*Saturday Review.*

XLVIII.—PHŒBE, JUNIOR.
BY MRS. OLIPHANT.

"This novel shows great knowledge of human nature. The interest goes on growing to the end. Phœbe is excellently drawn."—*Times.*

"This last 'Chronicle of Carlingford' not merely takes rank fairly beside the first which introduced us to 'Salem Chapel,' but surpasses all the intermediate records. Phœbe, Junior, herself is admirably drawn."—*Academy.*

XLIX.—LIFE OF MARIE ANTOINETTE.
BY PROFESSOR CHARLES DUKE YONGE.

"A work of remarkable merit and interest, which will, we doubt not, become the most popular English history of Marie Antoinette."—*Spectator.*

"This book is well written, and of thrilling interest."—*Academy.*

L.—SIR GIBBIE.
BY GEORGE MAC DONALD, LL.D.

"'Sir Gibbie' is a book of genius."—*Pall Mall Gazette.*

"This book has power, pathos, and humour. There is not a character which no lifelike."—*Athenæum.*

LI.—YOUNG MRS. JARDINE.
BY THE AUTHOR OF "JOHN HALIFAX, GENTLEMAN."

"'Young Mrs. Jardine' is a pretty story, written in pure English."—*The Times.*

"There is much good feeling in this book. It is pleasant and wholesome."—*Athenæum.*

"This story is charmingly told."—*The Queen.*

LII.—LORD BRACKENBURY.
BY AMELIA B. EDWARDS.

"A very readable story. The author has well conceived the purpose of high-class novel-writing, and succeeded in no small measure in attaining it. There is plenty of variety, cheerful dialogue, and general 'verve' in the book."—*Athenæum.*

"'Lord Brackenbury' is pleasant reading from beginning to end."—*Academy.*

THE NEW AND POPULAR NOVELS.
PUBLISHED BY HURST & BLACKETT.

SAM'S SWEETHEART. By HELEN MATHERS,
Author of "Comin' thro' the Rye," "Cherry Ripe!" "Land o' the Leal," &c. Second Edition. 3 vols.

"A new novel by Miss Mathers is a great treat."—*Athenæum.*

"'Sam's Sweetheart' is clever and amusing. It is superior to its predecessors from the same pen: the plot is closer, and better constructed."—*Graphic.*

IT WAS A LOVER AND HIS LASS. By Mrs.
OLIPHANT, Author of "Mrs. Margaret Maitland," "Agnes," &c. Second Edition. 3 vols.

"In 'It was a Lover and his Lass,' we admire Mrs. Oliphant exceedingly. Her story is a very pretty one. It would be worth reading a second time, were it only for the sake of one ancient Scottish spinster, who is nearly the counterpart of the admirable Mrs. Margaret Maitland. The reader is carried along very pleasantly in following the simple fortunes of a pretty country girl and her lover."—*Times.*

A MAID CALLED BARBARA. By CATHARINE
CHILDAR, Author of "The Future Marquis," &c. 3 vols.

"This story is stronger and more romantic than the author's previous works. She has drawn some good characters, and there is not a little pathos in the lives of the hero and heroine."—*Athenæum.*

"A bright, pleasant, and readable novel. The characters are lifelike and the scenes are well developed."—*John Bull.*

MONGRELS. By T. WILTON. 3 vols.

"A very clever novel. It shows much talent."—*Post.*

"A bright and diverting story, full of effective scenes and descriptions. There is a good deal of cleverness in it. The author's narrative is entertaining: it is told with point and spirit."—*Athenæum.*

WHAT HAST THOU DONE? By J. FITZGERALD
MOLLOY, Author of "Court Life Below Stairs," &c. 3 vols.

"This clever story is much above the average. The descriptions of Irish life are especially good."—*St. James's Gazette.*

"A bright, pleasant, and interesting novel. It contains scenes in Bohemia, scenes in high life in London, and scenes in Ireland."—*County Gentleman.*

WOODROFFE. By Mrs. RANDOLPH, Author of
"Gentianella," "Wild Hyacinth," &c. 3 vols.

"Mrs. Randolph's 'Woodroffe' is a clever description of a country house inhabited by ladies and gentlewomen, and so far sustains her reputation for easy and truthful writing. Constance Woodroffe and her sister are good specimens of English girls, with sufficient difference of character to give them reality."—*Athenæum.*

MISS CHEYNE OF ESSILMONT. By JAMES
GRANT, Author of "Romance of War," &c. 3 vols.

"A wholesome and entertaining romance of modern life. The plot is well-constructed and exceedingly dramatic, and the characters are sketched with that care and ability for which Mr. Grant is justly celebrated."—*Morning Post.*

SANGUELAC. By PERCY GREG, Author of "Ivy:
Cousin and Bride," &c. 3 vols.

"A most enjoyable book to read. In many respects it will be accounted Mr. Greg's best novel. On one side it is a story with a stirring plot and several very interesting and admirably drawn characters; on another it is a novel with a purpose."—*Spectator.*

FETTERED YET FREE. By ALICE KING, Author
of "Queen of Herself," &c. 3 vols.

"Miss King's new novel is brightly written."—*Athenæum.*

"A very readable story. Hope Millwood, the heroine, is a charming type of womanhood."—*Morning Post.*

THE NEW AND POPULAR NOVELS.
PUBLISHED BY HURST & BLACKETT.

JUNE. By Mrs. FORRESTER, Author of "Viva,"
"Mignon," "My Lord and My Lady," &c. 3 vols.

PEARLA. By M. BETHAM-EDWARDS, Author of
"Kitty," "Bridget," &c. 3 vols.

IN THE WEST COUNTRIE. By the AUTHOR OF
"QUEENIE," "Miss Daisy Dimity," &c. 3 vols.

ADRIAN BRIGHT. By Mrs. CADDY, Author of
"Artist and Amateur," &c. 3 vols.
"This novel will be read with avidity and keen pleasure by all epicures in fiction, who know how to enjoy what is good."—*Standard.*
"Those who are fond of the quiet domestic stories of modern life cannot do better than read 'Adrian Bright.' It is wholesome and readable."—*John Bull.*
"There is much to interest and amuse in this life-like picture of the home of Adrian Bright. The story increases in interest as it proceeds."—*Morning Post.*

SQUIRE LISLE'S BEQUEST. By ANNE BEALE,
Author of "Fay Arlington," &c. 3 vols.
"This novel can be recommended to those who are satisfied with an unaffected story gracefully told. It is healthy and high-toned throughout. The plot is well-imagined and neatly put together."—*Morning Post.*
"This story is pure and healthy in tone and agreeably written. The studies of character are excellent; the hero and heroine are admirably drawn."—*Academy.*

RED RIDING-HOOD. By FANNY E. MILLETT
NOTLEY, Author of "Olive Varcoe," &c. 3 vols.
"This story is well written, as well as conceived with something more than the ordinary success."—*Athenæum.*
"The best novel Mrs. Notley has written since 'Olive Varcoe,' and, in many respects, it is even better than that popular tale. It is a most exciting story."—*John Bull.*
"A very pretty and interesting romance."—*St. James's Gazette.*

A FALLEN FOE. By KATHARINE KING, Author of
"The Queen of the Regiment," &c. 3 vols.
"'A Fallen Foe' possesses all the qualities of the writer's former novels. The tone is refined and the principal characters carefully drawn."—*Morning Post.*
"This readable story is told with praiseworthy directness. The characters are fairly drawn, and there are some good scenes in the book."—*Pall Mall Gazette.*

FARMER JOHN. By GEORGE HOLMES. 3 vols.
"The author of 'Farmer John' knows the west-country people well, and writes their dialect with a care and uniformity which are really admirable."—*Athenæum.*
"As a study of character this book is not without merit. It is by no means an ordinary production."—*Morning Post.*

THE SENIOR SONGMAN. By the AUTHOR OF
"ST. OLAVE'S," "Janita's Cross," &c. 3 vols.
"The author of 'St. Olave's' gives us another readable story in 'The Senior Songman.' There is no lack of ability in the book."—*Athenæum.*
"This well-written story deserves the popularity assured to anything written by the author of 'St. Olave's.' There is not a page in the whole novel which fails to command attention or to repay it."—*Daily Telegraph.*

HER SAILOR LOVE. By Mrs. MACQUOID, Author
of "Patty," "Diane," &c. 3 vols.
"This is a good business-like novel of the homely sort. There is a great deal in the story to awaken interest, and not a little to afford pleasure and entertainment."—*Illustrated London News.*

www.ingramcontent.com/pod-product-compliance
Lightning Source LLC
Chambersburg PA
CBHW020301240426
43673CB00039B/663